COMPLETE GUIDE
TO U.S.
CIVIL SERVICE JOBS

Edited by

Hy Hammer, Chief of
Examining Service Division
New York City Department
of Personnel, (Ret.)

Prentice Hall
New York • London • Toronto • Sydney • Tokyo • Singapore

Tenth Edition

Copyright © 1991, 1988 by Arco Publishing, a division
of Simon & Schuster, Inc.

Prentice Hall General Reference
15 Columbus Circle
New York, NY 10023

An Arco Book

Prentice Hall and colophons are
registered trademarks of Simon & Schuster, Inc.

Manufactured in the United States of America

1 2 3 4 5 6 7 8 9 10

Library of Congress Cataloging-in-Publication Data

Complete guide to U. S. Civil Service jobs / edited by Hy Hammer.
   p. cm.
  ISBN 0-13-932658-8
  1. Civil service positions--United States. I. Hammer, Hy.
JK716.C597 1991   91-29319
353.001'03--dc20   CIP

CONTENTS

INTRODUCTION

The executive branch of the Federal Government includes the Office of the President, the departments with cabinet representation, and a number of independent agencies, commissions, and boards. This branch is responsible for such activities as administering Federal laws; handling international relations; conserving natural resources; treating and rehabilitating disabled veterans; conducting scientific research; maintaining the flow of supplies to the Armed Forces; and administering other programs to promote the health and welfare of the people.

The Federal Government employs several million white-collar workers. Entrance requirements for white-collar jobs vary widely. Entrants into professional occupations are required to have highly specialized knowledge in a specified field, as evidenced by completion of a prescribed college course of study or, in many cases, the equivalent in experience. Occupations typical of this group are attorney, physicist, and engineer.

Entrants into administrative and managerial occupations usually are not required to have knowledge in a specialized field but rather, they must indicate by graduation from a 4-year college or by responsible job experience, that they have potential for future development. The entrant usually begins at a trainee level, and learns the duties of the job after he is hired. Typical jobs in this group are budget analyst, claims examiner, purchasing officer, administrative assistant, and personnel officer.

Technician, clerical, and aid-assistant jobs have entry level positions that usually are filled by persons having a high school education or the equivalent. For many of these positions, no prior experience or training is required. The entry level position is usually that of trainee, where the duties of the job are learned and skill is improved. Persons with junior college or technical school training, or those having specialized skills, may enter these occupations at higher levels. Jobs typical of this group are engineering technician, supply clerk, clerk-typist, and nursing assistant.

Blue-collar jobs—service, craft, and manual labor—provide employment to over 600,000 workers. The majority of these workers are in establishments such as naval shipyards, arsenals, air bases, or army depots; or they work on construction, harbor, flood-control, irrigation, or reclamation projects.

The largest single group of blue-collar workers consists of mobile equipment operators and mechanics. Among these jobs are forklift operator, chauffeur, truckdriver and automobile mechanic. The next largest group of workers are general laborers, who perform a wide variety of manual jobs.

Many skilled occupations may be entered through apprenticeship programs. To qualify, experience normally is not required, but a test may be given to indicate whether an applicant has an aptitude for the occupation.

Federal employees are stationed in all parts of the United States and its territories and in many foreign countries. Although most Government departments and agencies have their headquarters in the Washington, D.C. metropolitan area, only 1 out of 11 Federal workers is employed there.

THE MERIT SYSTEM

The majority of Federal jobs in the United States are covered by the Civil Service Act. This act was passed by the Congress to hire Federal employees on the basis of individual merit and fitness. It provides for competitive examinations and the selection of new employees from among those who make the highest scores. The Office of Personnel Management (OPM), which administers the Civil Service Act, examines applicants and refers eligible persons to Federal agencies.

Some Federal jobs are excepted from Civil Service requirements either by law or by action of the OPM. However, most of the excepted positions are under separate merit systems of other agencies, such as the Foreign Service of the Department of State, the Department of Medicine and Surgery of the Veterans Administration, the Federal Bureau of Investigation, the Atomic Energy Commission, the Tennessee Valley Authority, and the Postal Service. These agencies establish their own standards for the selection of new employees.

In the United States, Civil Service competitive examinations may be taken by any resident. However, on the list of "Eligibles," priority will be given to U.S. citizens. To be eligible for appointment, an applicant must meet minimum age, training, and experience requirements for the particular position. A physical handicap will not in itself bar a person from a position if it does not interfere with his performance of the required duties. Examinations vary according to the types of positions for which they are held. Some examinations include written tests; others do not. Written examinations test the applicant's ability to do the job applied for, or his ability to learn how to do it. In nonwritten examinations, applicants are rated on the basis of the experience and training described in their applications and any supporting evidence required by the Office of Personnel Management.

OPM notifies applicants whether they have achieved eligible or ineligible ratings, and enters the names of eligible applicants on a list in the order of their scores. When a Federal agency requests names of eligible applicants for a job vacancy, OPM sends the agency the names at the top of the appropriate list. The agency can select any one of the top three available eligibles. Names of those not selected are restored to the list for consideration for other job openings.

Appointments to Civil Service jobs are made without regard to an applicant's race, color, religion, national origin, politics, or sex.

Pay rates of employees under the General Schedule are set by the Congress and are nationwide. This General Schedule provides a pay scale for employees in professional, administrative, technical, and clerical jobs, and for employees such as guards and messengers. General Schedule jobs are classified and arranged in 18 pay grades according to difficulty of the duties, and the responsibilities, knowledge, experience, or skill required. Employees in all grades to GS–12 receive within-grade increases after they have completed the required service periods, if their work is determined to be of an acceptable level of competence. Within-grade increases also may be given in recognition of high-quality service.

High school graduates with no related work experience are usually appointed to GS–2 positions, but some with special skills begin at GS–3. Graduates of 2-year junior colleges and technical schools can often begin at the GS–4 level. Most young people appointed to professional and administrative positions enter at grade GS–5 or GS–7 depending on their academic record. Those who hold a master's degree or the equivalent in education or experience usually enter at grade GS–7; they may enter at grade GS–9 if they are well qualified. In addition, the Federal Government also appoints very well-qualified, experienced people at the GS–11 level and above. These appointments are for such positions as psychologist, statistician, economist, writer and editor, budget analyst, accountant, and physicist.

New appointments usually are made at the minimum rate of the salary range for the appropriate grade. However, appointments in hard-to-fill positions frequently are made at a higher rate.

Advancement depends upon ability, work performance, and generally, upon openings in jobs at higher grades. Employees frequently get promotions by qualifying for jobs at higher grades. Promotions also may be obtained when jobs are reclassified to a higher grade to reflect more difficult work assignments and increased responsibilities.

Craft, service, and manual workers employed by the Federal Government are paid under the coordinated Federal wage system. Pay is fixed on the basis of prevailing rates paid by private employers for similar work.

Employees in agencies with separate merit systems are paid under acts other than those already mentioned.

The standard workweek for Federal Government employees is 40 hours, and the pay schedules are based on this workweek. If an employee is required to work overtime he is either paid overtime rates for the additional time worked or given compensatory time off at a later date. Most employees usually work 8 hours a day, 5 days a week, Monday through Friday, but in some cases, the nature of the work may call for a different workweek. Annual earnings for most full-time Federal workers are not affected by seasonal factors.

Federal employees earn 13 days of annual (vacation) leave during each of their first 3 years of service, then 20 days each year until they have completed 15 years; after 15 years, they earn 26 days of leave each year. In addition, they earn 13 days of paid sick leave a year. Nine paid holidays are observed annually. Employees who are members of military reserve organizations also are granted up to 15 days of paid military leave a year for training purposes. A Federal employee who is laid off is entitled to unemployment compensation similar to that provided for employees in private industry.

Other benefits available to most Federal employees include: A contributory retirement system; optional participation in low-cost group life and health insurance programs supported in part by the Government; and training programs to develop maximum job proficiency and help employees achieve their highest potential. These training programs may be conducted in Government facilities or in outside educational facilities at Government expense.

WHERE TO GO FOR MORE INFORMATION

Information on Federal employment opportunities is available from a number of sources. For college students, the college placement office is often a good source of such information. High school students in many localities may obtain information from their high school guidance counselors. Additional information may be obtained from State employment service offices.

Job Information Centers operated by the Office of Personnel Management are located in many large cities throughout the country. You can get complete information concerning Federal jobs by calling, visiting, or writing to the office in your area.

Information about a specific agency also may be obtained by contacting the agency directly.

PART ONE

Working for the Federal Government

HOW TO GET A JOB IN THE FEDERAL GOVERNMENT

The diagram below shows the steps involved in getting a government job:

Where and How to Obtain Information

A. The Office of Personnel Management (formerly the U.S. Civil Service Commission) maintains Federal Job Information Centers across the country to provide local job information. Look under "U.S. Government" in the blue pages of the metropolitan area phone directories for the center nearest you. If none is listed in your directory, dial 800-555-1212 for the toll free number of a Federal Job Information Center in your state.

B. Call or write the center in your state. You provide the following information:
   1. the level of education you have completed and the amount of paid and unpaid experience you have
   2. the kind of work that interests you
   3. the area or areas where you want to work
   4. the lowest salary you will accept
   5. whether you are a veteran
   6. a clearly written name and address to which forms may be sent

C. Request:
   1. a copy of examination announcements for which you qualify
   2. copies of blank application forms needed for the exam you will apply for

Hints on How to Apply

- Remember that jobs are located in Federal agencies.

- Job announcements are found in personnel offices at individual agencies.

- Check your telephone directory white pages under the heading "United States Government" to locate nearby Federal agencies.

- Call the number listed and ask for the address and phone number of the personnel offices.

- Visit personnel offices and ask for listing of vacancies.

- Submit application forms for jobs in which you are interested. Be sure to follow all procedures in the examination (job) announcement. The Office of Personnel Management will evaluate your application and issue a Notice of Results which may be a "Notice of Rating" telling you the grade level(s) and occupations for which you have qualified or a letter acknowledging the receipt of your application. A Notice of Rating or letter of acknowledgment is not an offer of a Federal job.

- Sources to locate vacancies include:
   1. newspapers
   2. employees of the agency
   3. agency officials
   4. special publications
   5. college or university placement offices or professors
   6. professional contacts

General Categories of Federal Jobs

Professional occupations are those requiring knowledge in a field of science or learning characteristically acquired through education or training equivalent to a bachelor's or higher degree with major study in or pertinent to the specialized field, as distinguished from general education, i.e., engineer, accountant, biologist, chemist.

Administrative occupations are those which are typically gained through progressive responsible experience or college level general education, i.e., personnel specialist, administrative officer.

Technical occupations are those involving work typically associated with, and supportive of a professional or administrative field, which is non-routine in nature, i.e., computer technician, electronic technician.

Clerical occupations are those involving structured work in support of office, business, or fiscal operations, i.e., clerk-typist, mail and file clerk.

Other occupations are those that cannot be related to the above, i.e., painters, carpenters, and laborers.

How to Fill Out Federal Application Forms

A. Upon receipt of SF-171 or other Federal application forms and job announcement, do the following:

1. Read job announcement thoroughly to familiarize yourself with the specific requirements listed in job announcement.

2. Begin the process of completing the SF-171 by remembering the following general guidelines:

   a. Make several photocopies of the blank form so that you can practice fitting your information into the categories and spaces provided and so that you can practice typing within the lines.

   b. Before you prepare your SF-171, review your life experiences, especially those which can enhance the position for which you are applying. Make a list of special activities, duties, knowledges, and work experience.

   c. Always use a typewriter. If this is not possible, write neatly and clearly in ink.

   d. Make a master copy and do not sign and date. Photocopy additional copies and sign and date each copy when necessary for distribution.

3. Begin with page 1 of the SF-171.

Standard Form 171

Personal Qualifications Statement

IMPORTANT
READ THE FOLLOWING INSTRUCTIONS CAREFULLY BEFORE FILLING OUT YOUR STATEMENT

● You must furnish all requested information. The information you provide will be used to determine your qualifications for employment. DO NOT SEND A RESUME IN LIEU OF COMPLETING THIS STATEMENT.

● If you fail to answer all questions on your Statement fully and accurately, you may delay consideration of your Statement and may lose employment opportunities. See the Privacy Act Information on the reverse of this sheet.

● So that it is understood that you did not omit an item, please write the letters "N/A" (Not Applicable) beside those items that do not apply to you, unless instructions indicate otherwise.

Personal Qualifications Statement
Read instructions before completing form

Form Approved:
OMB No. 50-R0387

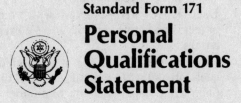

1. Kind of position (job) you are filing for (or title and number of announcement)

2. Options for which you wish to be considered (if listed in the announcement)

3. Home phone — Area Code / Number

4. Work phone — Area Code / Number / Extension

5. Sex (for statistics only)   ☐ Male   ☐ Female

6. Other last names ever used

Name (Last, First, Middle)

Street address or RFD no. (include apartment no., if any)

City / State / ZIP Code

8. Birthplace (City & State, or foreign country)

9. Birth date (Month, day, year)

10. Social Security Number

DO NOT WRITE IN THIS BLOCK
FOR USE OF EXAMINING OFFICE ONLY

Material ☐ Submitted ☐ Returned

Entered register:

Notations:

Form reviewed:

Form approved:

Option	Grade	Earned Rating	Preference	Aug. Rating
			☐ 5 Points (Tent.)	
			☐ 10 Pts 30% or More Comp. Dis	
			☐ 10 Pts Less Than 30% Comp. Dis	

ANNOUNCEMENT NO.

STATEMENT

Page 1 of the SF-171

1. **Position:** Fill in the position category or name and announcement number supplied on the job announcement.

2. **Options:** Fill in "Any job for which qualified."

3, 4. **Home and work phones:** Fill in your home phone and work phone numbers.

5. **Sex:** check one.

6. **Other last names:** This item is especially important for women who may have been married or remarried. Be sure to indicate maiden name and previous married name.

7–10. **Name, address, birthplace, birthdate, and Social Security number:** Fill in every block completely. If your address changes after you have applied for an evaluation at OPM, be sure to inform OPM by letter.

11. **Previous Federal employment:** Indicate where, when, and how long.

12. **Current application on file with OPM:** This is important. If this is your first time filling out a SF-171, you are obviously not on file with OPM.

13. **Pay or grade:** Fill in your desired salary.

14. **Availability:** Put whatever date you expect to be available.

15. **Temporary employment:** Willingness to accept a temporary assignment can be a good way of getting in the door. If this is offered, weigh the advantages and disadvantages as they apply to your situation.

16. **Other employment:** State kinds and titles.

17. **Where you will accept a job:** State location.

18. **Travel:** Check what is feasible for you and your circumstances.

19. **Part-time positions:** Willingness to accept a part-time position can be a good way of getting in the door.

20. **Veteran preference:** State whether or not you are a veteran. You may gain some added advantage by having 5 to 10 points added to numerical rating on an OPM exam.

Page 2 of the SF-171

21. **Experience:** The first question in this rather lengthy section on experience concerns whether or not personnel staff may contact your present employer. A "no" answer here will not affect your employment opportunities, but if you do answer "no," try to provide some form of evaluation, such as a performance evaluation or letter of recommendation.

   a. Use the word "I" instead of "the incumbent" or "he/she." Use "I" sparingly by indicating your responsibilities, i.e., "Was directly responsible for . . ."

   b. Use "active" verbs—a verb with a direct object is an active verb. *Example:* I typed letters.

   c. Be complete. Use all the lines allotted to each job and write more if you need to on plain white paper. Be sure to number the attachments with the item number, your birthdate, and name.

   d. Include all major duties of each job.

   e. Use your own words — not words from position descriptions.

   f. Be specific about what tasks you performed; do not summarize; explain fully.

   g. Include volunteer work.

   h. Note that the form asks you to list your present job first and then the one you had before that one, and so on. Experience acquired more than 15 years ago may be summarized in one block if it is not applicable to the type of position you are applying for.

   i. Write a draft of your experience first. Then rewrite your draft as many times as is necessary to produce a complete, well-written description of duties.

   j. Don't abbreviate. Don't use acronyms unless you explain the meaning in the first use.

   k. Include brief excerpts from official or unofficial letters in which your work was praised. Mention job-related awards.

l. Don't type your material into one long, unending paragraph, especially if you choose to use more space than that provided on the form. Break up your description into short sentences or paragraphs. Use headings. Aim for a clear, well-organized presentation to ensure that it will be read by the personnel specialist.

Page 3 of the SF-171

22. **Special qualifications and skills:** Include membership in professional organizations, title of any informational material written even if unpublished. Indicate examples of public speaking including Sunday School work, etc.; list hobbies relevant to positions for which you are applying; indicate typing skill.

23. **Education:** Be sure to show all the training you have had. Include the names of schools, location, dates attended, subjects studied, number of classroom or credit hours received, and any other pertinent data. (Credit hours refer to the number of units, whether quarter or semester, you earned for a college course.) As in other items, you may have to add separate sheets to be complete. You may also want to include a college transcript.

23-G. **Other schools and training:** Include in-service workshops, seminars, professional conferences, private study, correspondence courses, military training, leadership orientation, career specialty training, and others. Be sure to give all the details requested, including time involved, so that it may be properly rated. Do not neglect the area of personal development and study.

24. **Honors, awards, and fellowships:** Many people are modest about awards. Honors and awards don't have to be earth-shaking to be included. Cite scholarships, letters of commendation from your supervisor, safety awards, suggestion awards (you might describe the suggestion and its benefits briefly), community awards and nominations, and election to honorary societies or groups. Your most recent awards are usually the most relevant. However, if you received only a few awards list them all, even if all were presented some years ago.

25. **Foreign language:** Any familiarity with a foreign language should be mentioned. Be honest in evaluating your abilities.

26. **References:**
   - Use people who know you.
   - Use people who know your work.
   - Use people who can be reached and include their phone numbers.
   - Don't list people who are out of the country, have no phone, or whose whereabouts are unknown to you.
   - Ask your references for permission to use their names.

Page 4 of the SF-171

27–34. These questions are important. Read them carefully and answer yes or no as directed for each one. U.S. citizenship is required for most permanent civil service positions.

35. This space may be used to continue answers from any other question.

Read the closing information carefully. Make photocopies. Do not sign the original SF-171. Sign and date each copy as you submit it for a specific vacancy.

Part-Time Positions and Summer Jobs

Part-Time Positions

Part-time positions—16 to 32 hours per week—are available in agencies throughout the Federal

Government. Applications should be made directly to the personnel office in the agency of your choice.

Summer Jobs

Summer employment opportunities for high school, college, medical, and dental students are available but limited throughout the Federal Government. Contact your Federal Job Information Center in October or November for summer job announcements.

Information Applicable to All Summer Jobs

Summer jobs are located in Federal agencies and departments throughout the United States. The majority of jobs are in large metropolitan areas. If you wish information on employment opportunities in an agency, you should contact the agency directly to find out if applications are being accepted for summer employment. Agency addresses may be obtained from Federal Job Information Centers or from the blue pages of local telephone directories under the listing "United States Government."

Members of Family

You may not be considered for a summer job in the same department or agency in which your father or mother is employed unless you are selected for a job from an agency list of eligibles established in accordance with special procedures. Check with the agency regarding their procedures.

Who May Apply

If you meet the minimum qualification requirements for the job to be filled, age and citizenship requirements, and general standards for Federal employment, your name will be entered on the list of eligibles in the agency where you apply.

Special Placement Assistance for the Physically Handicapped

Persons who have severe physical handicaps which may limit their activity in performing a job may qualify for special placement assistance

from the Office of Personnel Management. For more information, contact a Federal Job Information Center. Handicapped applicants may also contact Federal agencies in which they would like to work.

Postal Service Jobs

Questions about Postal Service employment should be directed to the Post Office where employment is desired.

Jobs in Alaska, Guam, Hawaii, Puerto Rico, and the Virgin Islands

Because of the limited number of jobs in Alaska, Guam, Hawaii, Puerto Rico, and the Virgin Islands, residents of these areas will receive first consideration for employment. Other candidates will be considered only when there are no qualified residents available.

Working Conditions, Benefits, and Holidays

Hours of Work

The usual government workweek is 40 hours. Most government employees work 8 hours, 5 days a week, Monday through Friday, but, in some cases, the nature of the work may call for a different workweek. As in any other business, employees sometimes have to work overtime. If you are required to work overtime, you will either be paid for overtime or given time off to make up for the extra time you worked.

Advancement

Most agencies fill vacancies, whenever possible, by promoting their own employees.

Federal employees receive on-the-job training. They may also participate in individualized career development programs and receive job-related training in their own agency, in other agencies, or outside the government (for example, in industrial plants and universities). It is not always necessary to move to a new job in order to advance in grade. Sometimes an employee's work assignments change a great deal in the ordinary course of business. The job "grows." When that happens, it is time for a position classifier to study the job again. If he or she finds that the job should be put in a higher grade because of increased difficulty or responsibility of the duties, the change is made.

Efficiency Counts

At intervals, employees are rated on their job performance. In most agencies, the ratings are "outstanding," "satisfactory," and "unsatisfactory."

Employees with "outstanding" ratings receive extra credit for retention in layoffs. An employee whose rating is "unsatisfactory" may be dismissed or assigned to another position with duties which he or she can be expected to learn to do satisfactorily.

Incentive Awards

Government agencies encourage their employees to suggest better or simpler ways, or more economical ways, of doing their jobs. They may give a cash award to an employee for a suggestion or invention that results in money savings or improved service. They may also reward outstanding job performance or other acts that are deserving of recognition.

Vacation and Sick Leave

Most Federal employees earn annual leave for vacation and other purposes, according to the number of years (civilian plus creditable military service) they have been in the Federal service. They earn it at the rate of 13 days a year for the first 3 years of service and 20 days a year for the next 12 years of service. After 15 years, they earn 26 days of annual leave each year.

Sick leave is earned at the rate of 13 days a year. You can use this leave for illnesses serious enough to keep you away from your work and for appointments with a doctor, dentist, or optician. Sick leave that is not used can be saved for future use.

Injury Compensation

The government provides liberal compensation benefits, including medical care, for employees who suffer injuries in the performance of official duty. Death benefits are also provided if an employee dies as a result of such injuries.

Group Life Insurance

As a Federal employee, you may have low-cost term life insurance without taking a physical examination. Two kinds of insurance are provided: (1) life insurance, and (2) accidental death and dismemberment insurance.

Health Benefits

The government sponsors a voluntary health insurance program for Federal employees. The program offers a variety of plans to meet individual needs, including basic coverage and major medical protection against costly illnesses. The government contributes part of the cost of premiums and the employee pays the balance through payroll deductions.

Retirement

Seven percent of a career or career-conditional employee's salary goes into a retirement fund. This seven percent comes out of every paycheck. This money is withheld as the employee's share of the cost of providing him or her or his/her survivors with an income after the employee has completed his or her working career.

Federal employees hired after 1/1/83 are required to enroll in social security. Their retirement benefits will be based on a combination of social security benefits plus pension benefits. Your appointing officer will advise you of the amount of projected benefits and the percentage of your salary which will be deducted to provide for this retirement.

If you leave the government before you complete five years of service, the money you put into the retirement fund can be returned to you. If you leave after completing five years of service, you have a choice of having your money returned or leaving it in the fund. If you leave it in the fund, you will get an annuity starting when you are age 62.

Holidays

Government workers are entitled to the following ten regular holidays each year:

- New Year's Day, January 1
- Martin Luther King's Birthday, third Monday in January
- Washington's Birthday, third Monday in February
- Memorial Day, last Monday in May
- Independence Day, July 4
- Labor Day, first Monday in September
- Columbus Day, second Monday in October
- Veterans Day, November 11
- Thanksgiving Day, fourth Thursday in November
- Christmas Day, December 25

When Inauguration Day falls on a regularly scheduled workday, employees in the Washington metropolitan area get an extra holiday.

Glossary of Selected Federal Personnel Terms

Affirmative Action—A policy that requires Federal agencies to take positive steps to insure equal opportunity in employment, development, advancement, and treatment of all employees and applications for employment regardless of race, color, sex, religion, age, national origin, or physical or mental handicap. Affirmative Action also requires that specific actions be directed at the special problems and unique concerns in assuring equal employment opportunity for minorities and women.

Agency—Any department or independent estab-lishment of the Federal Government, including a Government-owned or controlled corporation.

Application forms—Documents, usually the Standard Form 171 and supplementary forms, completed by persons seeking Federal employment. The forms require information about the applicant's qualifications for the positions for which he or she is applying and about his or her suitability for Federal service.

Appointment—The process of selecting a person and assigning him or her to a position.

Appointment, career-conditional—The tenure of a permanent employee who has not yet completed three years of creditable, substantially continuous Federal service.

Appointment, competitive—Employment of a person after competition with others for the same position. Includes appointments from the register, some appointments from the applicant supply file, and most appointments under the Merit Promotion Program.

Appointment, noncompetitive—Employment without competing with others, in the sense that it is done without regard to OPM registers or the priorities of applicant supply files. Includes reinstatements, transfers, reassignments, demotions, and some promotions.

Career—Tenure of a permanent employee in the competitive service who has completed three years of substantially continuous creditable Federal service.

Certificate—A list of eligibles ranked, according to regulations, for appointment or promotion consideration. A more useful term is "candidate list."

Competitive service—Federal positions normally filled through open competitive examination (hence the term "competitive service") under civil service rules and regulations. About 62 percent of all Federal positions are in the competitive service.

Eligible—Any applicant for appointment or

promotion who meets the minimum qualification requirements.

Entrance level position—A position in an occupation at the beginning level grade.

Examination—A means of measuring, in a practical and suitable manner, qualifications of applicants for employment in specific positions.

Federal Personnel Manual (FPM)—The official publication containing Federal personnel regulations and guidance. Also contains the code of Federal civil service law, selected Executive orders pertaining to Federal employment, and civil service rules.

General Schedule (GS)—The graded pay system as presented by Chapter 51 of Title 5, United States Code, for classifying positions.

Grade—All classes of positions which, although different with respect to kind or subject matter of work, are sufficiently equivalent as to (1) level of difficulty and responsibility, and (2) level of qualification requirements of the work to warrant the inclusion of such classes of positions within one range of rates of basic compensation.

Job title—The formal name of a position as determined by official classification standards.

Journeyman level (full performance level)—The lowest level of a career ladder position at which an employee has learned the full range of duties in a specific occupation. All jobs below full performance level are developmental levels, through which each employee in the occupation may progress to full performance.

Leave, annual—Time allowed to employees for vacation and other absences for personal reasons.

Merit promotion program—The system under which agencies consider an employee for internal personnel actions on the basis of personal merit.

Personnel action—The process necessary to appoint, separate, reinstate, or make other changes affecting an employee (e.g., change in position, assignment, tenure, etc.).

Position—A specific job consisting of all the current major duties and responsibilities assigned or delegated by management.

Position classification—Analyzing and categorizing jobs by occupational group, series, class, and grade according to like duties, responsibilities, and qualification requirements.

Position description—An official written statement of the major duties, responsibilities, and supervisory relationships of a position.

Preference, Compensable Disability ("CP")—Ten-point preference awarded to a veteran separated under honorable conditions from active duty, who receives compensation of 10 percent or more for a service connected disability. Eligible "CP" veterans are placed at the top of civil service lists of eligibles for positions at GS-9 or higher.

Preference, 30 Percent or More, Disability ("CPS")—A disabled veteran whose disability is rated at 30 percent or more, entitled to special preference in appointment and during reduction in force.

Preference, Disability ("XP")—Ten-point preference in hiring for a veteran separated under honorable conditions from active duty and who has a service-connected disability or receives compensation, pension, or disability retirement from the VA or a uniformed service.

Preference, Mother ("XP")—Ten-point preference to which the mother of a deceased or disabled military veteran may be entitled.

Preference, Spouse ("XP")—Ten-point preference to which a disabled military veteran's spouse may be entitled.

Preference, Tentative ("TP")—Five-point veteran preference tentatively awarded an eligible who served on active duty during specified periods and was separated from military service under honorable conditions. It must be verified by the appointing officer.

Preference, Veteran—The statutory right to special advantage in appointment or separations;

based on a person's discharge under honorable conditions from the armed forces, for a service-connected disability. Not applicable to the Senior Executive Service.

Preference, Widow or Widower ("XP")—Ten-point preference to which a military veteran's widow or widower may be entitled.

Probationary period—A trial period which is a condition of the initial competitive appointment. Provides the final indispensable test of ability, that of actual performance on the job.

Promotion—A change of an employee to a higher grade when both the old and new positions are under the same job classification system and pay schedule, or to a position with higher pay in a different job classification system and pay schedule.

Promotion, career—Promotion of an employee without current competition when: (1) he or she had earlier been competitively selected from a register or under competitive promotion procedures for an assignment intended as a matter of record to be preparation for the position being filled; or (2) the position is reconstituted at a higher grade because of additional duties and responsibilities.

Promotion, competitive—Selection of a current or former Federal civil service employee for a higher grade position, using procedures that compare the candidates on merit.

Qualification Review Board (QRB)—A panel normally used to evaluate and group candidates for positions to be filled under the Merit Promotion Program.

Register—A list of eligible applicants compiled in the order of their relative standing for referral to Federal jobs, after competitive civil service examination.

Senior Executive Service—A separate personnel system for persons who set policy and administer programs at the top levels of the government (equivalent to GS-16 through Executive Level IV).

Standard Form 171 (Personal Qualifications Statement)—Used in applying for a Federal position through a competitive examination.

Office of Personnel Management Federal Job Information Centers

Contact the Federal Job Information Center which is nearest the location where you would like to work for information on the job opportunities in that area and the forms needed to apply.

Alabama
Huntsville:
Building 600, Suite 341
3322 Memorial Pkwy.,
South,
35801-5311
(205) 544-5803

Alaska
Anchorage:
222 W. 7th Ave., #22
99513-7572
(907) 271-5821

Arizona
Phoenix:
Century Plaza Bldg.,
Rm. 1415
3225 N. Central Ave.,
85012
(602) 640-5800

Arkansas
(See Oklahoma Listing)

California
Los Angeles:
Linder Bldg., 3rd Floor
845 S. Figueroa, 90017
(213) 894-3360

Sacramento:
4695 Watt Ave.,
North Entrance
95660-5592
(916) 551-1464

San Diego:
Federal Bldg.,
Room 4-S-9
880 Front St., 92188
(619) 557-6165

San Francisco:
P.O. Box 7405, 94120
(Located at 211 Main
St., 2nd Floor, Room
235)
(415) 744-5627

Colorado
Denver:
P.O. Box 25167, 80225
(303) 969-7050
(Located at 12345
W. Alameda Pkwy.,
Lakewood)

For Job Information
(24 hours a day) in the
following States, dial:

Montana:
(303) 969-7052

Utah:
(303) 969-7053

Wyoming:
(303) 969-7054

*For forms and local
supplements, dial:*
(303) 969-7055

Connecticut
Hartford:
Federal Bldg.,
Room 613
450 Main St., 06103
(203) 240-3096 or 3263

Delaware
(See Philadelphia
Listing)

District of Columbia
Metro Area:
1900 E St., N.W.,
Room 1416
20415
(202) 606-2700

Florida
Orlando:
Commodore Bldg.,
Suite 150
3444 McCrory Pl.,
32803-3701
(407) 648-6148

Georgia
Atlanta:
Richard B. Russell
Federal Bldg.,
Room 956, 75 Spring
St. S.W., 30303
(404) 331-4315

Hawaii
Honolulu (and other
Hawaiian Islands
and Overseas):
Federal Bldg.,
Room 5316

300 A'la Moana Blvd.,
96850
(808) 541-2791
Overseas Jobs - (808)
541-2784

Idaho
(See Washington
Listing)

Illinois
Chicago:
175 W. Jackson Blvd.,
Room 530
60604
(312) 353-6192
(For Madison and St.
Clair Counties, see St.
Louis, MO listing)

Indiana
Indianapolis:
Minton-Capehart
Federal Bldg.,
575 N. Pennsylvania St.,
46204
(317) 226-7161
(For Clark, Dearborn,
and Floyd Counties, see
Ohio listing)

Iowa
(816) 426-7757
(For Scott County see
Illinois listing; for
Pottawatamie County,
see Kansas listing)

Kansas
Wichita:
One-Twenty Bldg.,
Room 101
120 S. Market St.,
67202
(316) 269-6794
(For Johnson,
Leavenworth, and
Wyandotte Counties,
dial (816) 426-5702)

Kentucky
(See Ohio listing; for
Henderson County, see
Indiana listing)

Louisiana
New Orleans:
1515 Poydras St.,
Suite 608, 70112
(504) 589-2764

Maine
(See New Hampshire
Listing)

Maryland
Baltimore:
Garmatz Federal
Building
101 W. Lombard Street,
21201
(301) 962-3822

Massachusetts
Boston:
Thos. P. O'Neill, Jr.
Federal Bldg.
10 Causeway St., 02222-
1031
(617) 565-5900

Michigan
Detroit:
477 Michigan Ave.,
Rm. 565, 48226
(313) 226-6950

Minnesota
Twin Cities:
Federal Building,
Room 501
Ft. Snelling,
Twin Cities, 55111
(612) 725-3430

Mississippi
(See Alabama Listing)

Missouri
Kansas City:
Federal Building,
Rm. 134
601 E. 12th Street,
64106
(816) 426-5702
(For Counties west of
and including Mercer,
Grundy, Livingston,
Carroll, Saline, Pettis,
Benton, Hickory,

Dallas, Webster,
Douglas, and Ozark)

St. Louis:
400 Old Post Office
Bldg.
815 Olive St., 63101
(314) 539-2285
(For all other Missouri
Counties not listed
under Kansas City
above)

Montana
(See Colorado Listing)

Nebraska
(See Kansas Listing)

Nevada
(See Sacramento, CA
Listing)

New Hampshire
Portsmouth:
Thomas J. McIntyre
Federal Bldg.
Room 104
80 Daniel Street, 03801-
3879
(603) 431-7115

New Jersey
Newark:
Peter W. Rodino, Jr.,
Federal Bldg.
970 Broad Street, 07102
(201) 645-3673
*In Camden, dial (215)
597-7440*

New Mexico
Albuquerque:
Federal Building
421 Gold Avenue.
S.W., 87102
(505) 766-5583

New York
New York City:
Jacob K. Javits Federal
Bldg.
26 Federal Plaza, 10278
(212) 264-0422

Syracuse:
James M. Hanley
Federal Building
100 S. Clinton Street,
13260
(315) 423-5660

North Carolina
Raleigh:
P.O. Box 25069
4505 Falls of the Neuse
Rd.
Suite 445, 27611-5069
(919) 856-4361

North Dakota
(See Minnesota Listing)

Ohio
Dayton:
Federal Building,
Rm. 506
200 W. 2nd Street,
45402
(513) 225-2720
(For Van Wort,
Auglaize, Hardin,
Marion, Crawford,
Richland, Ashland,
Wayne, Stark, Carroll,
Columbiana Counties,
and all Counties north
of these, see Michigan
listing)

Oklahoma
Oklahoma City:
(Mail or phone only)
200 N. W. Fifth St.,
2nd Floor, 73102
(405) 231-4948
TDD- (405) 231-4614
For Forms, dial (405)
231-5208

Oregon
Portland:
Federal Bldg.,
Room 376
1220 S.W. Third Ave.,
97204
(503) 321-3141, or
326-3304

Pennsylvania
Harrisburg:
Federal Bldg.,
Room 168
P.O. Box 761, 17108
(717) 782-4494

Philadelphia:
Wm. J. Green, Jr.,
Federal Bldg.
600 Arch Street, 19106
(215) 597-7440

Pittsburgh:
Federal Building
1000 Liberty Ave.,
Rm. 119, 15222
(412) 644-2755

Puerto Rico
San Juan:
Federico Degetau
Federal Building
Carlos E. Chardon
Street
Hato Rey, P. R. 00918
(809) 766-5242

Rhode Island
(See Connecticut listing)

South Carolina
(See Raleigh, NC
Listing)

South Dakota
(See Minnesota Listing)

Tennessee
Memphis:
200 Jefferson Avenue
Suite 1312, 38103-2335
(901) 521-3956

Texas
Dallas:
(Mail or phone only)
1100 Commerce St.,
Rm. 6B12, 75242
(214) 767-8035

Houston:
(Phone recording only)
(713) 226-2375

San Antonio:
8610 Broadway,
Rm. 305, 78217
(512) 229-6611 or 6600

Utah
(See Colorado Listing)

Vermont
(See New Hampshire
Listing)

Virginia
Norfolk:
Federal Building,
Room 500
200 Granby St., 23510-
1886
(804) 441-3355

Washington
Seattle:
Federal Building
915 Second Ave., 98174
(206) 442-4365

West Virginia
Phone only:
(513) 225-2866

Wisconsin
For Dane, Grant,
Green, Iowa, Lafayette,
Rock, Jefferson,
Walworth, Milwaukee,
Waukesha, Racine, and
Kenosha Counties call
(312) 353-6189
(For all other Wisconsin
Counties not listed
above, see Minnesota
listing)

Wyoming
(See Colorado Listing)

**Career America College
Hotline**
1-900-990-9200 (A fee
call - 40 cents per
minute)

FEDERAL JOBS OVERSEAS

INTRODUCTION

United States citizens are employed by the Federal Government in Alaska, Hawaii, United States territories, and in foreign countries. They are found in almost every occupational field. They are construction and maintenance workers, doctors, nurses, teachers, technical experts, mining engineers, meteorologists, clerks, stenographers, typists, geologists, skilled tradesmen, social workers, agricultural marketing specialists, and agricultural and other economists.

Current needs of agencies with jobs to fill are generally limited to highly qualified and hard-to-find professional personnel, skilled technicians, and, in some cases, stenographers and clerical and administrative personnel. A few agencies are seeking experienced teachers, librarians, nurses, and medical personnel. However, a few vacancies occur in most fields from time to time because of normal turnover in personnel.

HOW JOBS ARE FILLED

In Alaska, Hawaii, and United States territories, most vacancies are filled by the appointment of local eligibles who qualify in competitive Civil Service examinations which are announced and held in the local area. Normally, there is a sufficient local labor market to fill the needs and examinations are not publicized outside the local areas. Some positions, however, may be filled by transferring career Government employees from the United States mainland.

When a vacancy is to be filled in a foreign country, determination is made whether to recruit from among persons in the area where the job is located or to seek qualified applicants residing in the United States. If the position is to be filled locally, the appointee may be a United States citizen residing or traveling in the area, the wife or dependent of a citizen employed or stationed in the area, or a foreign national.

In most instances where United States installations are established in foreign countries, either formal or informal agreements have been drawn up assuring the host government that local nationals will be employed wherever possible in order to be of maximum assistance to the economy of that country. Furthermore, it is almost always to the economic advantage of the United States to employ foreign nationals at local pay rates without responsibility for travel costs and overseas cost-of-living allowances. Positions held by foreign nationals are in the excepted service and are not subject to the competitive requirements of the Civil Service Act and Office of Personnel Management rules.

COMPETITIVE SERVICE POSITIONS

However, there are many thousands of technical, administrative, and supervisory positions in which United States citizens are employed in foreign countries. These positions are usually in the competitive service, and as vacancies occur they are filled in most cases by transferring career Government employees from the United States. This is the case in the Department of Defense, the largest employer of overseas personnel, and in most other agencies having overseas positions. When Government employees are not available for transfer overseas, and qualified United States citizens cannot be recruited locally, these vacancies are filled through the regular competitive examining process.

Approximately 30 examinations now open on a nationwide basis are being used, as recruiting needs require, to fill overseas positions. The examinations cover a variety of business and economics, engineering and scientific, medical, social and educational, and trades positions. Qualified persons interested in overseas assignments in these fields should establish eligibility under appropriate examinations. Applications and copies of examination announcements can be obtained from Federal Job Information Centers.

EXCEPTED SERVICE POSITIONS

Some positions are excepted from the competitive requirements of the Civil Service rules and regulations. Included in this group are positions in the Foreign Service of the Department of State, dependents' school teachers, positions in the attache offices, and most positions of clerk-translator, translator, and interpreter. Applications for these positions should be made directly to the agency in which employment is desired.

A description of the principal agencies which employ personnel outside the United States, with the addresses to which inquiries or applications should be sent, begins on page 17.

CONDITIONS OF EMPLOYMENT

PHYSICAL REQUIREMENTS

Applicants for most overseas positions must be able to pass rigid physical examinations, since employees may be required to serve under extremely difficult living conditions and, in some areas, at posts where complete medical facilities are not available. Physical standards are applied which are suitable for the location and occupation involved, and may include standards of mental and emotional stability and maturity.

Any physical defect which would make the employee a hazard to himself or to others, or prevent efficient performance of the duties of the position, is disqualifying. Conditions which require periodic medical care, hospitalization, special foods or medicine may be disqualifying for some areas.

Accompanying dependents may also be required to pass rigid physical examinations.

TOUR OF DUTY

Individuals selected in the United States for overseas employment generally are required to sign a transportation agreement for a definite period of service, which is usually for a minimum of 36 months. In certain areas the minimum period is 12 or 24 months.

INVESTIGATION

All appointments are subject to satisfactory security, character, and suitability investigations. Applicants considered for appointment are carefully screened, and only those possessing suitable qualifications are selected for overseas employment.

> Since most Federal jobs overseas are filled by local residents or by the transfer of people who already work for the Government, opportunities for appointment to an overseas position are extremely limited.

GENERAL INFORMATION

QUALIFICATIONS

Generally, the qualification requirements are the same as those established for like positions in the United States. Applicants may, however, be required to meet certain additional or higher standards. A foreign language capability, while not required in all, or even most, Federal jobs overseas, would obviously be a valuable qualification.

DEPENDENTS

For middle and upper-level positions in what may be broadly termed "professional occupations," most agencies permit employees to take their families with them. In certain other job categories, and in accordance with an established system of priorities, it is usually possible to arrange for dependents to follow from several months to a year after the employee has arrived at the overseas post.

For most clerical and secretarial positions abroad, agencies prefer single persons without dependents.

Appointments of both husband and wife are very infrequent, since there rarely are simultaneous vacancies in which their qualifications could be appropriately utilized at the same post. However, in foreign countries with a large American presence, both governmental and private-industrial, qualified U.S. citizens are sometimes needed for a variety of job openings. In the majority of cases, dependents of U.S. Government employees overseas are given priority consideration for such employment.

SALARY

Generally, overseas white-collar workers are paid the same base salaries as Federal employees in the United States occupying similar positions. In addition, where warranted by conditions at the post, they receive a post differential or cost-of-living allowance. In foreign areas, the wages of blue-collar workers are based upon continental United States rates plus, in some cases, a post differential or cost-of-living allowance; in United States areas overseas, their wages may be set in a similar way or they may be based on local rates.

QUARTERS ALLOWANCES

In foreign areas, employees are sometimes housed in Government quarters. If Government housing is not provided, a quarters allowance is paid which covers in large part the cost of rent and utilities. In most United States areas, Government quarters are not provided and no quarters allowance is paid.

FEDERAL EMPLOYMENT BENEFITS

In general, Federal employees are entitled to such liberal benefits as paid vacations, sick leave with pay, and retirement coverage. They are eligible for life insurance and health benefits partially financed by the Government. Employees serving overseas also normally receive special benefits such as free travel for themselves and their dependents, free transportation or storage for their household goods, and additional paid vacations with free travel to their homes in the United States between tours of duty. Also, the United States Government operates dependents' schools in many areas and provides educational opportunities for children which are comparable to those offered in the better schools in the United States.

VETERAN PREFERENCE

Veterans must be given consideration by appointing officers in the filling of overseas positions in accordance with the provisions of the Veterans' Preference Act.

AGENCIES EMPLOYING OVERSEAS PERSONNEL

This section indicates the kinds of positions for which these agencies may be recruiting and lists addresses to which inquiries about employment opportunities may be sent. (Persons who have never worked for the Government should also contact the Office of Personnel Management for information about competitive examinations.)

The largest employers of overseas personnel include the Departments of State, Army, Navy, Air Force, Interior, Commerce, and Agriculture, the International Communications Agency, the Agency for International Development, and the Panama Canal Company-Canal Zone Government.

DEPARTMENT OF AGRICULTURE

The Foreign Agricultural Service assigns agricultural attaches and secretaries to staff its offices at foreign posts. These personnel analyze and report on production, trade and consumption of agricultural commodities and work to develop foreign markets for U.S. farm products. Professional positions normally are filled by Department of Agriculture employees trained in agricultural marketing and agricultural economics. Appointments are initially made from the Administrative Careers with America (ACWA) exam and from specialized examinations for Agricultural Economist and Agricultural Marketing Specialist. Secretarial positions are generally filled by transferring persons already employed by the Department of Agriculture; otherwise, vacancies are filled by appointment from the Office of Personnel Management's list of eligibles in the clerk-stenographer examination, followed by a training program in Washington, D.C. Additional information may be obtained from the Personnel Division, Foreign Agricultural Service, Department of Agriculture, Washington, D.C. 20250.

DEPARTMENT OF THE AIR FORCE

The Air Force uses the Department of Defense Overseas Employment Program (OEP) as the primary source of candidates in filling its overseas positions. Although first consideration is given to qualified employees currently serving at Air Force installations in the United States, employees of other Federal agencies are also considered if sufficient well-qualified candidates are not available within the Air Force. Government employees or former employees having reinstatement eligibility and interested in registering in the OEP should contact the Civilian Personnel Officer at the nearest Department of Defense installation. When well-qualified employees are not available through the OEP, vacancies are filled from the appropriate Civil Service register through the regular competitive examining process.

DEPARTMENT OF THE ARMY

Civilian positions with the Army overseas are frequently filled through reassignment of current Army employees from the United States; however, employees of other Federal agencies, or former Federal service employees with reinstatement eligibility, may also submit applications. Administrative, technical and professional positions are those most often available. The U.S. Army Corps of Engineers accepts applications from career/career conditional employees with expertise in engineering design and construction. Department of the Army does not normally recruit for overseas positions in trades and crafts, equipment operation or general labor. These positions are normally filled by citizens of the host country or by private U.S. contractors. Clerical positions (including clerk typists/steno and secretarial) are also usually filled locally overseas. Dependents of military and civilian personnel stationed in the overseas area receive preferential consideration for these positions if qualified. Applications (completed Standard Form 171, Personal Qualifications Statement) or inquiries regarding employment should be submitted to the appropriate recruiting office below:

Europe, Middle East and Africa:
> USAREUR Civilian Recruitment Office
> Attention: AEAGA-CRC
> APO New York 09403

Far East:
> Civilian Personnel Center, Hawaii
> WESTPAC Support Office
> P.O. Box 50148
> Honolulu, Hawaii 96850

Alaska and Panama:
> Civilian Personnel Office
> HQ FORSCOM
> Attention: AFPR-CPS
> Fort McPherson, Georgia 30330

Army Corps of Engineers

Europe:
> Office, Chief of Engineers
> Attention: DAEN-PEC-E
> Pulaski Building
> 20 Massachusetts Ave. N.W.
> Washington, D.C. 20314

Far East:
> Civilian Personnel Center, Hawaii
> WESTPAC Support Office
> P.O. Box 50148
> Honolulu, Hawaii 96850

Saudi Arabia:
> U.S. Army Engineer Division, Middle East (Rear)
> Attention: MEDPO-S
> P.O. Box 2250
> Winchester, Va. 22601

Israel:
> U.S. Army Engineer Division, North Atlantic
> Attention: NADPE
> 90 Church Street
> New York, N.Y. 10007

DEPARTMENT OF THE NAVY

Vacancies are principally filled through the assignment of well-qualified Navy and Marine Corps career employees desiring to serve overseas. Primary recruitment sources are Department of the Navy career programs and the Department of Defense Overseas Employment Program (OEP). When recruitment from other sources is necessary, it is mainly for positions in engineering, science, skilled trades, accounting and auditing, and administration.

For information about appointment or assignment to overseas positions, see the Civilian Personnel Officer at the nearest Navy or Marine Corps installation.

DEPARTMENT OF DEFENSE

Employment opportunities are available for educators with the Department of Defense Dependents Schools.

The Department of Defense maintains a school system from kindergarten through grade 12 for the dependent children of military and civilian personnel stationed abroad. School year salaries for educators are comparable to the average rates for similar positions in school systems in U.S. districts having a population of 100,000 or more. Transportation and housing allowances are provided. Qualification requirements include completion of a baccalaureate degree with a minimum of 18 semester hours in the field of professional education to include student teaching and 1 full school year of professional employment as a teacher within the past 5 years. For information about teaching positions overseas, send a postcard to the Department of Defense Dependents, 2461 Eisenhower Avenue, Alexandria, Va. 22331.

U.S. DEPARTMENT OF COMMERCE

National Oceanic and Atmospheric Administration-Overseas positions are available for persons with meteorological or electronics backgrounds at weather stations maintained in Alaska, Puerto Rico, Mexico, Hawaii, Wake Island, Guam, Johnson Island, American Samoa, and the Trust Territories. Positions exist for persons with appropriate education or experience in geophysics at observatories located in Alaska, Hawaii, and American Samoa. There are a few positions available in the Antarctic for electronics engineers, technicians and physical scientists who have specialized experience in atmospheric research. Qualified persons interested in any of these positions should address inquiries to the Personnel Officer, National Oceanic and Atmospheric Administration, Washington, D.C. 20852.

DEPARTMENT OF TRANSPORTATION

Federal Highway Administration—Highway design, planning, construction, maintenance, and bridge engineers and specialists with experience in the administration and supervision of the operation and repair of highway construction equipment provide technical assistance to countries in connection with the Government's overseas technical aid program. Experienced persons interested in overseas employment should send inquiries to the Office of Personnel and Training, Federal Highway Administration, Washington, D.C. 20590.

DEPARTMENT OF THE INTERIOR

Most of the positions are in Alaska. Almost all of these positions have been brought into the competitive service. Vacancies occur from time to time in engineering, metallurgy, geology, forestry, and teaching (elementary) positions. The jobs are usually filled through competitive examinations announced by the Office of Personnel Management. For more information about employment opportunities, address inquiries to the Department of the Interior, Washington, D.C. 20240.

DEPARTMENT OF STATE

The Foreign Service of the United States, administered by the Department of State, recruits personnel for the career Foreign Service Officer Corps. Career Foreign Service Officers fill virtually all professional positions in the over 250 embassies and consulates maintained by the United States in more than 100 countries throughout the world. Officers serve primarily in one of the four functional specializations within the Department of State: Administration, consular affairs, economic/commercial, or political work. The Department of State is interested in personnel with training in diverse fields including political science, economics, public and business administration as well as experience in business, government and organizations involved in international activities. Appointments are made from among those who take competitive Foreign Service Officer examinations. Candidates for these examinations must be at least 21 years of age, except that candidates may apply at 20 years of age. Inquiries regarding these examinations should be addressed to the Board of Examiners for the Foreign Service, Department of State, Box 9317, Rosslyn Station, Arlington, Va. 22209.

There is a continuing need for secretaries, communications officers and communications technicians in the Foreign Service to staff the embassies and consulates throughout the world. Requests for information regarding opportunities and qualifications for employment in positions listed above should be addressed to the General Recruitment Branch, Recruitment Division, U.S. Department of State, Washington, D.C. 20520.

AGENCY FOR INTERNATIONAL DEVELOPMENT

The Agency for International Development (AID) is the principal administrator of U.S. economic and technical assistance to the developing countries of Africa, Asia, Latin America and the Near East.

To administer these development programs, AID relies upon a staff of highly skilled men and women with postgraduate degrees in a number of technical and professional disciplines. While employment opportunities vary from country to country and time to time, the most frequent needs are for agriculturists, public health physicians, economists, accountants, financial managers, auditors, contract specialists, family planning/population specialists, and nutritionists.

Many Foreign Service officers join AID in mid-level or senior-level positions. Others are recruited at the junior officer entry level as International Development Interns. The Interns are young men and women who have graduate degrees in the relevant disciplines and have had some working experience. Training is provided in Washington, D.C., and at overseas missions. Appropriate education and experience are the decisive criteria in the selection of candidates for both professional and intern positions. U.S. citizenship is a requirement.

Requests for information should be addressed to Chief, Recruitment Staff, Office of Personnel, Agency for International Development, Washington, D.C. 20523.

PANAMA CANAL COMMISSION

The efficient operation of the Panama Canal Commission is of vital importance to world trade. Applications are accepted from qualified ship pilots, towboat masters, towboat and dredge engineers and from most skilled craftsmen. Mail SF 171 or inquiries to U.S. Recruitment and Placement Assistance Section, Office of Personnel Administration, Panama Canal Commission, APO Miami 34011.

THE PEACE CORPS (ACTION)

The Peace Corps provides opportunities for skilled Americans to serve in developing nations overseas. Its purpose is threefold: to give help where help is needed, to promote a better understanding of the American abroad, and to sharpen the Americans' image of other peoples.

Tours of duty are approximately for 2 years, including several months of training received before overseas departure. Volunteers receive a living allowance to provide for food, housing, clothing and incidentals, and a readjustment allowance.

While most of the volunteers work in educational and community development programs, there are positions available in more than 300 separate skill areas. A college degree is not required. Beyond teaching and community development, demands are greatest for volunteers experienced in the fields of public health, agriculture, home economics, mechanics, construction, and social work.

Applicants must be at least 18 years of age and American citizens. Although the minimum age for volunteers is 18, very few applicants under 20 have the skills and experience to qualify. Married couples are eligible if they have no dependents under 18. There is no upper age limit.

For further information on opportunities for service, and instructions for application, contact the Peace Corps office in your state or write the Office of Recruitment and Communications, Peace Corps, Room p-305, Washington, D.C. 20525.

INTERNATIONAL COMMUNICATIONS AGENCY
(Formerly USIA)

Generally, all but a few specialized positions are filled from within the ranks of ICA's career Foreign Service. Entry into the Foreign Service Information Officer corps is open to individuals over 21 years of age under the Junior Officer Program. Candidates must participate in a competitive process involving both comprehensive written and oral examinations. Information about the next examination can be obtained from the Board of Examiners for the Foreign Service, Department of State, Box 9317, Rosslyn Station, Arlington, VA 22209.

As needed, the Agency may recruit experienced professionals for information and cultural work overseas. They are appointed as Foreign Service Limited Reserve Officers for a maximum of 5 years. They are eligible to apply for career status (FSIO) after 3 years in the Limited Reserve.

Candidates for the Foreign Service must have a knowledge of American foreign policy and international relations, and a solid background in the historical, political, economic and cultural development of the United States. They must possess an ability to communicate convincingly and tactfully, both orally and in writing. A good working command of a foreign language and an ability to learn foreign languages are useful. Candidates must be willing to serve in any country and at any post.

Opportunities for serving overseas also exist for secretaries. Applicants must be at least 21 years of age, be able to take shorthand at 80 words per minute, type at 50 words per minute, and have 3 years' secretarial or stenographic experience or 2 years of business school or college.

For additional information, write to the Recruitment and Examining Division, International Communications Agency, 1776 Pennsylvania Avenue, Washington, D.C. 20547. Standard Form 171 (Personal Qualifications Statement) should be submitted to this address when applying for a position with ICA (except for the Junior Officer Program; see above).

FEDERAL JOB INFORMATION CENTERS

The Office of Personnel Management offers Federal employment information through Federal Job Information Centers located in several major metropolitan areas across the country. They are listed under "U.S. Government" in the blue pages of local phone directories. In addition, Federal job opportunities are posted in local State Job Service (or State Employment Security) offices.

A call can save you time and unnecessary effort if you want to obtain application forms, announcements and other general types of information.

For specific information on possible openings in overseas areas, you should write:

For Pacific areas:

> Honolulu Area Office
> Office of Personnel Management
> 1000 Bishop Street, Suite 1500
> Honolulu, Hawaii 96813

For Atlantic areas:

> Washington Area Office
> Office of Personnel Management
> 1900 E Street, N.W.
> Washington, D.C. 20415

PATRONAGE AND "EXCEPTED" JOBS

Although the merit system for selecting employees is talked about a good deal, it is not practiced throughout the government. Patronage and political considerations control selection of certain public employees, particularly those in the more responsible and higher-paying positions. Patronage, or the spoils system, is not all bad. Employees and officials chosen by this method are frequently competent and often display a freshness of approach which some authorities maintain is not a common characteristic among competitive employees.

The 14 percent of Federal positions that are excepted from Civil Service requirements number 347,800. Of them, 136,400 are excepted by statute and the remainder by action of the Office of Personnel Management (OPM). Some people believe that all of these are patronage positions; actually, relatively few are true patronage jobs. The Federal Bureau of Investigation and the Central Intelligence Agency, for example, are not likely to be touched by the breath of patronage. And many thousands of temporary positions, and others filled for special duties outside the range of Civil Service requirements, must be maintained in order to uphold the continuity of government functions.

Examples of positions excepted by statute are those in the Foreign Service, on the Atomic Energy Commission, in the Library of Congress, and with the Tennessee Valley Authority.

Nevertheless, there are still left a considerable number of jobs under the spoils system. Several hundred top jobs are open whenever a new regime proceeds with its "housecleaning." A new cabinet is selected, along with Presidential assistants, various agency heads and subheads. The chiefs of commissions and boards are appointed to serve definite terms, but little difficulty is usually encountered if a new President should wish to oust some of these individuals and make room for his own appointees. A quiet Presidential request for resignation is likely in most cases to be honored.

Postmasterships are traditionally plums for the party in power, and all attorneys in the government are under patronage. The OPM has no control over such positions. The lawyer who wants a government job must get it by knowing his political leader or someone else who has political pull; many of the positions go to party workers. Not all the party workers selected for patronage positions are incompetent "clubhouse boys." The leader usually submits several names to the appointing officer, who then has a choice. And it is not common today for the name of a thoroughly incompetent person to be submitted.

The recommendation of college deans, professors, and prominent public figures with "contacts" in Washington are also helpful; knowing an official in an agency is often useful, since he may bring the applicant to the attention of the agency chief.

Appointments in the legislative branch of the Federal Government are not subject to Civil Service requirements. These appointments include all the workers in the Library of Congress, which hires directly, and the various aides—researchers, lawyers, secretaries, messengers, pages, clerks, and guards—to senators and congressmen. Those who want such jobs should get in touch with their representatives in Congress, or talk to their political leader.

Judicial positions in Federal courts are not under Civil Service. These positions include not only those of appointed judges, but marshals, bailiffs, court reporters, referees, probation and parole officers, auditors, and clerks. Here, too, "influence" counts.

RULE VI ("EXCEPTED" APPOINTMENTS)

There is a special rule concerning "excepted" appointments, that is, jobs which are not filled through the usual Civil Service methods. The rule sets down the kinds of positions which may be filled without examination. Rule VI states that certain positions shall be excepted from competitive service "because of their confidential or policy-making character, or because it is not practicable to make appointments through competitive examination." When it is decided (by the OPM) that a position should be "excepted," the title of that position is published in the Federal Register. At the end of each fiscal year the OPM submits to the White House a list of the jobs which have been thus freed of competitive requirements. An "excepted" position does not acquire competitive status.

Excepted positions (a long list of them) include all those which were excluded from competition by the original Civil Service Act of 1883, positions excepted by executive order of the President, positions which may be filled under personal service contract, and positions in government corporations. Veterans are entitled to preference in these positions, as in others, and each agency is supposed to set up proper standards for every excepted position, so that it is not filled by incompetents.

Positions excepted by action of the OPM are placed in 1 of 3 schedules—A, B, or C—after a study of all pertinent facts (such as the duties, pay, and location of the positions) has been made by OPM.

Schedule A is for positions for which it is not practicable to hold any examinations. Examples are: Chaplains, professional and technical experts for temporary consultation purposes, narcotics agents for undercover work, certain part-time positions at isolated localities, and many positions in foreign countries. There are 108,000 positions in this schedule.

Schedule B is for positions for which competitive examinations are impracticable but for which *non-competitive* examinations are given. Examples are positions assigned exclusively to Navy or Air Force Communications Intelligence activities. There are about 2,000 jobs in this schedule.

Schedule C is for positions whose occcupants serve in a policy-determining capacity to the politically appointed heads of agencies or in a confidential capacity to them and their key officials. It was established to more clearly define the career service by setting apart from it positions properly in the political area. It contains key positions which should be filled by the administration in power with persons who will fully support its political aims and policies.

No examination is required for appointment to Schedule C jobs. Departments and agencies have authority to assign duties to any position. They may recommend to OPM that a position be placed in Schedule C if they feel the duties assigned are either policy determining or require the incumbent to serve in a confidential relationship to a key official.

VETERANS' PREFERENCE

A large system of special advantages is available to veterans who seek work with the government, and to those already in Federal jobs. These advantages extend from preferential treatment in getting jobs to preferential treatment if layoffs should occur. Certain disabled veterans' wives, veterans' widows, and veterans' mothers are included in this system of advantages.

Here, in capsule form, are the major privileges which veterans enjoy.

Disabled veterans have 10 points added to the grade they earn on a Civil Service exam. Thus if a disabled vet gets a mark of 70, he or she is granted an additional 10 points—bringing him up to 80 and much closer to the job he or she wants. Non-disabled veterans are granted five additional points.

On any examination, the veteran must make 70 before 5- or 10-point preference is added.

A Federal employee who left his position to enter the armed forces is entitled to his old job back (unless it was a temporary job) or a position of like status, pay, and seniority.

In all positions except scientific and professional positions in grade GS-9 or higher, disabled veterans with a compensable service-connected disability of 10 percent or more go to the top of the lists of those to be appointed.

No appointing officer may pass over a veteran on an Office of Personnel Management certificate of eligibles to appoint a non-veteran without giving his reasons in writing to the OPM.

In making temporary appointments for which no examination is needed, agencies must give consideration first to disabled veterans with a compensable service-connected disability of 10 percent or more, second to other disabled veterans and then to non-disabled veterans before any consideration is given to non-veterans.

When layoffs take place the veteran must be retained longer than the non-veteran. Under the Veteran's Preference Act, veterans who have satisfactory or better performance (efficiency) ratings are retained in preference to all non-veterans, irrespective of their efficiency ratings or length of service, who rate "in competition with them" for retention.

Other privileges are given the veteran. In most examinations, he is granted a waiver of height, weight, and age requirements. He gets credit for experience and training in the armed forces. Under certain conditions an examination already "closed" will be opened for him. His protections against dismissal extend to other disciplinary actions—suspension, furlough without pay, demotion, debarment from future employment. If a veteran, after getting his extra points on an exam, has the same grade as a non-veteran, he is entered ahead of the non-veteran as a job prospect. The veteran isn't required to meet the "members-of-family" rule—the rule that not more than two members of the family living under one roof may hold permanent Federal positions. Nor will he be denied employment in case his state is "over-quota" in the number of its residents in armed forces.

Since January 1979, veterans with service-connected disabilities of 30% or more have received additional benefits, including:

- appointment without competitive examination, with a right to be converted to career apointments, and
- retention rights over other preference eligibles in reductions in-force.

Veterans with disabilities of 30% or more also have the right to be notified in advance and respond to any decision in which:

- they are considered ineligible for a position due to physical requirements of the position;
- they would be passed over by an agency in the course of filling a position from a Civil Service certificate; or
- they are deemed ineligible for retention in a position during a reduction-in-force due to the physical requirements of the position.

On October 1, 1980, veterans' preference was eliminated for non-disabled military retirees who retire from the service at or above the rank of major or its equivalent.

JOBS FOR VETERANS ONLY

Appointments to certain positions are restricted to veteran-preference eligibles. Persons not entitled to preference may file for and compete in examinations for these positions, but their applications will not be rated or referred to agencies for appointment as long as sufficient veterans are available.

Restricted positions include guard, elevator operator, messenger, and custodian.

Restricted positions in the "guard" category include: air corps patrolman; patrolman; building guard; mint guard; private and special officer (Secret Service); chief guard-fire marshall; guard chauffeur; guard-fire-fighter; guard-fireman; guard laborer; guard (U. S. Engineer Department); lieutenant of the guard (Post Office Custodial Service); housemaster (U. S. Naval Academy); parking lot attendant; customs enforcement officer; chief, project police (Public Housing Administration); safety and security chief, Terre Haute Ordnance Depot, Indiana; shipkeeper; and security officer (Bureau of Immigration and Naturalization).

Restricted examinations for custodial positions include: janitor and assistant foreman of janitors; engineman-janitor, head charwoman, laborer, matron, and window cleaner, Post Office Custodial Service; caretaker of abandoned Federal reservation, Federal cemetery, or small military reservation; caretaker-mechanic at inactive military reservation; charman; charwoman; clean-up man, Ordnance Department of the Army; dam tender; fireman-laborer; foreman of laborers (when duties are custodial); headwaiter, kitchen helper, and waiter, Veterans Administration; hospital attendant; hospital servitor; housekeeper (custodial); laborer (custodial); lockman; lockmaster; maid (custodial); matron (custodial); mess attendant; restroom matron; shipkeeper (custodial), U. S. Maritime Commission Reserve Fleets; supervisor of hospital attendants; ward attendant; ward orderly; bridge tender; and maintenance foreman (housing).

Those for elevator operator include elevator starter, Post Office Custodial Service.

Restricted messenger positions do not include special delivery messenger at first-class post offices.

BACKGROUND OF VETERANS' PREFERENCE

It is estimated that about 65 percent of the total number of men working for the government as civilians are veterans of the wars in which the United States has engaged. Eight per cent of all women workers are either veterans themselves or the widows of veterans or the wives of disabled veterans, or the mothers of deceased or disabled veterans. This is the result of a conscious move on the part of the government to grant preference in Federal employment to veterans. Serious concern has been voiced in many quarters concerning the effect of this policy upon the efficiency of the government. It is pointed out that the concept of veterans' preference runs contrary to the concept of merit and fitness in government service; that a veteran has only barely to pass an examination to go to the top of the list, if he has a compensable service-connected disability of 10 percent or more (except for professional and scientific jobs in grade GS-9 or higher) even though others may be far better qualified; that the Federal establishment is tending to become overloaded with veterans; that opportunities for younger people and women in the Federal service are being reduced.

On the other hand it is argued that veterans have lost out in economic competition with those who stayed at home during the wars and that the government owes them an opportunity to make up for this loss; that the number of veterans is so great that the government can be assured of quality personnel; that the need to help the veteran is an overriding consideration; that to get a Federal job the veteran must meet certain minimum standards—and that these standards should be sufficiently high so that those who meet them are qualified for the positions. Moreover it is argued that the nation overwhelmingly desires a system of veterans' preference, although this argument has never been proved.

The policy of granting preference is not a new one. Even before the first Civil Service Act was passed in 1883, when all public jobs were dispensed on a patronage basis, Congress granted job preference to war veterans. The first such statute came one month before the end of the Civil War, in March 1865, giving preference to qualified persons discharged from the armed forces because of disabilities incurred while in service.

During the next half century, Congress increased this preference so that veterans, along with their widows and orphans, received preferential treatment in the matter of discharge when a cut in personnel became necessary. After World War I, Congress granted preference in appointment to jobs in Washington to veterans and veterans' widows and also extended this preference to cover the wives of disabled veterans who could not qualify for appointment because of their disability. Each war has meant increased preference for veterans.

The present system of preference applies to veterans of all wars in which the United States has engaged and certain "peacetime" veterans.

WIVES, WIDOWS AND MOTHERS

The wife of a disabled veteran is entitled to ten-point preference on all examinations, and all other veterans' advantages. She must show these facts to obtain preference: (1) that she is presently married to the veteran; (2) that her husband served on full-time active duty in the armed forces of the United States and received a discharge under honorable conditions; (3) that her husband is disqualified by his existing service-connected disability for Civil Service appointment along the general lines of his usual occupation. Only a Federal medical officer acting for the Office of Personnel Management may make the determination that the veteran on whose service the preference claim is based is disqualified by his service-connected disability for Civil Service appointment along the general lines of his usual occupation. This determination is required for wife preference and for certain claims for mother preference.

The widow of a veteran is entitled to ten-point preference if she meets the following requirements:

1. That she was married to the veteran and was not divorced from him.
2. That the veteran is actually and legally dead and the widow has not remarried since his death, or her remarriage has been annulled.
3. That the veteran had served on full-time active duty in any branch of the armed forces of the United States:
   a. During a war or a national crisis, or
   b. In a campaign or expedition for which a campaign badge (service medal) has been authorized.
4. That the veteran had been separated from such active duty under honorable conditions.

The mother of a veteran who lost his life while serving on active duty during periods listed under 3 in the preceding paragraph may qualify for mother preference if she meets these additional qualifications:

1. That she is, or was, married to the father of the ex-service child and is the natural mother of the ex-service child.
2. That if she is presently living with her husband:
   a. That the father of her ex-service child or the husband of her remarriage, as the case may be, is totally and permanently disabled.
   b. If she is widowed, divorced or separated:
      1. That she is widowed by the death of, or is divorced or separated from, the father of her ex-service child and has not remarried, or
      2. That if she has remarried she has been widowed by the death of, or is divorced or legally separated from, the husband of her remarriage.

The mother of a disabled ex-service son or daughter must meet the following conditions in addition to those listed under 1 and 2 of the preceding paragraph:

1. That the ex-service son or daughter was separated under honorable conditions from full-time active duty performed in any branch of the armed forces of the United States at any time.
2. That her son or daughter is living and has an existing service-connected disability which disqualifies for Civil Service appointment along the general lines of his or her usual occupation.

SOMETIMES PREFERENCE CAN BE LOST

Conditions arise under which a person entitled to veterans' preference can lose it. Examples:

DIVORCE FROM VETERAN: The wife of a veteran loses preference based on his service when she is divorced from him.

REMARRIAGE OF VETERAN'S WIDOW: The widow of a veteran loses preference when she remarries.

RECOVERY FROM DISABILITY: A veteran loses disability preference when he recovers from his disability, or ceases to receive compensation, pension, or disability retirement benefits. The wife of a veteran loses preference when her husband recovers from a service-connected disability. A mother loses her preference when she reunites with the father of her ex-service child, unless said father is permanently and totally disabled, or when she remarries, unless the husband of her remarriage is permanently and totally disabled. The mother of disabled ex-service sons or daughters loses preference when the child dies or recovers from disability to such an extent that he or she is no longer disqualified for Federal employment.

HOW TO SECURE A TEMPORARY JOB

We have learned that veterans get "first crack" at the many temporary positions available in government service. Probably the simplest way to learn about such temporary positions is to write directly to the agency for which you wish to work. Some persons even write to all Federal agencies, asking that they be put on the list for consideration for temporary work in their occupations.

HOW TO CLAIM VETERANS' PREFERENCE

In order to obtain preference the veteran must submit evidence that he or she is entitled to it. A candidate must answer questions about military service when filling out the application and later, when he or she is being considered for appointment, he or she will be required to submit the DD214.

NON-DISABLED VETERAN WHO SERVED IN TIME OF WAR: Claim for five-point preference based on war service is filed by answering the questions on the application form. Later you'll be asked to submit proof of honorable separation from the armed forces.

NON-DISABLED VETERAN WHO SERVED IN CAMPAIGN OR EXPEDITION FOR WHICH CAMPAIGN BADGE WAS AUTHORIZED: Preference goes also to persons who served in various campaigns, as distinguished from wars. If you're among the veterans who served in a campaign or expedition, you'll need to fill out Standard Form 15, which you can obtain at the same office which gives out application blanks. In addition you'll need to submit proof of honorable separation and official notice of the award of the campaign badge.

DISABLED VETERAN: If you are disabled, you file the following documents: Standard Form 15; proof of honorable separation from the armed forces; either an official statement from the Veterans' Administration, Army, Navy, Air Force, Coast Guard, or Public Health Service certifying the existence of a service-connected disability, or an official statement from the Veterans' Administration that you are receiving compensation or an official statement from the Veterans' Administration, Army, Navy, Air Force, Marine Corps, Coast Guard, or Public Health Service certifying that you are receiving disability-retirement benefits.

WIFE: The wife of a disabled veteran must submit the same documents required of the disabled veteran. If the veteran is retired from military service, the official statement should contain information concerning the nature and extent of her husband's disability. This statement will be issued by the service department at the veteran's request.

WIDOW: A widow files the following information: Preference Form 15; proof of her husband's honorable separation from the armed forces.

When the claim is based on service in a campaign or expedition for which a campaign badge has been authorized, she must file with the Office of Personnel Management the veteran's official notification of the award by the military organization in which the service was performed.

She is not required to furnish proof of death except under these special circumstances: If he died in line of duty, she must submit the official notification. If he has disappeared and his death cannot be established she must submit two or more affidavits certifying that he has not been seen or heard from for at least seven years.

MOTHER: The mother of a disabled veteran must submit the same documents required of a disabled veteran.

The mother of a deceased veteran files the following information: Standard Form 15; official notification of the veteran's death in line of duty.

CIVIL SERVICE REFORM ACT

Personnel Practices and Actions in the Federal Government Require:

- Recruitment from all segments of society, and selection and advancement on the basis of ability, knowledge, and skills, under fair and open competition.
- Fair and equitable treatment in all personnel management matters, without regard to politics, race, color, religion, national origin, sex, marital status, age, or handicapping condition, and with proper regard for individual privacy and constitutional rights.
- Equal pay for work of equal value, considering both national and local rates paid by private employers, with incentives and recognition for excellent performance.
- High standards of integrity, conduct, and concern for the public interest.
- Efficient and effective use of the Federal work force.
- Retention of employees who perform well, correcting the performance of those whose work is inadequate, and separation of those who cannot or will not meet required standards.
- Improved performance through effective education and training.
- Protection of employees from arbitrary action, personal favoritism, or political coercion.
- Protection of employees against reprisal for lawful disclosures of information.

Officials and Employees Who Are Authorized to Take Personnel Actions Are Prohibited From:

- Discriminating against any employee or applicant.

- Soliciting or considering any recommendation on a person who requests or is being considered for a personnel action unless the material is an evaluation of the person's work performance, ability, aptitude, or general qualifications, or character, loyalty, and suitability.
- Using official authority to coerce political actions, to require political contributions, or to retaliate for refusal to do these things.
- Willfully deceiving or obstructing an individual as to his or her right to compete for Federal employment.
- Influencing anyone to withdraw from competition, whether to improve or worsen the prospects of any applicant.
- Granting any special preferential treatment or advantage not authorized by law to a job applicant or employee.
- Appointing, employing, promoting, or advancing relatives in their agencies.
- Taking or failing to take a personnel action as a reprisal against employees who exercise their appeal rights; refuse to engage in political activity; or lawfully disclose violations of law, rule, or regulation, or mismanagement, gross waste of funds, abuse of authority, or a substantial and specific danger to public health or safety.
- Taking or failing to take any other personnel action violating a law, rule, or regulation directly related to merit system principles.

The New Organization for Personnel Management

As a result of Reorganization Plan No. 2, the U.S. Civil Service Commission is abolished January 1979, and its functions divided between two new agencies. An Office of Personnel Management (OPM) is to

28

provide leadership in managing the Federal work force. An independent Merit Systems Protection Board (MSPB) is to resolve employee complaints and appeals. A third new agency, the Federal Labor Relations Authority (FLRA), is to administer the Federal labor relations program and investigate unfair labor practices.

The functions of the agencies are described below:

Office of Personnel Management

The Office of Personnel Management helps the President carry out his responsibilities for management of the Federal work force. The Office is headed by a director and deputy director appointed by the President and confirmed by the Senate.

OPM takes over many of the responsibilities of the Civil Service Commission. These include central examining and employment operations, personnel investigations, personnel program evaluation, executive development, and training. OPM also administers the retirement and insurance programs for Federal employees and exercises management leadership in labor relations and affirmative action.

As the central personnel agency, OPM develops policies governing civilian employment in Executive branch agencies and in certain agencies of the Legislative and Judicial branches, and helps agencies carry out these policies. Subject to its standards and review, OPM also delegates certain personnel powers to agency heads.

Merit Systems Protection Board

The Merit Systems Protection Board is the independent agency to safeguard both the merit system and individual employees against abuses and unfair personnel actions. The MSPB is headed by three board members, appointed on a bipartisan basis to 7-year nonrenewable terms. The Board hears and decides employee appeals and orders corrective and disciplinary actions against an employee or agency when appropriate. It also oversees the merit system and reports annually to Congress on how the system is functioning.

Within the MSPB is an independent Special Counsel, appointed by the President for a 5-year term. The Special Counsel has the power to investigate charges of prohibited personnel practices, including reprisals against whistleblowers; to ask MSPB to stop personnel actions in cases involving prohibited personnel practices; and to bring disciplinary charges before the MSPB against those who violate merit system law.

Federal Labor Relations Authority

The Federal Labor Relations Authority oversees the creation of bargaining units, supervises elections, and deals with labor-management issues in Federal agencies. The FLRA is headed by a chairman and two members, who are appointed on a bipartisan basis to staggered 5-year terms.

Within the FLRA, a General Counsel, appointed to a 5-year term, investigates alleged unfair labor practices and prosecutes them before the FLRA. Also within the FLRA and acting as a separate body, the Federal Service Impasses Panel resolves negotiation impasses.

Performance Appraisal Systems

Each agency is to develop and phase-in its own appraisal system(s). Performance appraisals are to be a basis for decisions to train, reward, assign, promote, demote, retain, or remove employees (for reasons other than misconduct). Agencies are encouraged to have employees participate in establishing performance objectives for their jobs.

Specifically, the appraisal systems must make it possible for agencies to:
- advise employees on what the critical elements of their jobs are;
- establish performance standards that will permit accurate evaluation of job performance on the basis of objective, job-related criteria;
- assist employees to improve unacceptable performance; and
- reassign, demote, or remove those employees whose performance continues to be unacceptable, but only after they have been given an opportunity to show that they can perform acceptably and have failed to improve.

Agencies are required to inform employees of the critical elements and performance standards of their jobs.

If any agency proposes to remove or demote an employee because of poor performance, and if that employee's performance becomes acceptable and remains acceptable for one year, the record of the poor performance will be removed from agency files.

Procedures for Adverse Actions and Appeals

Adverse actions, such as removals, suspensions for over 14 days, and reductions in grade or pay, may be appealed to the Merit Systems Protection Board. Employees in organized bargaining units may be able under their negotiated agreements to ask their union to seek arbitration instead of appealing to MSPB.

If an agency proposes to demote or remove an employee because of unacceptable performance, that employee is entitled to:
- receive written notice from the agency 30 days before the proposed action;
- be represented by an attorney or other representative;
- answer orally and in writing within a reasonable time; and
- receive a written decision (agreed to by a higher level supervisor than the one who proposed the action) which states the reason for the action.

An agency's final decision will be provided in writing within 30 days after the end of the notice period.

If an agency decides to demote or remove an employee at the end of the notice period, the employee may appeal to the MSPB for a hearing, or, if within a bargaining unit, the employee may use the grievance arbitration procedure. The agency's decision will be upheld if it is shown by substantial evidence that the employee failed to meet performance standards for one or more critical elements of the job. For adverse actions based on grounds other than poor performance, an agency's decision to remove an employee must be supported by a preponderance of evidence.

An agency's decision will not be upheld if an employee shows that the decision:
- was based on harmful procedural errors on the part of the agency;
- was based on any prohibited personnel practice; or
- was unlawful.

The same standards will apply whether the adverse action is appealed to MSPB or resolved by an arbitrator.

Agencies whose decisions are reversed may be required in certain cases to pay employees for reasonable attorney fees. These payments might occur in cases where agencies engaged in prohibited personnel practices.

Decisions or orders of MPSB are appealable to the U.S. Court of Appeals, or, in matters of pay, the Court of Claims.

Complaints Involving Discrimination

Procedures to handle discrimination complaints in two situations are established.

The first situation includes agency actions which the employee claims were discriminatory and which are of a type that may be appealed to MSPB (e.g. removals and demotions). These are called "mixed cases." An agency has 120 days to try to resolve the discrimination issue by using counseling and investigation. If an employee is not satisfied with the final agency decision, or if time runs out, that employee may appeal to MSPB. Instead of going to MSPB with a "mixed case," the union may call for grievance arbitration.

An employee may not directly appeal a "mixed case" to the Equal Employment Opportunity Commission (EEOC). However, an employee may ask EEOC to review the MSPB decision. Other steps would be followed if EEOC and MSPB do not agree.

The second type of situation includes discrimination complaints about actions or failures to act which are not appealable to MSPB (e.g. promotions or working conditions). In this case, an employee may appeal the final agency action to EEOC, or a union may call for grievance arbitration procedures. Appeals to EEOC will follow the current procedures for processing discrimination complaints. MSPB plays no part in these decisions.

Regardless of whether the decision is made by MSPB,

EEOC, or an arbitrator, an employee will have the right to appeal that decision to a U.S. District Court.

EEOC is also responsible for approving agency goals and timetables in affirmative action plans.

Special Counsel Protections

The Special Counsel to the Merit Systems Protection Board is, in effect, an independent investigator and prosecutor. This individual is appointed by the President for a 5-year term.

Specifically, the Special Counsel investigates charges that agency officials:
- undertook prohibited personnel practices, including reprisals against whistleblowers;
- engaged in prohibited political activity;
- withheld information under the Freedom of Information Act without just reason;
- discriminated in violation of law; or
- carried out activities prohibited by any other civil service law, rule, or regulation.

After these investigations, the Special Counsel may bring disciplinary charges before the MSPB against officials if the evidence shows a probable violation. They may be reprimanded, removed, fined, or barred from Federal employment.

The Special Counsel has authority to protect *whistleblowers*. Whistleblowers are those employees or applicants who expose practices which they reasonably believe to be a violation of law, rule, or regulation, or which they believe constitute mismanagement, gross waste of funds, abuse of authority, or a danger to public health or safety. Employees or applicants who make disclosures specifically prohibited by law or Executive order will not be protected.

The Special Counsel investigates charges of reprisal without revealing the identity of the whistleblower, and may petition any member of the MSPB to stop any personnel action while the matter is under investigation. The results of the investigation will be reported to the whistleblower.

Agencies may be required to conduct investigations and prepare reports on the substance of complaints made by whistleblowers. In such cases, the Special Counsel will review the agency reports to determine whether they contain sufficient information and whether the findings appear reasonable. Copies of the agency reports will be sent to the President and to Congress, and to the persons who filed the complaints.

Grade and Pay Retention

Pay retention provisions will make it possible for employees to retain their grades for two years and to avoid taking considerable cuts in salary as the result of downgrading actions for which they were not responsible.

Employees to be placed in lower-graded positions as the result of reductions-in-force or reclassification actions may, (if they have held their current positions for one year), retain their current grades for two years from the date of demotion. Pay for these employees will not be reduced.

At the end of the two-year period, the grades of these employees will be lowered. Should their pay at that time exceed the maximum rate of their new grades, they will retain their current rate of pay but will receive only 50% of their annual comparability pay increases. If or when their pay is lower than or equal to the maximum rate of their new grades, they will then receive full comparability pay increases.

These special benefits will continue only as long as the employees remain in their same positions and will apply to all reductions-in-force or reclassification actions taken on or after January 1, 1977.

Veterans' Preference and Benefits

Veterans with service-connected disabilities of 30% or more are entitled to receive additional benefits, including:
- appointment without competitive examination, with a right to be converted to career appointments, and
- retention rights over other preference eligibles in reductions-in-force.

Veterans with disabilities of 30% or more also have the right to be notified in advance and respond to any decision in which:
- they are considered ineligible for a position due to physical requirements of the position;
- they would be passed over by an agency in the course of filling a position from a civil service

certificate; or
- they are deemed ineligible for retention in a position during a reduction-in-force due to the physical requirements of the position.

On October 1, 1980, veterans' preference is eliminated for non-disabled military retirees who retire from the service at or above the rank of major or its equivalent.

Changes in Federal Labor Relations

The Civil Service Reform Act contains a number of new provisions which clarifies the roles and responsibilities of labor organizations and which, to an extent, expands the rights of employees in collective bargaining units.

The Act affirms the basic rights of Federal employees to form, join, and assist labor organizations (or to refrain from doing so). It prohibits strikes and work slowdowns, as well as picketing that interferes with government operations.

For most matters, employees working in organized bargaining units must use the grievance arbitration procedures negotiated by the union. However, an exception is made for adverse actions and discrimination complaints. In such cases, employees may use either the negotiated procedures *or* the appeals procedure. The union is required to represent all employees in the bargaining unit who choose the negotiated procedures, whether or not they are members of the union.

The issues subject to collective bargaining are to generally continue. However, departments and agencies (such as OPM, OMB, and GSA) which issue government-wide regulations affecting Federal employees, are required to consult with labor organizations representing a substantial number of employees over any substantive changes. In addition, a union that represents, in one bargaining unit, a majority of affected employees is able to negotiate without regard to their own agency's regulations on matters otherwise within the scope of bargaining.

The Act makes all types of management actions subject to collective bargaining unless specific "management rights" exist. These reserve to agency officials the authority to make decisions and take actions which are not subject to the collective bargaining

process, and exclude bargaining on Federal pay and benefits or nonvoluntary payments to unions by employees. The changes in the management rights area will: (1) *prohibit* agencies from bargaining on mission, budget, organization, number of employees, or internal security; and (2) *permit,* but not require, them to negotiate over the methods, means, and technology of conducting agency operations. Management has the right to determine whether vacant positions may be filled only by persons within the agency *or* by persons within and outside the agency.

Other provisions in the Act include:
- A time limit of 45 days for agency heads to decide if a proposed action is negotiable. This decision will be appealable to the Federal Labor Relations Authority.
- Court enforcement of FLRA decisions and orders, including judicial review in unfair labor practice cases.
- Provisions for back pay and attorney fees for employees subject to unjustified or unwarranted personnel actions.
- Dues withholding—based on voluntary allotments by employees—at the exclusive union's request. (Allotments are irrevocable for one year, and the withholding service is at no charge to the employee or labor organization.)
- Official time during regular working hours for employees representing unions in negotiations.

Trial Period for New Managers and Supervisors

First-time supervisors and managers will be required to serve a trial period before their appointments become final. Those who do not satisfactorily complete the trial period will be returned to positions of no lower pay and grade than those they occupied before assuming their managerial or supervisory assignments.

Previously, ineffective first-time supervisors and managers could normally be removed only through the application of adverse action procedures. Those who do not perform well during the trial period are to be removed from managerial responsibilities forthwith.

Merit Pay for Managers and Supervisors

A merit pay system is implemented in which the pay increases of managers and supervisors in grades GS-

13 through GS-15 will be directly linked to their performance, rather than to their length of service. Employees covered will no longer receive automatic within-grade increases, but will be eligible each year for merit pay increases.

Managers covered under the merit pay system will receive a minimum of one-half of the annual comparability pay increases authorized for white collar employees, but this minimum can be increased by OPM. The funds for merit raises are to be derived from a combination of the remainder of the annual comparability increases and from funds formerly used for step increases and quality step increases for these employees.

The amounts agencies award in merit increases will vary to recognize distinctions in the performance of individual managers and supervisors and of the organizations they direct. Agencies must base their decisions on a formal appraisal system. Factors taken into account in awarding merit pay increases will include cost efficiency; timeliness of performance; and improvements in efficiency, productivity, and quality of work or service.

All managers and supervisors in grades GS-13 through GS-15 are to be brought into the merit pay system. No employee will suffer a salary loss in the conversion to the new system.

Senior Executive Service

The Senior Executive Service (SES) is to include managers at GS-16 through Executive Level IV or their equivalents in the Executive branch. The SES will make it easier for the Federal Government to attract and keep top managers, to use their abilities productively, and to pay them according to their performance.

The large majority of SES executives are to be career managers. There is a 10% government-wide ceiling on the number who may be noncareer. In addition, about 45% of SES positions will be career-reserved; that is, they can be filled only by career executives.

SES executives may be reassigned to other positions within their own agencies, but may not be involuntarily transferred to other agencies.

Entry Into SES

OPM will determine the number of SES positions in each agency. Individuals who presently occupy those positions which their agencies designate to become a part of the SES have 90 days in which to choose either to enter the Service or to remain under their present appointment authorities. Those who choose not to join the SES will keep their present pay and benefits, but will not be eligible for promotions. Those who enter the SES at a later date must have their managerial qualifications evaluated by qualification review boards within the Office of Personnel Management, and must serve a trial period of one year. Veterans' preference will not apply in the SES.

Compensation and Benefits

Base pay for SES executives will be set at one of five levels, with the minimum at the equivalent of GS-16, step 1, and the maximum at the salary for Executive Level IV. In addition, performance awards may be given to 50% of the career executives in amounts up to 20% of base salary. Each year, up to 5% of SES executives may receive the rank of "Meritorious Executive," with a special award of $10,000. Up to 1% may receive the rank of "Distinguished Executive," with a special award of $20,000. A ceiling will be set on total compensation for SES members equal to the pay of Executive Level I (now $66,000). Only career executives in the SES will be eligible for performance awards and ranks.

Retention and Removal

Retention in the SES will be based on good performance. Executives will be evaluated annually by their supervisors, who will measure their individual performance and that of the organizations they direct. Among the evaluation criteria are improvements in efficiency and productivity; work quality; timeliness of performance; and success in meeting affirmative action goals.

Ratings will range from "fully successful," a rating which makes one eligible for performance awards, to "marginal" or "unsatisfactory," ratings which indicate a need for corrective action and improvement. Failure to improve would cause removal from the SES.

Career executives who are removed from the SES for

poor performance cannot appeal but may state their case in a hearing before the Merit Systems Protection Board. They are entitled to placement in non-SES positions at GS-15 or above, at no loss in base pay. Executives with 25 years of government service or with 20 years of service at age 50 may choose retirement under such circumstances.

Agencies are to conduct minority recruitment programs to help eliminate underrepresentation of minority groups in the Federal work force. The Office of Personnel Management and the Equal Employment Opportunity Commission will provide guidelines and assistance.

Nonpaid work by students in connection with educational programs is permitted, provided they do not reduce opportunities for regular employees.

Employees who would otherwise be separated under reductions-in-force may be retrained for jobs in other agencies.

Employees who are age 50 with 20 years of service, or who, regardless of age, have 25 years of service, may choose early retirement in major reorganizations, transfers of function, or reductions-in-force.

OPM must notify the U.S. Employment Service about competitive examinations it administers. Agencies must provide both OPM and the U.S. Employment Service employment information about positions for which they are seeking candidates outside of the civil service system.

The mobility program authorized by the Intergovernmental Personnel Act has been extended to include additional types of organizations and individuals. Federal employees who accept these assignments must return to the Federal Government for a period equal to that of the assignments.

Subject to its standards and review, OPM may delegate authority for personnel management functions, including certain competitive examinations, to the heads of agencies employing persons in the competitive service.

The combined retirement pay and federal civilian salary received by future retirees of the uniformed services may not exceed the pay for Executive Level V.

Federal agencies are authorized to adopt OPM's merit system standards as a personnel requirement for grants to state and local governments.

YOU BECOME AN "ELIGIBLE"

People who are found to meet the requirements in the announcement are called "eligibles." Their names are put on a "list of eligibles." An eligible's chances of getting a job depend on how high he stands on this list and how fast agencies are filling jobs from the list.

Federal agencies can fill jobs in several ways—for instance, by promoting an employee already within the agency or by hiring an employee from another Federal agency who wants to change jobs. But when a job is to be filled from a list of eligibles, the agency asks the Civil Service examiners for the names of people on the list of eligibles for that job.

When the examiners receive this request, they send to the agency the names of the three people highest on the list. Or, if the job to be filled has specialized requirements, the examiners send the agency, from the general list, the names of the top three persons who meet those requirements. An applicant who has said he would not accept appointment in the place where the job is located is, of course, not considered.

The appointing officer makes a choice from among the three people whose names were sent to him. If that person accepts the appointment, the names of the other persons are put back on the list so that they may be considered for future openings.

That is the rule in hiring from all kinds of eligible lists, whether they are for typist, carpenter, chemist, or something else. For every vacancy, the appointing officer has his choice of any one of the top three eligibles on the list. This explains why the person whose name is on top of the list sometimes does not get an appointment when some of the persons lower on the list do. If the appointing officer chooses the No. 2 or No. 3 eligible, the No. 1 eligible doesn't get a job at once, but stays on the list until he is appointed or the list is terminated.

S118

VETERANS GET PREFERENCE

If you are a veteran, you may be eligible for additional benefits in getting a Government job and also in keeping it after you are hired. For example, "veteran preference" will add extra points to your passing score.

Disabled veterans or their wives, widows of certain veterans, and widowed or divorced mothers of some veterans who died in service or who were totally and permanently disabled get 10 extra points. Most other honorably discharged veterans get 5 points, depending upon length or dates of service.

KINDS OF APPOINTMENTS

If you are offered a job, the letter or telegram will show what kind of appointment is involved. Most appointments are either temporary, term, career-conditional, or career. You should know what these mean.

A *temporary* appointment does not ordinarily last more than 1 year. A temporary worker can't be promoted and can't transfer to another job. He is not under the retirement system. Persons over 70 can be given only temporary appointments, but they can be renewed.

A *term* appointment is made for work on a specific project that will last more than 1 year but less than 4 years. A term employee can be promoted or reassigned to other positions within the project for which he was hired. He is not under the retirement system.

If you accept a temporary or term appointment,

your name will stay on the list of eligibles from which you were appointed. This means that you will remain eligible for permanent jobs that are normally filled by career-conditional or career appointments.

A *career-conditional* appointment leads after 3 years' service to a career appointment. For the first year, the employee serves a probationary period. During this time, he must demonstrate that he can do a satisfactory job and may be dismissed if he fails to do so. A career-conditional employee has promotion and transfer privileges. After a career-conditional employee completes his probation, he cannot be removed except for cause. However, in reduction-in-force (layoff) actions, career-conditional employees are dismissed ahead of career employees.

A *career* employee also serves a probationary period, as described above, and has promotion and transfer privileges. After he completes his probation, however, he is in the last group to be affected in layoffs.

WHY YOU MAY BE BARRED

Applicants may be denied examinations and eligibles may be denied appointments for any of the following reasons:

1. Dismissal from employment for delinquency or misconduct.

2. Physical or mental unfitness for the position.

3. Criminal, infamous, dishonest, immoral, or notoriously disgraceful conduct.

4. Intentional false statements, deception, or fraud.

5. Refusal to furnish testimony which the Commission may require.

6. Drunkenness.

7. Any legal or other disqualification.

An old conviction for civil or criminal offense will not of itself bar an applicant from U. S. government employment. Ordinarily a person who has been convicted of a felony must wait two years after release before his application will be considered. Exceptions can be made by the Office of Personnel Management, which also decides whether or not to accept applications from persons who have been convicted of misdemeanors or who are under suspended sentence or on probation.

PART TWO

Representative
Civil Service Jobs

GENERAL INFORMATION FOR PART II

The following list of terms applies to most of the positions discussed in PART II. It is a good idea, therefore, to read through this list before you embark upon this highly informative section of U.S. CIVIL SERVICE JOBS. Exceptions to and/or qualifications of any of these terms will be indicated and described at length for relevant positions.

ACADEMIC YEAR: Consists of approximately 36 weeks of full-time study, 30 semester hours, 45 quarter hours, or the equivalent. One academic year equals approximately nine months of experience.

CREDITING EDUCATION or TRAINING: Study completed in an institution above the high school level is evaluated as evidence of ability in terms of its relatedness to the knowledges, skills, and abilities required to assume the position of interest successfully. Study completed in a business or secretarial school or other comparable institution above the high school level is creditable provided subjects related to the position of interest were studied. Study completed in a junior college, college, or university is creditable provided such study included a minimum of six semester hours, or the equivalent, per year in subjects which equipped the candidate with the knowledges, skills, and abilities required at the level of the position of interest.

FULL-TIME STUDY: In the case of business and commercial schools, it is the equivalent of at least 20 classroom hours of instruction per week, plus necessary outside study. Part-time study is pro-rated on this basis also but is creditable only in amounts equivalent to one-half academic year or multiples thereof.

INTERVIEWS: The purpose of interviews is to observe and evaluate personal characteristics and qualifications which are essential to the successful performance of the duties of the position.

PHYSICAL REQUIREMENTS: Applicants must be physically and mentally able to efficiently perform the essential functions of the position without hazard to themselves or others. Depending on the essential duties of a specific position, usable vision, color vision, hearing or speech may be required. However, in most cases, a specific physical condition or impairment of a specific function may be compensated for by the satisfactory use of a prosthesis or mechanical aid. Reasonable accommodation may also be considered in determining an applicant's ability to perform the duties of a position. Reasonable accommodation may include but is not limited to: the use of assistive devices, job modification or restructuring, provision of readers and interpreters, or adjusted work schedules. Also, all positions involving Federal motor vehicle operation carry the additional medical requirements.

QUALITY OF EXPERIENCE: For positions at any grade, the required amount of experience will not in itself be accepted as proof of qualifications. The candidate's record of experience and training must show that he/she has the ability to perform the duties of the position.

QUALITY RANKING FACTORS: A quality ranking factor is a knowledge, skill, or ability which could be expected to significantly enhance performance in a position, but could not reasonably be considered necessary for satisfactory performance. Quality ranking factors may be used to distinguish the better qualified candidates from among those who meet all other requirements, including selective factors.

SELECTIVE FACTORS: Selective factors must be job related, represent an extension of the basic knowledges and skills required of the position and be essential to successful performance of the position. Selective factors are knowledge and skills of a kind and level which reasonably could not be acquired on the job without undue interruption of the organization's production. Selective factors for positions at higher grades typically will be more narrowly defined and/or set at a higher level than is necessary at lower grades. What may be appropriate as a quality ranking factor at a lower grade may have to be a selective factor in a higher graded position.

* Alternative definition: a knowledge, skill, or ability that is essential for satisfactory performance in a position, and represents an addition to the basic minimum requirements in this standard.

CLERICAL POSITIONS

Clerk (various positions) GS–1/3

DESCRIPTION OF WORK

Clerical positions involve the orderly processing of the papers and performance of the routine work supporting an office or organization. Within a framework of procedures, regulations, precedents, and instructions, clerks process and maintain the records and written materials which represent the transactions or business of the office or organization served. Among the basic duties which may be performed are, for example: (1) maintaining records; (2) receiving, screening, reviewing, and verifying documents; (3) searching for and compiling information and data; (4) providing a central source of information on the activities of the organization orally or by correspondence; (5) preparing and/or verifying the validity of documents with which the organization is concerned; etc.

REQUIREMENTS

A. GENERAL BACKGROUND

In order to be considered for appointment the applicant's overall background, work history, personal characteristics, work habits, and general behavior and reputation in his/her community, school, and previous employment must be of such nature as to provide positive evidence that he/she can and will perform clerical or office type work in a successful and productive manner in an office type of environment.

B. EXPERIENCE

For grade GS–1, no written test, experience, training, or education is required.

GS–2.—Six months of general experience; or graduation from a full 4-year or senior high school or possession of a General Educational Development High School Equivalency Certificate (GED).

GS–3.—One year of general experience; or 1 academic year of business or secretarial school, junior college, or college which is in addition to graduation from high school.

WRITTEN TESTS

Applicants for positions at grades GS–2 and GS–3 are required to pass written tests.

For some positions, only applicants who receive suitably high scores on parts of the test specifically pertinent to the particular kind of work to be done will be considered.

BASIS OF RATING

For GS–1: An evaluation of the applicant's willingness to do simple and repetitive clerical work, dependability, and the ability to perform work safely.

For GS–2 and GS–3: The score on the written test *and* an evaluation of the extent and quality of experience, education, and training.

APPLICABLE STANDARDS FOR CLERICAL POSITIONS ALSO REQUIRING SKILL IN TYPING OR STENOGRAPHY

Some positions requiring typing or stenographic skill as high as that required under the competitive standard for typing or stenographic work, are so constituted that other work skills or abilities, rather than typing or stenographic skills, form the main qualification requirements for the positions. An appropriate means should be used to assure that applicants possess sufficient skill in typing or stenography to perform the duties of all such positions (i.e., a performance test, certificate of proficiency, or some method of certification acceptable to the Office of Personnel Management).

REQUIREMENTS FOR CLERICAL POSITIONS INVOLVING PUBLIC CONTACTS

Some clerical positions (e.g., information receptionists) which involve substantial contact with others, require a clear speaking voice, tact, courtesy, and capacity for effective public contacts. In filling such positions competitively and noncompetitively, appointing officers will assure themselves by reference checks, personal interviews, or other appropriate means that applicants possess these qualities to the degree necessary for satisfactory performance of the duties of such positions.

Office Machine Operator (various positions) GS–1/3

DESCRIPTION OF WORK

Persons employed in these positions have as their primary responsibility the operation of the specific office machine described in the individual job title, although clerical work of varying degrees is also involved in many such positions.

EDUCATION AND EXPERIENCE REQUIREMENTS

GS–1.—No experience or education required; however, the appropriate tests must be passed.

GS–2.—Must pass the appropriate written test and—

Alternative 1. Pass appropriate performance test (if any);

or

Alternative 2. Have had six months of office clerical experience or office machine operation experience;

or

Alternative 3. Have completed a specialized course of instruction in the operation of the appropriate machine and either

a. had three months of general or specialized experience

or

b. have graduated from high school.

The specialized course of instruction on appropriate machines may have been completed as part of the high school curriculum. Evidence of successful completion of such courses will be required.

GS–3.—Must pass the written test *and* the appropriate performance test (if any) and have had either (a) one year of acceptable experience of which at least six months is specialized experience, or (b) one academic year of business or secretarial school or junior college. For occupations for which no performance test is available, education offered under (b) must have included training in the operation of appropriate office machines.

WRITTEN TESTS

All applicants are required to pass tests covering (a) verbal abilities and clerical abilities (alphabetizing and arithmetic) and (b) eye-hand coordination and perception of differences. All applicants for positions of operators of machines equipped with an alphabetic keyboard will be required to pass a performance test on a typewriter-style keyboard. Applicants for positions of EAM Operator must pass a test of abstract reasoning ability.

Higher scores may be required for the higher grades.

BASIS OF RATING

Applicants will be ranked on the basis of (a) their score on the verbal abilities test, and (b) the extent and quality of their experience and education. Other required tests must be passed but are not used to rank the eligibles.

GENERAL NOTE AS TO
APPLICABLE STANDARDS FOR
POSITIONS ALSO REQUIRING SKILL
IN TYPING OR STENOGRAPHY

Some office machine operator positions may require typing or stenographic skill at or above the level of proficiency required under the competitive standard for entry-level clerk-typist or clerk-stenographer positions, but may be so constituted that the machine operator skills, rather than the typing or stenographic skills, form the main qualification requirements for the positions. Positions so constituted are classified in the office machine operator series appropriate for the main requirement and are identified by the parenthical addition of the words "typing" or "stenography" to the titles otherwise prescribed for those series.

Secretary, All Grades
Secretary (Stenography), All Grades
Secretary (Typing), All Grades

DESCRIPTION OF WORK

This series includes all positions the duties of which are to assist one individual, and in some cases the subordinate staff of that individual, by performing general office work auxiliary to the work of the organization. To be included in this series, a position must be the principal clerical or administrative support position in the office, operating independently of any other such position in the office. The duties require a knowledge of clerical and administrative procedures and requirements; various office skills; and the ability to apply such skills in a way that increases the effectiveness of others. The duties do not require a technical or professional knowledge of a specialized subject-matter area.

EXPERIENCE REQUIREMENTS

The requirements at all levels discussed below are purposely stated in terms of knowledges, skills, and abilities, rather than specific duties. A candidate may demonstrate possession of the knowledges, skills, and abilities through various means. For example, a candidate with extensive writing experience could perhaps demonstrate the ability to compose nontechnical correspondence without ever having performed that specific duty. Volunteer work for organizations such as civic groups or church groups may be used to fulfill experience requirements to the degree that such work can be verified and evaluated when such work demonstrates possession of the knowledges, skills, and abilities applicable to secretarial work.

For positions at GS–3
A general background in the performance of routine clerical duties which demonstrates that a candidate has *all* of the following:
1.—basic knowledge of office routines and functions sufficient to refer visitors and telephone calls and to route correspondence by name or functional area.
2.—knowledge of clerical practices and filing procedures.
3.—knowledge of spelling, punctuation, and syntax.

Experience acquired through the performance of most kinds of clerical work in an office setting is normally considered qualifying.

For positions at GS–4
A background in the performance of a variety of clerical duties which demonstrates that a candidate has *all* of the following:
—working knowledge of many different office procedures such as those needed to request a variety of office equipment, supplies, publication material, and maintenance services, when each of these requires a different procedure;

AND
—ability to understand an organization and its

functions sufficient to establish file systems for classifying, retrieving, and disposing of materials; refer telephone calls and visitors; distribute and control mail; maintain leave records; and provide general and non-technical information.

For positions at GS—5 and above

Experience in administrative or clerical work which demonstrates possession of the knowledges, skills, and abilities required to serve as a principal office assistant at these levels, including *all* of the following:

1.—ability to organize effectively the flow of clerical processes in an office;
2.—ability to organize and design a filing system;
3.—ability to make arrangements for such things as travel, conferences, and meetings;
4.—ability to locate and assemble information for various reports, briefings, and conferences;
5.—ability to compose non-technical correspondence.

Length of experience will not necessarily in itself be considered qualifying. The candidate's record must show the ability to perform the duties of the position to be filled.

For positions at GS—3

A candidate must have had six months of qualifying experience at GS—2 in the General Schedule or equivalent experience outside the General Schedule.

For positions at GS—4 or GS—5

A candidate must have had one year of qualifying experience at the next lower grade in the General Schedule or equivalent experience outside the General Schedule.

For positions at GS—6

A candidate must have had six months of qualifying experience at GS—5 in the General Schedule or equivalent experience outside the General Schedule.

For positions at GS—7 through GS—11

A candidate must have had six months of qualifying experience at the next lower grade in the General Schedule or equivalent experience outside the General Schedule *OR* one year of qualifying experience at the second lower grade in the General Schedule or equivalent experience outside the General Schedule.

For positions at GS—12 and above

A candidate must have had one year of qualifying experience at the next lower grade in the General Schedule or equivalent experience outside the General Schedule.

SUBSTITUTION OF EDUCATION FOR EXPERIENCE

Except for any requirement for passing performance tests to demonstrate skill in shorthand and/or typing (when required), the following will apply:

For positions at GS—3

All of the experience requirements for the GS—3 level may be met by completion of 1 academic year of full-time business school or 1 academic year of education above the high-school level.

For positions at GS—4

All of the experience requirements for the GS—4 level may be met by completion of 2 academic years of full-time business school or 2 academic years of education above the high-school level.

For positions at GS—5

All of the experience requirements for the GS—5 level may be met by completion of 4 academic years of education in an accredited college or university.

NOTE: Academic study alone is not creditable as qualifying experience for positions above the GS—5 level; i.e., no more than 4 years of academic study is creditable towards meeting experience requirements.

Combination of education and experience may be used to meet the minimum qualification requirements.

Courses that are not measurable in terms of credit hours (e.g., "certificate courses") should be treated as if they were work experience. However, no credit will be allowed for training which has been obtained only or primarily in the basic skills of shorthand or typing or refresher courses.

TYPING AND STENOGRAPHIC SKILLS

When secretary positions require skill in typing or stenography at or above the level of proficiency required under the competitive standards for these skills, the qualification standard for the skill should be used in conjunction with this standard to assure that candidates possess at least the minimum degree of skill required to perform the typing or stenographic duties of the position.

The level of stenographic proficiency required by positions classified as Secretary (Stenography) is based on the classification of the *stenography* duties and not necessarily on the grade level of the position. Therefore, before applying for positions of this type, first determine the skill level required by the stenographic duties.

WRITTEN TESTS

No written test will be required at any grade level to establish basic qualifications of candidates, or to rank candidates. Performance tests may be required to demonstrate possession of stenographic or typing skill.

BASIS FOR RATING AND RANKING CANDIDATES

Candidates who meet the minimum qualification requirements will be rated on a scale of 70 to 100 based on an evaluation of the quality and extent of their experience, education, training, or other achievements pertinent to the duties of the positions to be filled.

Some kinds of training and experience which enhance the candidate's qualifications may be treated as factors to award extra credit for rating and ranking purposes. These include, but are not limited to, the following:

—Possession of a certificate as a "Certified Professional Secretary";
—Successful completion of in-service courses which offered training in areas related to the secretarial function, general management or administration, or the program area with which the supervisor is concerned;
—Successful completion of work-related educational courses in excess of those used to meet minimum requirements;
—Recognition for exceptional work performance.

Personnel Clerk
Staffing Clerk
Classification Clerk
Employee Development Clerk
Employee Relations Clerk
GS–4/6

Personnel Assistant
Staffing Assistant
Classification Assistant
Employee Development Assistant
Employee Relations Assistant
GS–6/10

DESCRIPTION OF WORK

Personnel clerks perform a variety of clerical tasks in connection with processing paper work, compiling and presenting data for reports, and providing basic information on personnel matters. Individual assignments may involve such duties as processing personnel actions; maintaining registers and issuing certificates of eligibles; compiling data for and preparing periodic and special personnel reports; providing basic information about personnel regulations, procedures, programs, or benefits to employees, management officials, or the general public; or providing clerical support in a personnel office or specialized unit within a personnel office where the work requires substantial knowledge of civilian personnel rules, regulations, procedures, and program requirements.

Personnel assistants perform a variety of technical support work which is usually related to one of the recognized personnel management specialties. This work may take the form of assisting one or more fully qualified personnel specialists in a limited area of assignment. It also may involve independent performance of assignments in a prescribed segment of a personnel program where a fully qualified personnel specialist is not required.

EXPERIENCE AND EDUCATION

Except for the substitution of education or training provided for below, applicants must have had the kind and amount of experience shown in the following table, and as described in the statements immediately following:

Grade	Total (years)	General (years)	Specialized (years)
GS–4	2	1	1
GS–5	3	1	2
GS–6	4	1	3
GS–7 and above	5	1	4

NOTE: The work of *clerical* positions (as distinguished from *assistant* positions) at grades GS–5 and above requires the application of specialized knowledge gained through experience in civilian personnel operations. These positions are generally filled through noncompetitive action.

These requirements for directly related experience will ordinarily apply. However, the requirement may be waived under certain circumstances where a lateral reassignment is involved, as provided elsewhere in this stand-

ard. In addition, the requirement for directly related experience may be waived for individuals under consideration for promotion in the relatively few instances where it can be clearly shown that the candidate's background gives positive evidence that he possesses to a superior degree the essential skills and abilities needed for the position.

Substitution of Education and Training for Experience.

For a maximum of three years of the required experience (one year of general plus two years of specialized experience) study successfully completed in a resident school or institution may be substituted as follows:

General experience only:

a. Study completed in a college, university, or junior college, above the high school level may be substituted on the basis of one-half an *academic year* of study for *six months* of experience.

b. Full-time study completed in a business or secretarial school or other comparable institution above the high school level may be substituted on the basis of one-half an *academic year* of study for *six months* of experience provided such subjects as business English, office machines, filing and indexing, office practices, business mathematics, bookkeeping or accounting were studied. No credit will be allowed for training which has been obtained only or primarily in the basic skills of shorthand or typing or refresher courses.

Specialized experience:

a. For the first year of specialized experience, study successfully completed in a resident school above the high school level may be substituted at the rate of one-half an *academic year* of study for *six months* of specialized experience provided the study included a minimum of six semester hours, or the equivalent, per year in subjects closely related to the personnel field. Such subjects include statistics; psychology; sociology or other social sciences; courses where primary emphasis is on writing skill; public administration; personnel administration, industrial relations, or similar courses dealing directly with subjects in the personnel field; organization and management; and management analysis.

b. For the second year of specialized experience, study of the type described in item a, above, may be substituted at the rate of one academic year of study for six months of specialized experience. Therefore, a full 4-year course of this type of study may be substituted for a maximum of three years of the required experience and is fully qualifying for grade GS−5.

COMPUTER POSITIONS

Computer Clerk, GS−2/4
Computer Assistant, GS−5/9

DESCRIPTION OF WORK

Computer Clerks and Computer Assistants perform a variety of work in support of specialists and computer operators engaged in the design and operation of computer systems. Employees in this occupation also support functional users of computer systems by accepting processing requirements, preparing them for execution, and in some cases performing or directing program execution through remote terminals, distributing the products and performing related control and processing support duties. These tasks are complementary to and support such specialized computer systems work as analysis, design, programming, installation, operations and system management.

Computer Clerks perform such tasks as: (1) labeling, maintaining and controlling tapes, disks and other storage media and documentation in tape libraries; (2) preparing processing schedules for jobs that are executed in simple sequence and have dependencies that are readily accommodated; (3) maintaining a variety of computer program files, records, manuals and related documents; or, (4) tracing sources of procedural errors in documents, data and control records.

Computer Assistants perform limited phases of computer specialist functions in addition to project control and scheduling work such as: (1) translating program routines and detailed logic steps designed by others into instructions, codes, or languages that machines can accept; (2) preparing charts showing the flow of documents and data in assigned subject areas; (3) preparing daily or longer schedules for program processing sequences where multiple systems, multiprocessing, dependencies, contentions and similar conditions affect the scheduling processes; (4) assembling, modifying controls, annotating instructions and staging the materials and documentation required for machine processing; and/or, (5) tracing and identifying the sources of processing failures, correcting those associated with system controls, introducing new or revised schedules of program processing and providing control stream modifications to take advantage of alternative operating system hardware configurations and processing techniques.

EXPERIENCE REQUIREMENTS

Applicants must have the kind, quality and amount of experience indicated in the following table and explanatory information.

Grade	General Experience (years)	Specialized Experience (years)	Total Experience (years)
1	0	0	0
2	½	0	½
3	1	0	1
4	2	0	2
5	2	1	3
6	2	2	4
7 and above	2	3	5

General Experience—any experience which includes work associated with following written directions, procedures, or systematic work methods such as in classifying and maintaining records, or comparable clerical support work which gives evidence of the ability to perform this kind of work.

Specialized Experience—any experience in computer clerical or other computer related support work requiring knowledge of computer terminology, processing methods, controls, media and data flow. OR: Experience requiring proficiency in translating actions into a computer programming language (COBOL, FORTRAN,

ALGOL, etc.); preparing and interpreting program and system charts and instructions; or other work requiring comparable knowledges of computer processing techniques.

Substitution of Education for Experience

Education may be substituted for work experience according to the following criteria:

GS–2 Graduation from a 4-year high school or GED equivalent.

GS–3 Successful completion of a 2-year course, including instruction and practice in data processing in high school which provides knowledge of electronic computer systems, programming, media (tape, disks, and/or drum), input and retrieval methods. Specific knowledge or ability as computer operators is not essential to this occupation and is not required when crediting high school ADP training. OR: Successful completion of 1 year of education above the high school level that includes at least six semester hours, or equivalent, in data processing courses. OR: Successful completion of a full time concentrated course of study of at least 6 months' duration which includes systems design and programming instruction and practice in a technical school above the high school level.

GS–4 Successful completion of two years of study above the high school level which includes at least 12 semester hours (or equivalent) in courses such as computer mathematics, basic and advanced programming, data processing, computer operations, or other ADP related courses of study and practice.

GS–5 Successful completion of four years of study above the high school level which includes at least 24 semester hours (or equivalent) in courses such as those described above for GS–4.

QUALITY OF EXPERIENCE

In evaluating combinations of experience, education and training, one academic year of study may be substituted for one year of general experience or six months of specialized experience. Academic study may be substituted for a maximum of one year of specialized experience.

The applicant's record of experience and training must show the ability to perform the duties of the positions. In addition:

For grade GS–5, except for those who qualify on the basis of education alone, the 1 year of required specialized experience must have been comparable in difficulty and responsibility to the GS–4 level in the same or closely related work.

For grade GS–6 and above, at least 1 year of the required specialized experience must have been comparable in difficulty and responsibility to the next lower grade in the Federal service or 2 years comparable to the second lower grade in the Federal service.

WRITTEN TEST

Applicants for competitive appointment to grades GS–2/4 must pass a written test. The written test is waived for applicants who qualify on the basis of specialized training or experience in the data processing field.

BASIS FOR RATING

GS–2/4 applicants will be rated on the basis of written test scores except for applicants for whom the written test is waived. For such applicants and for positions at grade GS–5 and above, applicants will be rated on an evaluation of the quality and extent of their experience, education or training.

For Supervisory and Nonsupervisory Positions
GS−2/13 in the Computer Operation Series

DESCRIPTION OF WORK

Computer Operators are primarily responsible for the operation of the control console of a computer and all elements of the system which are directly connected with it. This involves readying the equipment for operation, starting it, monitoring its operation, and taking prompt action in response to machine commands or unscheduled halts.

EXPERIENCE, EDUCATION, AND TRAINING REQUIREMENTS

Applicants must have the kinds, quality, and amounts of experience indicated in the following table and explanatory information.

Grade	General Experience (years)	Specialized Experience (years)	Total Experience (years)
2.................	½	0	½
3.................	1	0	1
4................	2	0	2
5.................	2	1	3
6.................	2	2	4
7 & above	2	3	5

General Experience—experience in the operation of electric accounting machines; *or* clerical experience; *or* experience in the operation of office business machines and other machines such as card punch, verifier, and the like.

Specialized Experience—experience in the operation of a computer system or peripheral device used in support of computer operations.

Specialized experience also may be experience in other computer-related occupations such as those involving programming, systems analysis, production control, scheduling, or others that are directly related.

Substitution of Education for Experience

In crediting education above the high school level, one year of study is equal to 30 semester hours or the equivalent. Education may be substituted for work experience according to the following criteria.

GS−2—Graduation from a 4-year high school or GED equivalent.

GS−3—Successful completion of 1 year of study in a school above the high school level in any field of study,

OR

Successful completion of a full-time, or equivalent part-time, course of study in computer operations in an accredited vocational or technical school above the high school level.

GS−4—Successful completion of 2 years of study in a school above the high school level.

GS−5—Completion of 4 years of study above the high school level which includes at least 12 semester hours in any one or a combination of the following: mathematics, statistics, data processing, or other pertinent or related fields.

In evaluating combinations of experience, education and training, 1 academic year of study may be substituted for 1 year of general experience or 6 months of specialized experience. Academic study may be substituted for a maximum of 1 year of specialized experience.

QUALITY OF EXPERIENCE

For positions at any grade the amount of experience will not in itself be accepted as proof of qualification. The applicant's record of experience and training must show that he/she has the ability to perform the duties of the position. In addition:

For grade GS−5, except for those who qualify on the basis of education alone, at least 6 months of the required specialized experience must have been comparable in difficulty and responsibility to the GS–4 level in the same or related work.

For grade GS–6 and above, in addition to education, training, and/or experience credited at lower levels, at least 1 year of the required specialized experience must have been comparable in difficulty and responsibility to the next lower grade in the Federal service or 2 years comparable to the second lower grade in the Federal service.

WRITTEN TEST

Applicants for competitive appointment to grades GS–2/4 must pass a written test.

BASIS FOR RATING

For GS–2/4, applicants will be rated on the basis of written test scores. For positions at grade GS–5 and above, applicants will be rated on an evaluation of the quality and extent of their experience, education, or training.

RELATING QUALIFICATIONS OF CANDIDATES TO JOBS HAVING SPECIAL REQUIREMENTS

The numbers and kinds of computers, and the primary purposes they serve, differ among various work situations and may vary widely. Consequently, the particular demands of positions in these different work situations may vary widely. Referral of candidates for these positions may be limited to those whose records show evidence of the required capabilities.

Computer Systems Analyst GS–5/15
Computer Programer GS–5/15
Computer Programer Analyst GS–5/15
Computer Systems Programer GS–5/15
Computer Equipment Analyst GS–5/15
Computer Specialist GS–5/15

DESCRIPTION OF WORK

Positions in this series advise on, supervise, or perform work necessary to design or implement systems for solving problems or accomplishing work processes by the use of digital computers. Except for entry level positions, the primary requirement is knowledge of computer requirements and techniques.

Computer Systems Analysts are concerned with analysis of problems or processes and design of computerized systems for accomplishment of the work. Representative assignments include performance of feasibility studies for proposed computer applications in a subject matter area, development of an application's programing specifications, or analysis of existing applications systems to correct problems.

Computer Programers are concerned with translating system designs into the plans of instructions and logic by which computers can produce the desired actions or products. Knowledge of a particular programing language is an important consideration in recruitment for these positions.

Computer Programer Analysts perform work which is a combination of Computer Systems Analyst and Computer Programer duties.

Computer Systems Programers are concerned with systems software. This typically involves maintenance and modification of assemblers, compilers, debugging routines, and similar internal computer programs necessary for the processing of other programs.

Computer Equipment Analysts are concerned with the selection or utilization of computer equipment. These positions do not involve design or repair of equipment; concern is with the relative merits of equipment items (e.g., mainframe computers, disk memory devices, printers, terminals) and the arrangement of the items into equipment systems appropriate to an organization's needs.

Computer Specialists perform work of a kind or combination of duties that does not fall under one of the above specializations but does have as the main requirement knowledge of computer requirements and techniques.

Further information about the nature of the work performed by employees in the Computer Specialist Series may be obtained from the position classification standard.

KNOWLEDGES, SKILLS AND ABILITIES

KNOWLEDGES AND SKILLS

The requirements in this standard reflect the fact that proficiency in application of knowledges and skills at a given level indicates probability of success in similar work at the next higher level. The requirements are keyed to the progression of grade levels set forth in the classification standard. Successful accomplishment of assignments at the next lower grade in the normal line of promotion to the position being filled demonstrates capability to do work of the required level of difficulty and responsibility. Work in other fields which has provided the same kind and level of knowledges and skills similarly is qualifying. Education is substitutable for practical experience when the education has provided the knowledges and skills.

The GS−5 and GS−7 levels require basic analytic and communicative skills combined with broad general knowledges. The knowledges and skills required for GS−9 and above are more specialized. Persons typically gain and demonstrate the more specialized knowledges and skills through a) successful performance in lower grade level positions in this series, b) related work experience in other fields, or c) graduate study in

fields such as data processing or computer science.

SELECTIVE FACTORS

Selective factors are knowledges and skills of a kind and level which reasonably could not be acquired on the job without undue interruption of the organization's production. Selective factors must be job related, represent an extension of the basic knowledges and skills required of the position and be essential to successful performance of the position.

Owing to the diversity of work in the Computer Specialist Series, the use of selective factors normally will be required in filling positions above the developmental level. Some factors, such as knowledge of a certain level of mathematics, may be appropriate for positions at any level. At the GS−9 and higher grades, knowledges and skills typically will be needed which relate to both the specialty of the position and the particular duties and responsibilities involved. For example, patterns of selective factors for a sample of full performance positions might be:

—For a Computer Programer Analyst position, a) proficiency in the use of a particular higher level programing language (e.g., COBOL), b) skill in development and implementation of specifications for applications programs, and c) knowledge of techniques pertinent to the appropriate broad category of subject matter applications (i.e., scientific applications or bussiness applications).

—For a Computer Systems Programer position, a) proficiency in the use of a particular assembly level programing language (e.g., ALC), b) knowledge of general techniques for analysis of system software requirements, and c) skill in development and implementation of specifications for system software programs.

—For a Computer Equipment Analyst position, a) knowledge of techniques for analysis of computer equipment requirements, b) knowledge of techniques for evaluation of computer equipment, c) skill in development of specifications for procurement of computer equipment, and d) knowledge of a broad category of equipment (e.g., telecommunications related computer equipment).

Positions at GS–12 and above commonly involve very demanding and responsible roles, often with little or no "back up" expertise available in the organizational unit. Therefore, selective factors for positions at these grades typically will be more narrowly defined. What may be appropriate as a quality ranking factor at a lower grade may have to be a selective factor in a higher graded position. For example, knowledge of statistical methods and accounting techniques normally would be a quality ranking factor in filling positions concerned with an automation project involving such methods and techniques. However, this knowledge normally would constitute a selective factor in filling the position of the project leader responsible for planning the overall approach and integrating segments of the system where these methods and techniques were of critical importance.

MINIMUM QUALIFICATION REQUIREMENTS

For the GS–5 Level
  A. A background which includes one year of work at no lower than GS–4 or equivalent and demonstrates:
    1. Skill in analyzing problems, to include identifying relevant factors, gathering pertinent information and recognizing solutions,
    2. Skill in doing thorough, accurate work that requires planning a logical sequence of steps, and
    3. Skill in communicating, both orally and in writing.

Such skills typically are gained in administrative, technical, or investigative lines of work. It is also possible to acquire these skills through a variety of other means, such as volunteer work, vocational training, or substantive clerical work.
OR
  B. Completion of a four year course in an accredited college leading to a bachelor's degree in any field.
AND
(In the case of A or B)
  C. Evidence of possession of any selective factors appropriate to the position to be filled.

For the GS–7 Level
  A. A background which includes one year of work at no lower than GS–5 or equivalent and demonstrates skills related to the computer field through performance of tasks such as:
    —translating detailed logical steps developed by others into language codes that computers accept where this requires understanding of procedures and limitations appropriate to use of a programing language.
    —interviewing subject matter personnel to get facts regarding work processes and synthesizing the resulting data into charts showing information flow.
    —operating computer consoles where this involves choice among various procedures in responding to machine commands or unscheduled halts.
    —scheduling the sequence of programs to be processed by computers where alternatives must be weighed with a view to production efficiency.
    —extracting and compiling information concerning an equipment feature where this involves selecting pertinent data from catalogs, manufacturer's literature, and previous studies.
    —preparing documentation on cost/benefit studies where this involves summarizing the materials and organizing them in logical fashion.

Such skills typically are gained as a trainee in the Computer Specialist Series, as a Computer Operator or Assistant, or through performance of work where the primary concern was the subject matter of the computer application (e.g., supply, personnel, chemical process control) and one or more of the above types of computer related efforts were required to facilitate the basic duties. Also, work in management analysis, program analysis, or a comparable field often provides such skills.
OR
  B. Superior Academic Achievement.
OR
  C. Completion of one full academic year of graduate study in any field.
AND
(In the case of A, B, or C)
  D. Evidence of possession of any selective

factors appropriate to the position to be filled.

For the GS—9 Level

A. A background which includes one year of work at no lower than GS—7 or equivalent and demonstrates knowledges of computer requirements and techniques in carrying out project assignments consisting of several related tasks. To be qualifying for the GS—9 level the assignments must have shown completion of the following, or the equivalent:

1. Analysis of the interrelationships of pertinent components of the system,
2. Planning the sequence of actions necessary to accomplish the assignment, and
3. Personal responsibility for at least a segment of the overall project.

Such knowledges and skills typically are gained in the Computer Specialist Series or through performance of work where the primary concern was the subject matter of the computer application, and the above types of computer related efforts were required to facilitate the basic duties. Also, work in management analysis, program analysis, or a comparable field often provides such knowledges and skills.

OR

B. Completion of two full academic years of graduate study, or all requirements for a master's or equivalent degree, in a computer related field such as computer science, data processing, or information processing science.

AND

(In the case of A or B)

C. Evidence of possession of any selective factors appropriate to the position to be filled.

For the GS—11 Level

A. A background which includes one year of work at no lower than GS—9 or equivalent and demonstrates accomplishment of computer project assignments that required a range of knowledges of computer requirements and techniques. For example, this level would be shown by assignments where, on the basis of general design criteria provided, the person developed modifications to parts of a system that re-

quired significant revisions in the logic or techniques used in the original development. In addition to the characteristics noted for the GS—9 level, qualifying accomplishments for the GS—11 level involve the following, or the equivalent:

1. Knowledge of the customary approaches, techniques, and requirements appropriate to an assigned computer applications area or computer specialty area in an organization,
2. Planning the sequence of actions necessary to accomplish the assignment where this has entailed a) coordination with others outside the organizational unit and b) development of project controls, and
3. Adaptation of guidelines or precedents to the needs of the assignment.

Such knowledge and skills typically are gained in the Computer Specialist Series or through performance of work where the primary concern was the subject matter of the computer application (e.g., supply, personnel, chemical process control) and the above types of computer related efforts were required to facilitate the basic duties. Also, work in management analysis, program analysis, or a comparable field occasionally provides such knowledge and skills.

OR

B. Completion of three full academic years of graduate study, or all requirements for a doctoral degree (Ph.D or equivalent), in a computer field such as computer science, data processing, or information processing science when 1) the position to be filled involves highly specialized work and 2) the graduate work is directly pertinent to the duties and responsibilities of the position.

AND

(In the case of A or B)

C. Evidence of possession of any selective factors appropriate to the position to be filled.

For GS—12 and above

A. A background which includes one year of work at no lower than the next lower grade or equivalent and demonstrates accomplishment of computer project assignments that required a wide range of knowledges of computer requirements and techniques pertinent to the position to be filled. This normally will have included knowledges of how the work is carried out in other organizations. In addition to the characteristics noted for the GS–9 and GS–11 levels, to be qualifying for the GS–12 and above the assignments will have involved performance of studies, such as feasibility studies, where alternatives were evaluated, reports prepared, and recommendations made.

Such knowledges and skills typically are gained in the Computer Specialist Series.

AND

B. Evidence of possession of any selective factors appropriate to the position to be filled.

RANKING QUALIFIED CANDIDATES

A suggested procedure is to analyze the requirements of the position and determine, in addition to selective factors essential to satisfactory performance, quality ranking factors which would distinguish the better qualified candidates among those who meet the minimum requirements. (Where appropriate, selective factors may also serve as quality ranking factors.)

Positions at GS–5 and GS–7

Evaluation of candidates for positions at GS–5 and GS–7 should be based on evidence indicating probable success at higher level assignments.

Other things being equal, candidates who can be expected to achieve full performance competence most quickly usually will be distinguished by:

1. The quality of achievements that indicate ability in analyzing problems,
2. The caliber, job relatedness, and extent of education or experience which provided familiarity with data processing concepts, terminology and techniques, and
3. For applications oriented positions (e.g., computer programer), the degree of subject matter knowledge of the work process to be automated.

Positions at GS–9 and above

Evaluation of candidates for positions at GS–9 and above should be based on:

1. Knowledges and skills specific to the position vacancy, and
2. Evidence of the capacity to accept change and keep pace with the rapidly evolving computer technology.

Examples of quality ranking factors specific to a position, when supported by the position description, could be the degree of: a. skill in planning, developing, and conducting training, b. knowledge of a specific application, c. familiarity with a specific model of computer, d. knowledge of techniques for development of ADP standards, e. knowledge of data base design, f. skill in simulation of new applications, and/or g. familiarity with specific operating modes.

Considerations in evaluating the capacity to accept change and keep pace with the technology could include the extent to which the candidate's background shows: a. success in a diversity of work in the computer field, b. development of systems or programs for which no precedents exist, c. accomplishments which involved the use of advanced design or programing techniques, and/or d. evidence of continuing self development, such as pertinent course work or publication of papers in ADP society journals.

ACCOUNTING, BUDGETING, AND FISCAL MANAGEMENT POSITIONS

Accounting Clerical, Supervisory, and Administrative Positions GS–7/15

EXPERIENCE, TRAINING, AND RELATED REQUIREMENTS

This standard is considered appropriate for filling such positions as Cash Accounting Assistant; Voucher Examiner; Time, Leave, and Payroll Supervisor; Benefit-Payment Roll Supervisor; etc.

A. LENGTH AND KIND OF TRAINING AND EXPERIENCE REQUIRED

Except for the substitutions provided for below, applicants must have had as a minimum the length of experience specified in the following table.

Grade of position	Total (years)	Length of experience required	
		General (years)	Specialized (years)
GS–7	4	2	2
GS–8	4½	2	2½
GS–9	5	2	3
GS–10	5½	2	3½
GS–11 and above ...	6	2	4

General experience is work in (1) accounting, auditing, or bookkeeping of a commercial type in such fields as cost accounting, financial accounting, etc., or (2) maintaining or examining fiscal records for the issuance, collection, safekeeping, or disbursing of money and securities by municipal, State, or Federal government agencies, or commercial, industrial, or eleemosynary concerns and institutions, or (3) supervising work described in (1) and (2) above with re-

sponsibility for the technical adequacy thereof, including supervision of machine accounting groups.

Specialized experience is experience in the kind of work which is to be done in the position for which the examination is held and for which application is made. (Specialized experience in excess of the required length may be accepted as general experience.)

B. PROVISION FOR SUBSTITUTION OF EDUCATION FOR EXPERIENCE

For a maximum of 2 years of the required general experience and 1 year of the specialized experience, applicants may substitute the following:

1. Study successfully completed in a resident school above high-school level with a major in the field of accounting or business administration on the basis of 1 academic year of study for 9 months of experience; *or*

2. Teaching of any of the fields named in (1) above in a resident school above high-school level on the basis of 1 academic year of teaching for 9 months of experience; *or*

3. Any time-equivalent combination of (1) and (2) above; *or*

4. The possession of a certificate as a Certified Public Accountant in a State, Territory, or the District of Columbia, provided the certificate number, date, and place of issuance are clearly stated in the application.

5. In addition, applicants who offer a bachelor's degree within 24 semester hours, or its equivalent, in any of the fields named in (1) above as a substitution for 2 years of the required general experience and 1 year of the specialized experience may substitute a master's degree in any of the fields named for 1 ad-

ditional year of specialized experience. Under this provision, an applicant with a master's degree in the named fields of study may qualify at the GS–7 level.

C. OTHER REQUIREMENTS

Quality of experience. Applicants must have had progressively responsible experience of a scope and quality sufficient to demonstrate conclusively the ability to handle the duties of the position. The degree of fiscal responsibility involved must have been proportionately greater for each successively higher grade for which the applicant is being considered. The prescribed lengths and levels of experience must be met, but meeting them does not of itself entitle one to an eligible rating. The measure of total performance must be so full as to give promise of at least satisfactory performance at the grade or grades for which he is being considered.

For grades GS–12 and above, at least 1 year of the required specialized experience must have been at a level of difficulty comparable at least to that of the next lower grade in the Federal service. For grades GS–11 and below, at least 6 months of the required specialized experience must have been at a level of difficulty comparable to that of the next lower grade in the Federal service, or 1 year must have been at a level comparable at least to that of the second lower grade.

Budget and Accounting Officer GS–11/15

DESCRIPTION OF WORK

Budget and accounting officers are typically responsible for the day-to-day supervision over the budget and the accounting operations and may also be responsible for auxiliary areas such as credit and finance, internal audit, contractor accounts, etc. As specialists, budget and accounting officers serve as technical experts for the organization's management staff on budget and on accounting matters, provide specialized accounting and budget advice, interpret the results and needs of the budget and of the accounting programs, and coordinate these two separate functions (within the subordinate staff supervised) to the extent required for the effective conduct of each function.

To perform this work, the budget and accounting officer should have a high degree of knowledge of budget and/or accounting functions and operations, plus ability to manage and direct the accounting, budgeting, and auxiliary staffs so as to provide the organization's management staff with the necessary specialized accounting and budget information and advice which that staff needs.

EXPERIENCE

All applicants must have had a total of 6 years of progressively responsible administrative, technical, or specialist experience which provided a thorough knowledge of methods of supervision, administration, and management; a demonstrated ability to deal with others. Of the 6 years, at least 3 years must have been *specialized* experience as defined below. The applicant's experience must include significant supervisory or administrative responsibilities, and also responsible technical or specialist experience in either the budget or accounting field, but *preferably in both*. If actual experience has been obtained in only one of these fields, the applicant must demonstrate possession of basic knowledge of the other area.

For some positions the services of a professionally-qualified accountant are desirable. For such positions only those applicants will be considered who also meet the qualification requirements for the Accounting Series (including, where required, passing a written test). (Some types of experience may satisfy the requirements of both the Accounting Series and this standard and may be credited accordingly.)

Eligibility in any grade level will be based upon a clear showing that the applicant has had experience of a scope and quality sufficient to give him the ability to handle technical and/or supervisory problems commensurate with the duties of the grade for which he is being considered.

SPECIALIZED EXPERIENCE

Specialized experience is progressively responsible experience in the fields of budget administration and/or accounting, or in any of the major kinds of work which are to be supervised and/or managed in the position for which the applicant is being considered. Experience in closely related fields is also acceptable, provided that the experience demonstrated competence in and knowledge of budget or accounting functions and also demonstrated:

1. Ability to plan, direct, and coordinate a budget and accounting program, and to provide service thereon;
2. Ability to select, develop, and supervise a subordinate staff;
3. Ability to establish and maintain effective working relationships with all levels of key management officials and subordinate staff.

The degree of technical ability involved must be proportionately greater for each successively higher grade for which the applicant is considered. Among the kinds of work which may be accepted as specialized experience are the following:

a. The development, direction, evaluation, or revision of budgetary control systems;
b. Budget preparation and presentation, budget analysis and/or program analysis;
c. Supervision or maintenance of commercial type accounts in such fields as cost accounting, financial accounting, etc.;
d. Supervision of the maintenance or examination of records for the issuance, collection, safekeeping, or disbursing of money and securities by municipal, State, or Federal Government agencies or private industry (including such records as cost, time, payroll, expenses, revenues, expenditures, appropriations, revolving funds, working capital, trust funds, or other fiscal records);

e. Planning, directing, or supervising a program for collecting, classifying, compiling or evaluating accounting data;
f. Planning, developing, or installing new accounting systems, or revising existing accounting systems;
g. Preparing financial or cost statements and reports used to evaluate performance or to determine status of activities or programs;
h. Auditing or examining accounting systems, records, or financial statements;
i. Examining or appraising organizational procedures, operations, or internal controls which involve financial systems or are accomplished primarily for budget or accounting purposes;
j. Preparing or reviewing reports of financial audits;
k. Experience as an office manager, owner, etc., which has involved direct supervision of accountants, auditors, or budget analysts provided that budget and accounting responsibilities comprised a major part of the position.

QUALITY OF EXPERIENCE

For grade GS–11, at least 6 months of the required specialized experience must have been at a level of difficulty comparable to that of the next lower grade in the Federal service, or 1 year must have been at a level comparable at least to that of the second lower grade. For grades GS–12 and above, at least 1 year of the required specialized experience must have been at a level of difficulty comparable at least to that of the next lower grade in the Federal service.

EDUCATIONAL AND OTHER SUBSTITUTIONS

1. Successfully completed study in a residence school above high school level in any field may be substituted for a maximum of 3 years of general experience at the rate of 1 academic year of study for 9 months of experience.
2. Full-time graduate education may be sub-

stituted for experience on the following basis. The education must have equipped the candidate with the knowledge and ability to perform fully the work of the position for which he is being considered.

a. *For 1 year of specialized experience.*—One full academic year of graduate education in business administration, public administration, economics, industrial engineering or industrial management, government, political science, or in other directly related fields.

b. *For 2 years of specialized experience.*—

Completion of all requirements for a master's or an equivalent degree, or 2 full academic years of graduate education, which is in the fields described in paragraph "a" above.

3. The possession of a certificate as a Certified Public Accountant obtained through written examination in a State, Territory, or the District of Columbia, provided the certificate number, date, and place of issuance are clearly stated in the application, may be substituted for 3 years of general experience.

Accounting Series, GS–5/15
Auditing Series, GS–5/11–5/15

DESCRIPTION OF WORK

Accountants and auditors perform professional work in any of several capacities depending upon the accounting system involved, the organizations and operating programs served, the financial data sought, and the needs of management. Accountants classify and evaluate financial data; record transactions in financial records; develop and install new accounting systems, revise existing accounting systems; and prepare and analyze financial statements, records and reports. Auditors examine accounts for the purpose of certifying or attesting that as of a certain date or for a stated period various financial statements fairly present the financial position of the activity audited in terms of assets, liabilities, net worth, and income and expenses. Auditors evaluate such matters as (a) the degree of compliance with laws, regulations and principles of sound financial management; (b) the effectiveness, economy, and efficiency of resource utilization and management systems; and (c) the extent to which desired results or benefits are being achieved. Audit emphasis includes evaluating internal controls to determine the reliability of reported results; and assuring that generally accepted accounting principles have been consistently applied by the activity audited.

BASIC REQUIREMENTS FOR ALL GRADES

Candidates for all grades must meet the requirements of paragraph A, B, or C below:

A. A full 4-year course of study in an accredited college or university which meets all of that institution's requirements for a bachelor's degree with an accounting major.

B. A full 4-year course of study in an accredited college or university that meets all requirements for a bachelor's degree and that included or was supplemented by at least 24 semester hours in accounting.[1]

C. At least 4 years of experience in accounting, or an equivalent combination of accounting experience, college-level education, and training that provided professional accounting knowledge equivalent in type, scope, and thoroughness to that acquired through successful completion of a 4-year college curriculum in accounting as in A above. → The background of candidates who meet the requirements of this paragraph must also include one of the following: ←

[1]Generally, for editorial convenience, the term "accounting" is used in lieu of "accounting and/or auditing." Similarly "accountant" should be interpreted, generally, as "accountants and/or auditors."

1. Twenty-four semester hours in accounting or auditing courses of appropriate type and quality. Note: Resident or home-study academic courses conducted by a Federal agency or a nonaccredited institution that are determined to be fully equivalent to accounting and auditing courses in an accredited college may be accepted.
2. A certificate as Certified Public Accountant or a Certified Internal Auditor, obtained through written examination.
3. Recognized, well-established professional stature in accounting or auditing based on a combination of (a) successful experience in a variety of highly responsible accounting functions in positions equivalent to GS–12 or higher, and (b) significant documented contributions to the accounting or auditing profession through publications, leadership in professional organizations, development of new methods and techniques, or comparable achievements.
4. Completion of the requirements for a bachelor's or higher degree with major study in accounting, auditing or a related field which includes substantial course work in accounting or auditing, e.g., 15 semester hours, but which does not fully satisfy the 24 semester hour requirement of paragraph B provided that (a) the candidate has successfully demonstrated the ability to perform work of the GS–12 or higher grade level in accounting, auditing or a related field, e.g., valuation engineering or financial institution examining; (b) a panel of at least two higher level professional accountants or auditors have determined that the candidate has demonstrated a good knowledge of accounting and of related and underlying fields that equals in breadth, depth, currency, and level of advancement that normally obtained with successful completion of the 4-year course of study in paragraph A; and (c) except for literal nonconformance to the requirement of 24 semester hours in accounting, the candidate's education,

training, and experience fully meet the specified requirements.

GS–5.—The basic requirements are fully qualifying for grade GS–5.

ADDITIONAL EXPERIENCE AND TRAINING REQUIREMENTS

Candidates for grades GS–7 and above must have had either professional experience or graduate education, or an equivalent combination of both, in addition to meeting the basic requirements. This professional experience or graduate education must have been in or directly related to accounting or auditing or in a field closely related to the position to be filled.

1. EXPERIENCE

In addition to the basic requirements, the following amounts of professional experience are required for grades GS–7 and above:

Grade:	Years
GS–7	1
GS–9	2
GS–11 and above	3

For grades GS–11 and below at least 6 months of the required experience must have been at a level of difficulty comparable to that of the next lower grade or 1 year comparable to the second lower grade in the Federal service. For grades GS–12 and above at least 1 year of the required experience must have been at a level of difficulty comparable to that of the next lower grade in the Federal service.

2. EDUCATION

In addition to the basic requirements, the following amounts and levels of education are qualifying for grades GS–7 and above. This education must have been either in accounting and auditing or in directly related fields.

GS–7 .... One full academic year of graduate education.

GS–9 .... Completion of all requirements for a master's or equivalent degree; or two full academic years of graduate education.

Equivalent combinations of professional experience and graduate education of the type described above are acceptable at each grade.

3. ALTERNATE REQUIREMENTS

a. Superior academic achievement at the baccalaureate level or 1 year of student trainee experience in accounting or auditing is qualifying at grade GS–7. A combination of superior academic achievement at the baccalaureate level and 1 year of appropriate professional experience is qualifying at grade GS–9.

b. Technician experience: For positions at GS–7 only, candidates who have completed the required 24 semester hours in accounting and who have experience—in addition to that needed to satisfy the basic requirement for all positions—as an accounting technician equivalent to grade GS–5 or higher may have that experience credited for GS–7 on a month-for-month basis up to a maximum of 12 months.

SELECTIVE AND QUALITY RANKING FACTORS

In general, candidates who meet the "Basic Requirements For All Grades" are qualified for positions at the entrance and lower levels in any specialized branch of accounting such as cost, systems, staff, and auditing. Specific knowledges, skills, and/or abilities will be used as quality ranking factors under justification that shows: (a) how the quality ranking factor is directly related to the duties and responsibilities of the position; and (b) why possession of the desired knowledge, skill and/or ability would predict superior performance.

For other specialized positions, only candidates who possess specific job-related knowledges, skills, and/or abilities may be qualified. Justification for selective placement factors must show: (a) how the selective factor is directly related to the duties and responsibilities of the position; and (b) why possession of the knowledges, skills, and/or abilities identified as selective factors are necessary for successful performance in the position.

The Office of Personnel Management Position-Classification Standard for the Accounting Series and the Auditing Series includes a great deal of valuable information on the various specialized branches of accounting.

BASIS OF RATING

No written test is required. Candidates will be rated on a scale of 100 on the extent and quality of their experience and training. Ratings will be based upon candidates' statements in their applications and upon any additional information that may be secured by the Office of Personnel Management.

Professional knowledge of accounting is defined as (a) a thorough knowledge of the concepts, theories, principles and practices of general and cost accounting; public industrial and/or governmental accounting; auditing, taxation, budgeting and analysis of financial statements; and trends and current developments in the accounting profession in government, industry and public accounting firms; (b) an understanding of the legal principles that govern financial transactions and relationships in government or industry; and (c) a basic foundation in related fields such as banking, mathematical analysis, statistics, automatic data processing systems and techniques, business organization, and the principles and processes of management.

Professional ability to apply accounting knowledge is defined as the ability to (a) apply fundamental and diversified professional accounting concepts, theories, and practices to achieve financial management objectives with versatility, judgment, and perception; (b) adapt and apply methods and techniques of related disciplines such as economics and statistical analysis; and (c) organize, analyze, interpret, and evaluate financial data in the solution of management and accounting problems.

Positive and continuing development of professional knowledge and ability is defined as an action program involving activities such as the following as appropriate to the circumstances:

(a) Developing new approaches, methods or techniques for the solution of problems in accounting or auditing;

(b) Formal or informal training and guidance on the job by specialists or more mature professionals;

(c) College-level academic study;

(d) Participations in seminars, conferences, and technical committees of professional societies and other organizations;

(e) Review and study of the professional literature of accounting and related fields;

(f) Publication of professional papers.

Professional work in accounting, like that of other professions, is marked by continuing personal effort to keep abreast of the advancing and changing discipline. Continuing education in accounting and related fields is an important element of full professional competence as an accountant which should be considered in evaluating the qualifications of candidates for professional accountant positions. Accounting technicians who desire to make the upward mobility transition to professional accountant must not only satisfy the essential requirement of 24 semester hours in accounting, but should plan on continued academic course work.

EDUCATION IN ACCOUNTING

UNDERGRADUATE EDUCATION

Most accounting majors consist of 24 semester hours of accounting courses that have easily recognizable titles such as elementary accounting, intermediate accounting, advanced accounting, auditing, Federal tax accounting, cost accounting, CPA problems, accounting systems, internal auditing, government accounting, accounting theory, accounting seminar, and the like. However, not all professional accounting courses have the words accounting or auditing in their titles. Courses entitled, for example, analysis of financial statements, business budgeting, cost analysis and control, investment analysis, and statement and report presentation and analysis are considered professional accounting courses when they: (a) have as a prerequisite one or more clearly identifiable professional accounting courses such as principles of accounting; and (b) are primarily concerned with the development, analysis, and presentation of financial data and/or the interpretation and evaluation of financial information and its application to management problems.

GRADUATE EDUCATION

Graduate education may have been either in accounting or in directly related fields such as business administration, finance, comptrollership, and management. Normally such study includes one or more courses in accounting.

ACCEPTANCE OF TECHNICIAN EXPERIENCE

At grade GS−7, for competitive appointment and for inservice placement accounting technician experience at the grade GS−5 level and above may be accepted toward meeting the professional experience requirements as described on page 60, provided the candidate meets the basic requirements for all grades on page 59.

Accounting Technician GS−4/9

DESCRIPTION OF DUTIES

Accounting technicians perform nonprofessional work necessary to insure the effective operation of established accounting systems. They apply a basic understanding of accounting concepts and procedures in performing such functions as classifying accounting transactions; maintaining, balancing and reconciling accounting records; examining accounting records to verify accuracy; determining appropriate adjustments and special entries; preparing and verifying accounting statements and reports; and performing prescribed analyses of accounting data and reports. These functions may involve a narrow range of accounts or may encompass the entire accounting system of the activity, depending on the nature and level of assignments.

EXPERIENCE REQUIREMENTS

Except for the substitutions provided for below, candidates must have had the kind and amount of experience shown in the table and described in the statements immediately following.

Grade	General experience (years)	Specialized experience (years)	Total experience (years)
GS–4	2	0	2
GS–5	2	1	3
GS–6	2	2	4
GS–7	2	3	5
GS–8 and above	2	4	6

1. *General experience* is clerical work which has demonstrated arithmetic aptitude and ability, accuracy and attention to detail, and the ability to apply established procedures for recording and compiling data. Such work may have involved—
   (a) maintaining various types of records requiring accuracy in selecting, posting, and consolidating pertinent data;
   (b) coding, compiling, or verifying statistical data;
   (c) making arithmetic computations, applying formulas or conversion tables, etc.;
   (d) screening various types of documents to verify the accuracy of codes, amounts, or similar data in numeric form against related documents or guides;
   (e) operating various calculating or posting machines provided this work included responsibility for verifying accuracy; or
   (f) similar work which demonstrated the relevant abilities.

2. *Specialized experience* is work which required the candidate to acquire and apply a knowledge of established accounting procedures and techniques in the performance of such functions as—
   (a) analyzing and classifying or recording transactions;
   (b) balancing, reconciling, adjusting, or examining accounts;
   (c) developing or verifying accounting data for reports, statements, and schedules; or
   (d) performing prescribed analyses of accounting data.

Directly related specialized experience is defined as experience gained in the same specialized area of accounting technician work as the position for which application is made.

3. *Quality of experience.*—Candidates for any grade must have at least 1 year of experience at a level of difficulty comparable to the next lower grade or 2 years of experience at the level of difficulty comparable to the second lower grade in the Federal service.

SUBSTITUTIONS ALLOWED

1. Study successfully completed in a resident college, university, or junior college may be substituted for *general* experience on the basis of *one-half academic year* of study for *6 months* of experience provided it included at least 3 semester hours per year in the fields of bookkeeping or accounting.
2. Study successfully completed in a resident business or commercial school or other comparable institution above the high school level may be substituted for *general* experience on the basis of *one-half academic year* of study for *6 months* of experience provided such study included accounting or bookkeeping as well as other subjects such as business English, office machines, filing and indexing, office practices or business mathematics. No credit will be allowed for training which has been obtained only or primarily in the basic skills of shorthand or typing or refresher courses.
3. Study of the nature described in 1 and 2 above may be substituted for the *first year* of specialized experience on the basis of *1 academic year* of study for *6 months* of specialized experience.

Under these provisions a 2-year course of study of the above nature meets the experience requirements for grade GS–4 and a full 4-year course of study meets the experience requirements for grade GS–5.

WRITTEN TEST

A written test of abilities necessary to learn and perform the duties of these positions is required for positions at grade GS–4.

BASIS OF RATING

Competitors for all positions will be rated on a scale of 100. Rankings are made:
1. For competitive appointments at GS–4: on the basis of the written test.
2. For competitive appointments above GS–4 and for in-service placement actions at all grades: on the basis of the extent and quality of experience and training relevant to the duties of the position.

IN-SERVICE PLACEMENT PROVISIONS

1. SUBSTITUTION FOR SPECIALIZED EXPERIENCE

Responsible work in closely related occupations which has demonstrated potential for advancement and aptitude for accounting technician work may be substituted for a *maximum of 1 year* of specialized experience. Experience in related work may be credited provided it involved—
(a) demonstrated analytical ability in interpreting and applying a body of regulations and procedures under varying conditions;
(b) substantial responsibilities for verifying the accuracy and completeness of data in source and supporting documents or reports and for tracing and correcting discrepancies; *and*
(c) reconciling records maintained with related accounting data *or* performing prescribed analyses of the records maintained.

Work in related areas which does not fully meet the above conditions is creditable as *general* experience only.

2. WAIVER OF DIRECTLY RELATED EXPERIENCE REQUIREMENT

The requirement for directly related experience may be waived under the following conditions:
(a) For lateral reassignments when:
(1) The candidate has had experience that provided a general familiarity with the work of the position for which he is being considered; *and*
(2) A review of the candidate's experience and performance discloses possession of the necessary skills and abilities, and evidences potential for successful performance of the work.
(b) For promotion actions, where it is clearly shown that:
(1) Despite the lack of directly related experience, the candidate's background gives positive evidence that he possessed to a superior degree the essential skills and abilities needed for the position; *and*
(2) The candidate has had experience that has provided a general familiarity with the work of the position for which he is being considered; *and*
(3) The overall evaluation of the candidate's background provides strong evidence that he can successfully perform the higher grade work without prolonged training.

3. SUGGESTIONS FOR EVALUATING EMPLOYEES FOR IN-SERVICE PLACEMENT

In evaluating candidates for in-service placement to accounting technician jobs, it is suggested that inquiries be made of former supervisors of the candidate to elicit detailed information concerning demonstrated abilities, type of work experience and past responsibilities.

Inquiries should develop information on:
(a) The kind and extent of knowledges of double entry accounting processes or of closely related recordkeeping techniques. (NOTE: The accounting and finance unit is not the only place where such pertinent experience can be gained);
(b) The degree of responsibility for interpreting guidelines and procedures, and the relative degree of supervision; and
(c) Such personal characteristics and interests as—
• interest and aptitude in working with figures;
• ability to maintain a high level of accuracy in work requiring close attention to detail;

- interest in the purpose and effect of prescribed procedures; or
- initiative in questioning unusual actions or in obtaining information to support or verify questionable actions.

In ranking individuals, other things being equal, the greatest credit should be given to those with the greatest amount of directly related experience, and to those who have had the great-

est responsibility and freedom from supervision. Extra credit may be given for a broader range of experience (in addition to any required directly related experience) when the broader experience will be of benefit in the position and if it gives evidence of greater potential for development. Extra credit may also be given for completion of correspondence courses or part-time study, not credited under educational substitution provisions, in accounting or bookkeeping.

Budget Analyst, GS–5/15
Budget Officer, GS–11/15
Budget Examiner, GS–5/15 (OMB only)

DESCRIPTION OF WORK

Positions in this series perform, advise on, or supervise work in the phases or systems of budget administration currently in use in the Federal service. Such work primarily requires knowledge and skill in the application of related laws, regulations, policies, precedents, methods and techniques of budgeting.

Budget Analysts perform a segment, but less than the full range of the budget administration work done in the employing component or installation. The work requires a knowledge of the particular phase(s) of budgeting, analytical methods, processes, and procedures used in budgeting for assigned organizations, programs or activities. Budget analysts analyze the relative costs and benefits of alternate courses of budget and program action, check the propriety of obligations and expenditures, establish standard rates and charges to customers of industrially-funded activities, or develop budgetary policy and regulatory guidance.

Budget Officers are responsible for the full complement of budgetary operations which support the programs and personnel of the employing organizational component and level. At a minimum a budget officer's responsibilities include formulation and execution of the annual operating budget for the employing component. However, most budget officers also provide expert staff advice and assistance to managers by developing budget plans and estimates, inter-

preting budget laws, policies, and regulations, analyzing the cost effectiveness of program operations, and recommending alternate sources of program funding.

Budget Examiners are budgetary experts in the Office of Management and Budget (OMB) actively engaged in the review, analysis, and control of the budgetary operations of Federal agencies and departments. Budget examiners approve, disapprove, or adjust agency requests for funds in proposed and approved annual budgets and provide budgetary guidance to Federal agencies. These positions are established only in OMB.

For a more complete description of the work performed by budget analysts, budget officers, and budget examiners, refer to the position classification standard for the Budget Analysis Series.

EXPERIENCE REQUIREMENTS

Applicants must show that they have met the general and specialized experience requirements summarized in the following chart:

Grade	Specialized (years)	General (years)	Total (years)
GS–5	0	3	3
GS–7	1	3	4
GS–9	2	3	5
GS–11 and above	3	3	6

General experience is experience from which the applicant gained a general knowledge of financial and management principles and practices applicable to organizations. Experience in specialized fields which are closely related to budget analysis or excess specialized experience is acceptable as general experience.

Specialized experience is experience which provided specific knowledge and skill in the application of budgetary principles, practices, methods and procedures directly related to the work of the position to be filled. Such experience must have included substantially full-time work or its part-time equivalent in one or more of the following budgetary functions.

—budget preparation, justification, and presentation;

—budget execution (i.e., monitoring and control of obligations and expenditures);

—development of budgetary policies, procedures, and guides;

—development, evaluation, or revision of budgetary control systems; or

—planning and budgeting for the operations of a working capital fund.

QUALITY OF EXPERIENCE

Applicants must demonstrate progressively responsible experience of a scope, quality, and degree such as to have equipped them with the capability to perform duties at the grade level of the position for which application is made. Typically, this is demonstrated by accomplishment of assignments of the difficulty and responsibility described in the position classification standard used to evaluate positions at the next lower grade in the normal line of promotion to the position being filled.

Specialized experience which involved less than the majority of the candidate's time is to be prorated and credited on a month-for-month basis. In crediting experience gained in the Federal service, the grade of specialized experience may or may not be equivalent to the grade level of the position in which it was gained. Whenever possible, determination of the grade level of specialized experience should be based upon the

classification evaluation of the budget work performed.

SUBSTITUTION OF EDUCATION

Education may be substituted for the required experience as follows:

1. Undergraduate Education
   a. Successful completion of a four year course of study in an accredited college or university leading to a bachelor's degree or the equivalent is acceptable as meeting all requirements for the GS–5 level.
   b. Part-time undergraduate education of the type described above may be substituted at the rate of 1 year of education for 9 months of general experience.
2. Graduate Education
   a. Successful completion of one full academic year of relevant graduate education in business administration, economics, accounting, governmental budgeting, public administration, industrial engineering, political science, or an equally relevant field with comparable course work meets all requirements for grade GS–7.
   b. Successful completion of all requirements for a master's or equivalent degree, or 2 full years of graduate education which is in one of the fields described in paragraph (a) above meets all requirements for grade GS–9.
   c. For some positions, notably those which also require intensive knowledge of the Congressional budget process, economics, or statistics, completion of all requirements for a doctoral degree in a field directly related to the work of the position to be filled is accepted as qualifying for grade GS–11.
   d. Part-time graduate education of the type described above may be substituted at the rate of 30 semester hours for 1 year of specialized experience, or 15 semester hours for ½ year of specialized experience.
3. Education may not be substituted for the required experience above the GS–11 level.

SPECIAL PROVISIONS FOR INSERVICE PLACEMENT

Positions covered by this standard may be filled at the GS–5 and GS–7 levels without regard to experience or educational requirements of Part I of this standard by inservice lateral reassignment of employees from positions in the Budget Clerical and Assistance Series, the Accounting Technician Series, the General Accounting Clerical and Administrative Series, or other series which provided comparable financial skills. Unless otherwise qualified under experience and educational requirements described in other parts of this standard, employees reassigned under this provision must serve at least 1 year in the position at the grade level at which reassigned before promotion within this series.

This provision is not to be used to promote an employee from a clerical, assistant, or technician occupation directly into a position in this series.

BASIS OF RATING

Candidates for competitive appointment to all positions will be rated on the basis of their experience and/or education as it relates to the work or the position to be filled.

GUIDE FOR EVALUATING CANDIDATES

Positions at all grade levels in this series require:
1. Ability to effectively express ideas and recommendations orally and in writing;
2. Ability to reason in quantitative terms (e.g., in numerical concepts);
3. Analytical ability which includes the ability to conceptualize, generalize, and draw meaningful inferences and conclusions from financial and narrative data;
4. Ability to work effectively under pressure of tight time frames and rigid deadlines;
5. In addition, some positions in this series require skill in presenting and gaining the acceptance of budgetary requests, recommendations, and decisions during formal negotiations with fund granting and reviewing authorities.

For positions at the entry level (GS–5 and GS–7) credit should be given for experience and education which has demonstrated the candidate's ability to communicate effectively, both orally and in writing.

Analytical ability of the type required in this series is often demonstrated through completion of college-level courses in logic, philosophy, economics, mathematics (e.g., probability and statistics), computer science, chemistry and physics. In ranking candidates, courses which included analytical methods and techniques commonly used in budget analysis may also be considered. While courses in business mathematics, financial management, statistics, economics, and accounting are highly desirable, they have not been specified as minimum educational requirements because to do so could possibly exclude some candidates who would otherwise be well-qualified to do the work.

SELECTIVE PLACEMENT FACTORS

In filling positions at grades above the entry levels, selective factors may be appropriate for screening candidates. If selective factors are used, the requirements must be job related, and need for them must be reflected in the official position description or other official communication. These will vary considerably, depending upon the nature of the position to be filled.

QUALITY RANKING FACTORS

Candidates who meet or exceed the basic requirements, including any selective factors, may be ranked according to their degree of proficiency on quality ranking factors which have been identified for use. Examples of quality ranking factors could include:
1. Knowledge of the programs and work processes of organizations for which budgetary services are provided.
2. Skill in developing and presenting briefings on budgetary matters.

Volunteer service (e.g., in charitable, religious, or service organizations) is to be counted toward meeting experience requirements of this standard.

Savings and Loan Examiner GS–5/15
Farm Credit Examiner GS–5/15
Investment Company Examiner GS–5/15
Savings and Loan Examining Officer GS–12/15
Farm Credit Examining Officer GS–12/15
Investment Company Examining Officer GS–12/15

DESCRIPTION OF WORK

Examiners in positions of these kinds make examinations and audits of savings and loan associations, farm credit associations, cooperative banks, investment institutions, national banks, or other financial institutions to determine financial condition, soundness of operations, compliance with regulatory laws and provisions, integrity of accounts, and other pertinent matters.

Examining Officers in positions of these kinds plan, manage, and direct the work of examiners of financial institutions.

EXPERIENCE REQUIREMENTS

Except for the substitutions provided for below, applicants must have had experience of the kinds and amounts specified below:

Grade	Total (years)	General (years)	Specialized (years)
GS–5	3	3	....
GS–7	4	3	1
GS–9	5	3	2
GS–11 and above	6	3	3

GENERAL EXPERIENCE

(1) Experience in positions requiring a thorough knowledge and the application of commercial accounting or auditing principles and practices (but less than full professional accounting knowledges), i.e., experience which has provided an understanding of debits and credits, the principles of journalizing, balance sheets, and operating statements; or

(2) Experience with a savings and loan association, savings or commercial bank, or other financial institution, requiring knowledge of accounting or auditing principles as applied to such institutions; or

(3) Any time-equivalent combination of (1) and (2) above.

SPECIALIZED EXPERIENCE—TYPE A (USUAL REQUIREMENT)

(4) Progressively responsible experience requiring a thorough knowledge and the application of accounting or auditing principles and practices (but less than full professional accounting knowledge) with a financial institution engaged in mortgage lending operations, with the mortgage loan department of an insurance company, or with a Federal agency making, insuring, guaranteeing, or supervising mortgage lending; *or*

(5) Progressively responsible experience in the examining or auditing of such financial institutions as savings and loan associations, savings or commercial banking institutions or trust companies, Federal Reserve Banks, farm credit associations, or Federal or State credit unions; *or*

(6) For up to a *maximum of 2 years* of experience, professional accounting or auditing work which provided a broad knowledge of the application of accounting or auditing principles and practices; *or*

(7) Any time-equivalent combination of (4), (5), and (6) above.

SPECIALIZED EXPERIENCE—TYPE B (OPTIONAL REQUIREMENT)

(8) Experience which has provided a thorough knowledge of Federal and State laws ap-

plicable to the type of financial institution involved and of the operations and practices of such institutions.

Specialized experience, Type B may be required for some positions but when required, this will not increase the total length of required experience. The specialized experience, Type B may be required, therefore, in lieu of part of the above stated requirement for either general experience or specialized experience, or both. For grade GS–7, specialized experience, Type B may be the sole specialized experience which is required.

Specialized experience, Type A in excess of that required may be substituted for general experience.

SUBSTITUTION OF EDUCATION FOR EXPERIENCE

1. Study successfully completed in a resident institution above the high school level may be substituted for general experience at the rate of 1 academic year of study for 9 months of experience provided that such study included an average of 6 semester hours (or the equivalent) in either one or two of the following, or directly related fields: accounting, banking, business administration, commercial or banking law, economics, or finance. For some positions 12 semester hours of this study must have been in accounting. A total of 4 academic years of study as described in this paragraph is qualifying for grade GS–5.

2. Full-time graduate education may be substituted for experience on the following basis.

a. *For 1 year of specialized experience.*—One full academic year of graduate education in one of the following: accounting, banking, business administration, economics, finance, or other directly related fields. (This amount and kind of education meets all the requirements for grade GS–7.)

b. *For 2 years of specialized experience.*— Completion of all requirements for a master's or an equivalent degree, or 2 full academic years of graduate education, which is in the fields described in paragraph "a" above. (This amount and kind of education meets all the requirements for grade GS–9.)

3. Applicants may substitute the possession of a certificate as a Certified Public Accountant in a State, Territory, or the District of Columbia for all of the 3 years of general experience, provided the certificate number and date of issuance are clearly shown.

QUALITY OF EXPERIENCE

The prescribed lengths and levels of experience must be met, but meeting them does not of itself entitle one to an eligible rating unless the quality of the applicant's total background gives promise of satisfactory performance at the grade level for which the applicant is being considered.

For grades GS–11 and below, at least 6 months of the required specialized experience must have been at a level of difficulty comparable to that of the next lower grade in the Federal service, or 1 year must have been at a level of difficulty comparable at least to that of the second lower grade. For grades GS–12 and above, at least 1 year of the required specialized experience must have been at a level of difficulty comparable to that of the next lower grade in the Federal service.

ADDITIONAL REQUIREMENTS

All applicants must demonstrate ability to meet and deal successfully and effectively with the public.

WRITTEN TEST

Applicants for grade GS–5 and GS–7 positions must pass an appropriate written test.

Applicants for all positions at grades GS–9 and above will not be required to take a written test.

BASIS OF RATING

Applicants for GS-5 and GS-7 positions will be rated on the basis of their test scores and an evaluation of their education and experience.

Applicants for all positions at GS-9 and above will be rated on the basis of the quality, diversity, and extent of their experience and its relevance to the duties of the position to be filled. Such ratings will be based on the competitors' statements in their applications and on any additional evidence which is obtained.

LAW ENFORCEMENT POSITIONS

Investigator
Supervisory Investigator
Criminal Investigator
Supervisory Criminal Investigator
GS-5/15

COVERAGE

These standards are intended to be used primarily in filling investigator and criminal investigator positions which involve the performance of factfinding and reporting duties and related responsibilities described below, and other positions in these series for which actual investigative experience is essential. All parts of these standards apply to positions in both the General Investigating Series and the Criminal Investigating Series; where variations exist involving differences in investigating duties, specialized experience, physical standards, and minimum age requirements, these are so indicated.

DESCRIPTION OF WORK

INVESTIGATORS

Investigators plan and conduct investigations relating to the administration of, or compliance with, Federal laws and regulations. The duties performed typically include: Collecting facts and obtaining information by observing conditions, examining records, and interviewing individuals; writing and securing affidavits; administering oaths; preparing investigative reports to be used as a basis for court or administrative action; testifying before administrative bodies, courts, or grand juries, or serving as a witness for the Government. The work occasionally may involve criminal investigations.

Performance of these duties may require work at irregular hours and considerable travel. In-

vestigators may also be required to operate motor vehicles.

CRIMINAL INVESTIGATORS

Criminal investigators plan and conduct investigations relating to alleged or suspected violations of Federal laws. The duties typically performed include: obtaining physical and documentary evidence; interviewing witnesses; applying for and serving warrants for arrests, searches, and seizures; seizing contraband, equipment and vehicles; examining files and records; maintaining surveillance; performing undercover assignments; preparing investigative reports; testifying in hearings and trials; and assisting U.S. Attorneys in the prosecution of court cases. Most criminal investigators are required to carry firearms and to be proficient in their use. The work may occasionally involve noncriminal investigations.

Performance of these duties frequently requires irregular unscheduled hours, personal risks, exposure to all kinds of weather, considerable travel, and arduous exertion, under adverse environmental conditions. Criminal investigators may also be required to operate motor vehicles.

TYPES OF POSITIONS

The kind of investigative work performed varies in respect to the investigative jurisdiction and functions of the employing agencies. The grade levels of the positions vary with the scope, complexity, and importance of investigations and the degree of individual responsibility required. At the higher grade levels, investigators may also serve as team leaders, group supervisors, case reviewers, unit coordinators, or in similar capacities, with responsibility for supervising the work of other investigators; or they may be responsible for the management or direction of an investigative program or program segment.

The duties of some positions require experience or equivalent educational backgrounds (*a*) which have been obtained in or are closely related to particular industries, business operations, commercial enterprises, professions, or other occupational areas; or (*b*) which have been obtained in both the investigative and the criminal investigative areas.

EXPERIENCE REQUIREMENTS

Except for the substitutions provided for below, applicants must have had experience of the length shown in the table and of the nature described in the paragraphs following:

Grade	General experience (years)	Specialized experience (years)	Total experience (years)
GS–5	3	0	3
GS–7	3	1	4
GS–9	3	2	5
GS–11 and above ...	3	3	6

GENERAL EXPERIENCE

This must have been progressively responsible experience which has required (1) ability to work or deal effectively with individuals or groups of persons, (2) skill in collecting and assembling pertinent facts, (3) ability to prepare clear and concise reports, and (4) ability and willingness to accept responsibility. Acceptable general experience may have been gained in types of work such as the following:

(1) Adjustment or investigation of claims arising under law, contract, or governmental order;

(2) Analysis of reports or data or the preparation of surveys, studies, or reports, requiring the development, organization, evaluation and interpretation of substan-

tive program, technical, or similar information;

(3) Examining, administrative, or professional experience with Government regulatory bodies requiring review of regulatory material or reports on compliance with regulations;

(4) Experience requiring ability to determine applicability of laws, rules, and regulations, and to explain legal requirements;

(5) Responsible auditing and accounting work which included analyzing books and records, and preparation of statements and reports in accordance with recognized accounting standards, procedures, and principles;

(6) Adjudication or examination of claims which required the collection and analysis of pertinent data and the preparation of written reports and recommendations on such claims;

(7) Performance of preliminary record inspection, verification and procurement of documents required to establish prima facie cases from courts and law enforcement agencies and securing of related information from records of such courts and agencies;

(8) Experience as a teacher of accounting or law in a resident college or university;

(9) Experience described below under "Specialized Experience" for either Investigator or Criminal Investigator;

(10) Any time-equivalent combination of any of the above or comparable types of experience.

SPECIALIZED EXPERIENCE

This must have been progressively responsible investigative experience which demonstrated (1) initiative, ingenuity, resourcefulness, and judgment required to collect, assemble, and develop facts and other pertinent data; (2) ability to think logically and objectively, to analyze and evaluate facts, evidence, and related information, and arrive at sound conclusions; (3) skill in written and oral reports and presentation of investigative findings in a clear and concise manner; and (4) tact, discretion, and capacity for obtaining the cooperation and confidence of others.

For Investigator positions, this may be either investigative or criminal investigative experience, or comparable experience. For Criminal Investigator positions, this must have been criminal investigative experience, or comparable experience.

INVESTIGATOR POSITIONS

Acceptable investigative experience may have been obtained in types of work such as the following:

(1) Investigations of difficult casualty or insurance claims;

(2) Investigations conducted for a private detective agency which involved responsible factfinding and reporting on substantial issues;

(3) Newspaper reporting where the major responsibility involved personal investigations of facts pertaining to violations of law;

(4) Investigations in connection with the prosecution or defense of civil or criminal cases;

(5) Investigations for a Federal, State, county, or municipal agency;

(6) Investigations of important cases for practicing attorneys; or practice of law involving a substantial amount of investigative work or analysis of issues of fact and law;

(7) Legal experience involving such activities as personal participation in court cases and interviewing of suspects or witnesses;

(8) Investigations concerning compliance with, or violations of, governmental law, rules, and regulations;

(9) Investigations of individuals for character, conduct, suitability, and fitness for employment;

(10) Any of the types of specialized experience described for Criminal Investigators, below;

(11) Any time-equivalent combination of the above types or similar types of experience.

CRIMINAL INVESTIGATOR POSITIONS

Acceptable criminal investigative experience may have been gained in types of work such as the following:

(1) Investigative experience as a member of a military intelligence or criminal investigative component in any of the branches of the Armed Forces or in any of the various intelligence or investigative branches of the public service, in which the principal duties consisted of the supervision of or the independent conduct of investigations of security, intelligence, or criminal cases, the preparation of comprehensive documented reports, and responsibility for testifying in court;

(2) Investigation of complex casualty or insurance claims which included a substantial number of cases involving suspected crimes or alleged fraud;

(3) Investigation of criminal cases for practicing attorneys requiring the use of recognized investigative methods and techniques;

(4) Experience in the general practice of criminal law which required appearing in court and interviewing suspects and witnesses, or which required a substantial amount of complex criminal investigative work;

(5) Experience as a uniformed law officer where the principal duties (at least 50% of the time) were criminal investigations requiring the use of a variety of investigative methods and techniques such as surveillance, assuming an undercover role, etc. (Investigative experience of this nature which has been acquired on less than a full-time basis will be pro-rated for credit.);

(6) Any time-equivalent combination of the above types or similar types of experience.

NONQUALIFYING EXPERIENCE

There are some types of experience which are related to investigative work but which are not acceptable as either general or specialized experience for either the Investigator positions or the Criminal Investigator positions. Applicants who offer only these kinds of experience will be disqualified. Experience is not acceptable if (*a*) it has not afforded training in, or required the application of the knowledges, abilities and skills described above, or (*b*) it has been acquired in essentially clerical tasks or assignments. Examples of the kinds of experience which are not qualifying are:

(1) Experience in performing the normal duties of policeman, guard, watchman, or private detective assigned principally to the protection of life or property, or similar experience in other kinds of positions;

(2) Experience as a probation or parole officer which did not require pre-sentence investigations, investigations of parolees, objective development of facts, preparation of reports, or appearance in court to defend investigative findings;

(3) The investigation of minor insurance damage claims or of the financial standing of individuals or firms for credit associations or for collection agencies;

(4) Clerical work performed incidental to the adjudication of claims;

(5) Experience generally acquired in such positions as payroll clerk or reviewer, or voucher clerk or reviewer; cash accounting clerk; cashier; teller; time and leave clerk; disbursing clerk; fiscal clerk; administrative clerk; and similar positions;

(6) Experience as an inspector whose principal duties were to examine materials, plant facilities, or equipment to determine whether they conformed to prescribed specifications or standards.

QUALITY OF EXPERIENCE

Length of experience is of less importance than demonstrated success in positions of a responsible nature, and of less importance than the breadth and scope of the pertinent knowledges, skills, and abilities possessed by the applicant and applied by him in the performance of the duties of such positions. Although no additional amount of experience beyond that required for grade GS–11 is required for grades GS–12 through GS–15, applicants for these higher grade

levels must have had a progressively higher quality of experience.

For all grades through GS–11, at least 6 months of the required specialized experience must have been of a level of difficulty and responsibility comparable to that of the next lower grade, or at least 1 year of the specialized experience must have been at a level of difficulty and responsibility comparable to that of the second lower grade in the Federal service. For the GS–12 level and above, at least 1 year of the specialized experience must have been at a level of difficulty and responsibility comparable to that of the next lower grade in the Federal service.

EDUCATIONAL AND OTHER SUBSTITUTIONS

1. *For a maximum of 3 years of general experience* (for both Investigator positions and Criminal Investigator positions):

a. Study successfully completed in an accredited college or university may be substituted at the rate of 1 year of study for 9 months of experience. (Four years of study in a college or university or completion of all requirements for a bachelor's degree qualifies for positions at grade GS–5.)

b. Possession of a certificate as a Certified Public Accountant in a State, Territory, or the District of Columbia.

2. Full-time graduate education may be substituted for experience on the following basis:

a. *For 1 year of specialized experience.—For Investigator and Criminal Investigator positions:* One full academic year of graduate education. (This amount and kind of education meets all the requirements for both types of positions at grade GS–7.)

b. *For 2 years of specialized experience.—For Investigator positions:* Completion of all requirements for a master's or an equivalent degree, or 2 full academic years of graduate education in public administration, industrial relations, political science, government, business administration, law enforcement, police administration, criminology, or directly related fields. (This amount and kind of education meets all the requirements for these positions at grade GS–9.)

For Criminal Investigator positions: Completion of all requirements for a master's or an equivalent degree, or 2 full academic years of graduate education in law enforcement, police administration, criminology, or directly related fields. (This amount and kind of education meets all the requirements for these positions at grade GS–9.)

3. Completion of a total of at least 6 years of legal and pre-legal education which meets all the requirements for an LL.B. or J.D. degree will provide eligibility in full at grade GS–9 for both Investigator positions and Criminal Investigator positions.

PERSONAL QUALITIES

In addition to meeting all other requirements, applicants for these positions must possess certain personal qualities essential for investigative work. Among these qualities are ability in oral expression; poise and self-confidence; good personal appearance; tact; initiative and drive; capacity for effective public relations; and practical intelligence.

WRITTEN TEST

Competitors for positions at the GS–5 and GS–7 levels must pass an appropriate written test.

No written test is required for positions at GS–9 and above.

BASIS OF RATING

Competitors for GS–5 and GS–7 will be rated on the basis of the written test and an evaluation of their experience and education.

Competitors for GS–9 and above will be rated on the basis of an evaluation of their experience, education, and investigative skills.

INTERVIEW

Competitors who pass the written test, as required, and who meet the experience and training requirements may be requested to appear for an interview at the time of consideration for appointment.

SPECIAL PHYSICAL REQUIREMENTS

INVESTIGATOR POSITIONS

Applicants must be physically able to perform efficiently the duties of the position for which application is made. Good distant vision in one eye and ability to read without strain printed material the size of typewritten characters are required, glasses permitted. Ability to hear the conversational voice, with or without a hearing aid, is required. In most instances, an amputation of arm, hand, leg, or foot will not disqualify an applicant for appointment, although it may be necessary that this condition be compensated by use of satisfactory prosthesis. Applicants must possess emotional and mental stability. Any physical condition which would cause the applicant to be a hazard to himself or to others will disqualify him for appointment.

CRIMINAL INVESTIGATOR POSITIONS

The duties of the positions require moderate to arduous physical exertion involving walking and standing, use of firearms, and exposure to inclement weather. Manual dexterity with comparatively free motion of finger, wrist, elbow, shoulder, hip, and knee joints is required. Arms, hands, legs, and feet must be sufficiently intact and functioning in order that applicants may perform the duties satisfactorily. Applicants must possess sufficiently good vision, with or without glasses, each eye, in order that they may perform the duties satisfactorily. Near vision, glasses permitted, must be acute for the reading of printed material the size of typewritten characters. The ability of applicants to hear the conversational voice and whispered speech without the use of a hearing aid is required. Since the duties of the position are exacting and responsible, and involve activities under trying conditions, applicants must possess emotional and mental stability. Any physical condition which would cause the applicant to be a hazard to himself or to others will disqualify for appointment.

MOTOR VEHICLE LICENSE

For some positions, applicants (*a*) must possess a valid automobile license at the time of appointment, and (*b*) must also qualify after appointment for authorization to operate motor vehicles in accordance with applicable Civil Service regulations and with related requirements of the employing agency.

AGE

INVESTIGATOR POSITIONS

Minimum of 18; see standard paragraph.

CRIMINAL INVESTIGATOR POSITIONS

Minimum of 21; not waived for any applicants including those persons entitled to veterans' preference.

EVALUATION OF EXPERIENCE AND EDUCATION FOR COMPETITIVE AND IN-SERVICE PLACEMENT PURPOSES

(1) Education which has been acquired in fields directly or closely related to the positions to be filled should be rated at a higher level than that which has been acquired in less closely or unrelated fields.

(2) Quality levels for rating investigator and criminal investigator experience should be established in accordance with the following guides:

(a) experience which has concerned matters involving substantial ramifications or elements of investigative complexity should be rated at a higher quality level than experience which did not involve such ramifications or elements (ordinarily investigative complexity can be gauged by such indicators as the size, diversity, and interrelationships of operations and activities investigated; the numbers of investigative matters growing out of the original case assignment; the numbers, size, and complexity of structure and subsidiary activities of the organizations involved; the geographic dispersion of the operations investigated; the degree of involvement of other principals; the degree of controversy surrounding the case; the potential deterrent value in successfully bringing the case to a conclusion; the delicacy of the legal issues involved; the absence of precedents; etc.);

(b) experience which has required individual responsibility on the part of the investigator for complete investigations should be rated at a higher quality level than experience which has involved responsibility for a segment or phase of an investigation, or which has involved limited responsibility for a complete investigation;

(c) experience which has required the exercise of sound independent decision-making and judgment while working under general technical and administrative supervision and direction should be rated at a higher quality level than experience which has been acquired while working under closer supervision;

(d) experience which has required the exercise of a high degree of ingenuity, resourcefulness, and creative thinking should be rated at a higher quality level than experience which called for these qualities to a lesser degree.

RATING PROCEDURE

Evaluation of the scope and level of the applicants' knowledges, skills, and abilities is of greater importance than evaluation of length of experience in individual types of positions.

Police Officer GS–2/5
Detective GS–6/7
Supervisory Police Officer GS–5/9
Supervisory Detective GS–7/8

DESCRIPTION OF WORK

Police perform or supervise performance of law enforcement work involved in the protection of life, property, and the rights of individual citizens. They enforce Federal, State, county, and municipal statutes, laws, and ordinances, and agency rules and regulations. They preserve the peace; prevent, detect, and investigate accidents and crimes; arrest violators; and aid citizens in emergency situations.

EXPERIENCE, TRAINING, AND RELATED REQUIREMENTS

All candidates for positions in grade GS–2 must take a written test to demonstrate their abilities to understand the written word, and to follow oral directions.

Candidates for positions at GS–3 and above are required to show experience of the length and nature described below:

MINIMUM EXPERIENCE AND TRAINING

Grade	Total experience required (years)
GS–2	None
GS–3	1
GS–4	2
GS–5	3
GS–6	4
GS–7 and above	5

ACCEPTABLE EXPERIENCE

For positions at GS–3, acceptable experience is that which clearly demonstrates that the candidate possesses a knowledge of general law enforcement methods and techniques that could be applied in performing police functions. This experience must have included protecting property, equipment, or materials; and person-to-person relationships in enforcing various rules and regulations.

For positions at GS–4 and above, acceptable experience is that which has given the candidate a broad knowledge of police operations, practices, and techniques. The experience must have included making arrests, protecting life and property, maintaining law and order, investigating accidents, preventing crime, and preserving the peace. Experience of this type normally may be acquired through regular, active service as a member of a Federal, state, county, municipal, or local police force or similar organization; or through service as a military police officer in the Armed Forces or Coast Guard.

QUALITY AND LEVEL OF EXPERIENCE

For nonsupervisory positions, at least 6 months of the required experience must have been at a level of difficulty and responsibility comparable to that of the next lower grade, or at least 1 year of required experience must have been at a level of difficulty and responsibility comparable to that of the second lower grade in the Federal service.

NONQUALIFYING EXPERIENCE

Experience as a prison or jail guard, night watchman, or other position which did not provide knowledges and skills in general law enforcement methods and techniques that could be applied in the performance of police functions, will not be considered as acceptable experience.

SUBSTITUTIONS

(1) Successful completion of police recruit training in a large civilian police force, a police academy, or police school, may be substituted for the experience requirements at GS–3.

(2) Successful completion of a Reserve-Police training course which included a minimum of 36 hours of actual lecture or training in police department procedures and methods, and local laws and regulations; and which led to the award of a certificate of proficiency or issuance of a badge, may be substituted for a maximum of 6 months of the experience →required for GS–3←.

(3) Successful completion of 1 year of study in a resident school above high school level may be substituted in full for the GS–3 requirements, provided each semester of study included 3 semester hours, or the equivalent, in one or more of the following subjects: police administration, police law and evidence, police investigation, criminology, law enforcement, general law, or similar subjects pertinent to police work.

(4) Successful completion of 2 years of study in a resident school above high school level may be substituted in full for the GS–4 requirements, provided each semester of study included 3 semester hours, or the equivalent, in one or more of the following subjects: police administration, police law and evidence, police investigation, criminology, law enforcement, general law, or similar subjects pertinent to police work.

(5) Successful completion of a full 4-year course of study required for a B.S. degree in Police Science from a resident school above high school level may be substituted in full for the GS–5 requirements.

MOTOR VEHICLE OPERATOR QUALIFICATIONS

For positions requiring the operation of a Government-owned motor vehicle, candidates must:
—Pass a practical road test, driving the appropriate type vehicle supplied by the agency to which the candidate is provisionally certified;
—Possess a valid State or territory motor vehicle operator's license or obtain one within 30 days after entry on duty;
—Have a satisfactory safe driving record.

BASIS OF RATING

Competitors for all positions will be rated on a scale of 100. The basis of rating will be:
For GS–2: Competitors will be rated only on the basis of the written test. They will be rated on a scale of 100. A rating of at least 70 must be obtained on the test as a whole.
For GS–3 and above: An evaluation of experience and training. Candidates must present evidence of ability to discharge the duties of the position.

PERSONAL QUALITIES

Candidates, in addition to other qualifications, must demonstrate that they possess traits and characteristics which are important to success in police work. Among these are: alertness, ability to work in stress situations, ability in oral expression, tact, integrity, capacity for effective public relations, practical intelligence, and good judgment.

AGE LIMITS

Persons appointed to police positions must be at least 21 years of age. This requirement may be waived only for veterans. Persons between the ages of 20 and 21 may file applications for examinations. Such persons will be examined but only veterans may enter on duty before attaining the age of 21 years.

PHYSICAL REQUIREMENTS

Applicants must be physically able to perform efficiently the duties of the position, which are described elsewhere in this standard. →For most positions, applicants must have binocular vision correctible to 20/20 (Snellen). Uncorrected vision must test at least 20/70 (Snellen) in each eye. Near vision corrected or uncorrected must be sufficient to read Yaeger Type 2 at 14 inches. However, there may be some positions suitable for persons with good vision in one eye only.← Ability to distinguish basic colors is essential. Ability to hear the conversational voice, without the use of a hearing aid, is required. Persons with an amputation of arm, hand, leg, or foot should not apply. Applicants must possess emotional and mental stability. Any physical condition which would cause the applicant to be a hazard to himself or to others will disqualify for appointment.

Correctional Officer GS−6/13

DESCRIPTION OF WORK

Correctional Officers supervise and perform work concerned with the correctional treatment, supervision, and custody of criminal offenders in correctional institutions or community-based treatment or rehabilitation centers. They have primary responsibility for guiding inmate conduct, supervising work details, carrying out plans for the correctional treatment and modification of attitudes of inmates, instructing and counseling inmates on institutional and personal problems, and generally ensuring the custody, safety, and well-being of inmates. On occasion, Correctional Officers are required to carry firearms.

Supervisory Correctional Officers have either (*a*) responsibility for planning, directing, coordinating and implementing programs to accomplish the work described above, and for supervising a force of Correctional Officers on all shifts, or (*b*) responsibility for the immediate supervision of correctional officers assigned to a shift or to a physical area or activity of an institution.

Grade	General experience (years)	Specialized experience (years)	Total experience (years)
GS−6	3½	None	3½
GS−7	3½	1	4½
GS−8	3½	2	5½
GS−9/13	3½	3	6½

NOTE: When positions are to be filled at grades below the normal GS−6 level, the qualification requirements should be determined by a downward extension of the criteria in this standard, e.g., 3 years of general experience is qualifying for grade GS−5.

GENERAL EXPERIENCE

Experience, paid or voluntary, full or part time, that demonstrates the applicant's aptitude for acquiring the skills and knowledges needed for correctional work, and in addition, demonstrates the possession of personal attributes important to the effectiveness of correctional officers, such as:

—ability to meet and deal with people of differing backgrounds and behavioral patterns;

—ability to be persuasive in selling or influencing ideas;

—ability to lead, supervise, and instruct;

—sympathetic attitude towards the welfare of others;

—capacity to adapt to new ideas and changing conditions;

EXPERIENCE AND TRAINING

Except for the substitution of education provided below, applicants must have had the following kinds and length of experience:

—ability to reason soundly and to think out practical solutions to problems;

—ability to pay attention to detail;

—ability to make decisions and act quickly, particularly under stress;

—poise and self-confidence, and ability to remain calm during emergency situations.

The following types of experience are illustrative of acceptable general experience, providing they meet the above criteria (this list is not intended to be all inclusive).

(1) Social case work in a welfare agency;

(2) Classroom teaching or instructing;

(3) Responsible rehabilitation work, e.g., in an alcoholic rehabilitation program;

(4) Supervision of planned recreational activities;

(5) Active participation in community action programs;

(6) Employment with a counseling service in interviewing and counseling people;

(7) Management of, or supervising work in, a business or other organization that included personnel management responsibilities in addition to directing work performance;

(8) Sales work (other than taking and filling orders as in over-the-counter sales);

(9) Active participation, as an officer or member, in extracurricular activities in college, such as student government, service organizations, college magazines or newspapers, fraternal organizations, etc.

SPECIALIZED EXPERIENCE

This is experience in the correctional custody and supervision, in accordance with modern penological concepts, of inmates of a penal or correctional institution or community based correctional treatment facility. This experience must satisfy all of the following requirements:

(a) must have included satisfactory completion of a federally operated inservice training course for correctional officers, or completion of a comparable training course covering modern correctional concepts and techniques;

(b) must have demonstrated the ability to supervise and control inmates in groups of 20 or more, and to make sound decisions in critical circumstances;

(c) must have shown the capacity to relate successfully to inmates with respect to matters such as close and continuous counseling, singly and in groups; and

(d) must have shown the ability to work independently and to assume responsibility for the correctional custody and supervision of inmate activities; to direct, observe, and correct inmate behavior; and to take precautionary measures to ensure control in situations relatively critical to the security of the institution.

In addition:

For grade GS–8, the applicant must have demonstrated the ability and knowledge necessary to perform difficult post assignments that require the judgment, maturity, and knowledge of inmate behavior developed through experience gained in performing a variety of correctional assignments; to use, and to make reports and recommendations based on the use of techniques such as informal counseling, guidance, interview, and observation, and to deal adequately with special problems of correctional custody made difficult by unusual conditions of supervision and control.

For grade GS–9 nonsupervisory positions, the applicant must have demonstrated the knowledge of, and ability to apply technical treatment and/or counseling skills and techniques acquired through formal classroom and supervised practical training. These skills may have been utilized in a variety of assignments, typically as part of structured treatment or rehabilitation programs under the guidance of professionals in the behavioral sciences or social work.

QUALITY OF EXPERIENCE

The applicant's record of experience and training must show that he has the ability to perform the duties of the position.

In addition:

For grade GS–6, applicant must have had at least 6 months of general experience comparable in difficulty and responsibility to that of the next lower grade, or 1 year comparable to the second lower grade in the Federal service.

For grades GS–7 through GS–11, at least 1 year of the specialized experience must have been comparable in difficulty and responsibility to the next lower grade, or 2 years comparable to the second lower grade in the Federal service.

For grades GS–12 and above, at least 1 year of the specialized experience must have been comparable in difficulty and responsibility to the next lower grade in the Federal service.

SUBSTITUTION OF EDUCATION AND TRAINING FOR EXPERIENCE

To be acceptable as substitution for general or specialized experience, the level and quality of the education and/or training (or of the combined experience and education and/or training) must have equipped the candidate to perform correctional duties at the grade level of the position to be filled.

GENERAL EXPERIENCE

(1) Two years of study successfully completed in a resident school above high school level may be substituted for two years of general experience.

(2) Successful completion of a full 4-year course of college study may be substituted for three years of general experience.

(3) One full semester of graduate study successfully completed in an accredited college or university, except as noted below, may be substituted for six months of general experience, and is fully qualifying for grade GS–6.

At any grade, post-high school education may be partially substituted for required experience at the rates of substitution indicated above.

SPECIALIZED EXPERIENCE

One full semester of graduate study in correctional administration, criminology, penology, sociology, or social work successfully completed in an accredited college or university may be substituted for six months of specialized experience, up to a total of 18 months.

Credit for appropriate education and training

other than that outlined above (such as manpower development programs, "New Careers" programs, rehabilitated offender programs, or inservice training programs) will be granted depending on the nature, extent, and applicability of the training in relation to the position to be filled.

SELECTIVE PLACEMENT

Additional knowledges and abilities may be required for some positions because of the concentration of inmates in distinct age, ethnic, cultural, or other specific groups in certain institutions. It is desirable for these institutions to have sufficient numbers of correctional officers who can successfully relate to the members of these groups. Selective placement consideration may be given to applicants having a thorough knowledge and understanding of the customs, language patterns, and problems of specific groups of inmates.

BASIS OF RATING

Applicants for all grades will be rated on the basis of an evaluation and appraisal of experience, education, and training.

EMPLOYMENT INTERVIEW

The personal qualities and characteristics of the applicant are the most critical of all the requirements for positions of Correctional Officer. He must be willing to perform arduous and prolonged duties on any of the three shifts. He must possess certain personal qualities in order to effectively relate to inmates in a correctional setting. These qualities include: empathy, objectivity, perceptiveness, resourcefulness, adaptability and flexibility, stability and maturity.

Before appointment, candidates may be required to appear before a panel of specialists in correctional administration for an employment interview. The interview will also serve to acquaint the applicant with further details of, and the environment surrounding, the position. A determination by the panel that a person who is otherwise qualified does not possess such personal characteristics to the required degree may result in removal of his application from further consideration. Notice will be given, in advance, of the date and place of the interview.

PHYSICAL REQUIREMENTS

The duties of these positions involve unusual mental and nervous pressure and require arduous physical exertion involving prolonged walking and standing, restraining of prisoners in emergencies, and participating in escape hunts. Applicants must be physically capable of performing efficiently the duties of the position, be free from such defects or disease as may constitute employment hazards to themselves or others, and have no deformities, disfigurements, or abnormalities which tend to be conspicuous. Persons having remediable defects or curable diseases, and who are otherwise qualified, will be admitted to the examination but must submit proof, during the time the list of eligible competitors exists, that the defects or diseases have been remedied or cured before they may be considered for appointment.

No height or weight limits are specified, but weight must be in proportion to height. Male applicants under 66 inches and female applicants under 63 inches in height will be especially evaluated for stamina and vigor.

Vision: Uncorrected vision must be no less than 20/100 (Snellen) in each eye, capable of full correction to 20/30 (Snellen) in each eye, provided that defective vision is not due to active or progressive organic disease.

Hearing: Hearing in each ear must be normal, that is, 15/15 in each ear by the whispered voice test. Hearing aids are not acceptable.

General: Hernia (with or without truss); organic heart disease (whether or not compensated); severe varicose veins; serious deformities, or disabilities of extremities (including weak feet); chronic constitutional disease; marked abnormality of speech; facial disfigurement; or other serious physical defect or disease will disqualify for appointment. Disease of the nervous system or history or presence of mental disease or emotional instability may disqualify an applicant for appointment. Before entrance on duty, appointees will be given, without expense to them, a physical examination by a Federal medical officer, and will be rejected if they do not meet the standards specified above. Persons who are offered appointment must pay their own expenses in reporting for duty. Any person reporting for duty at the place of assignment and found ineligible because of physical defects cannot be appointed, and no part of his expense for reporting and returning home can be borne by the Government.

PROFESSIONAL POSITIONS

Paralegal Specialist, GS–5 and above

DESCRIPTION OF WORK

Paralegal specialist positions involve such activities as (a) legal research, analyzing legal decisions, opinions, rulings, memoranda, and other legal material, selecting principles of law, and preparing digests of the points of law involved; (b) selecting, assembling, summarizing, and compiling substantive information on statutes, treaties, contracts, other legal instruments, and specific legal subjects; (c) case preparation for civil litigation, criminal law proceedings or agency hearings, including the collection, analysis, and evaluation of evidence, e.g., as to fraud and fraudulent and other irregular activities or violations of laws; (d) analyzing facts and legal questions presented by personnel administering specific Federal laws, answering the questions where they have been settled by interpretations of applicable legal provisions, regulations, precedents, and agency policy, and in some instances preparing informative and instructional material for general use; (e) adjudicating applications or cases on the basis of pertinent laws, regulations, policies and precedent decisions; or (f) performing other paralegal duties requiring discretion and independent judgment in the application of specialized knowledge of particular laws, regulations, precedents, or agency practices based thereon. These duties may or may not be performed under the direction of a lawyer.

EXPERIENCE AND TRAINING REQUIREMENTS

Except for the substitution of education provided for below, candidates must have had both general and specialized experience as follows:

| Grade | Experience | | |
	General (years)	Specialized (years)	Total (years)
GS–5	3	0	3
GS–7	3	1	4
GS–9	3	2	5
GS–11 and above	3	3	6

GENERAL EXPERIENCE

This is progressively responsible experience which demonstrated the ability to explain, apply or interpret rules, regulations, procedures, policies, precedents, or other kinds of criteria. Such experience may have been gained in administrative, professional, investigative, technical, high level clerical, or other responsible work.

SPECIALIZED EXPERIENCE

This is legal, quasi-legal, paralegal, legal technician, or related work that demonstrated:
- —Ability to evaluate pertinent facts and evidence;
- —Ability to interpret and apply laws, rules, regulations, and precedents;
- —Skill and judgment in the analysis of cases;
- —Ability to communicate effectively orally and in writing;
- —As required, ability to deal effectively with individuals and groups;
- —As required, knowledge of the pertinent subject area.

Qualifying specialized experience may have been acquired in positions which involved, for example:
(1) Preparation, development, examination, review, or authorization of action on claims in accordance with applicable laws, rules, regulations, precedents, policies, office practices and established procedures; or

(2) Examination and/or preparation of contracts, legal instruments, or other documents to assure completeness of information and conformance to pertinent laws, rules, regulations, precedents, and office requirements which has required the application of a specialized knowledge of particular laws, or of regulations, precedents or practices based thereon; or

(3) Analysis of legal decisions, opinions, rulings, memoranda, and other legal material and preparation of digests of the points of law involved for the internal use of the agency; or

(4) Interpretation and application of laws and related regulations in determining individual or agency responsibility; or

(5) Selection, compilation, and summarization of substantive information on statutes, treaties, and specific legal subjects for the use of others; or

(6) Conduct of hearings or adjudication of appeals arising under statute or regulations of a Government agency; or

(7) Investigation and analysis of evidence of alleged or suspected violations of laws or regulations.

QUALITY OF EXPERIENCE

The candidate's record of experience and training must show the ability to perform the duties of the position. For positions at grades GS–11 and below, at least six months of the required specialized experience must have been at a level of difficulty and responsibility equivalent to that of the next lower grade, or one year of such experience at a level equivalent to the second lower grade in the Federal service. For positions at grades GS–12 and above, at least one year of the required specialized experience must have been at a level equivalent to the next lower grade in the Federal service.

SUBSTITUTION OF EDUCATION FOR EXPERIENCE

(1) Successful completion of a full 4-year course in an accredited college or university leading to a bachelor's degree may be substituted for three years of general experience. Such education successfully completed in a residence school above high school level may be substituted at the rate of one academic year of study for nine months of experience up to a maximum of four years of study for three years of general experience.

(2) Completion of all requirements for an LL.B., J.D., or higher degree from a recognized law school, including at least six full years of resident college work, will meet the requirements for grade GS–9.

(3) Successful completion of one full academic year of study in a paralegal or legal curriculum may be substituted for one year of specialized experience required for grades GS–7 and above; less than one full year of study will be credited on a pro rata basis.

WRITTEN TEST

Candidates for competitive appointment to grades GS–5 and GS–7 must pass an appropriate written test. In addition, the test may *not* be used in evaluating or ranking eligible employees unless the test is approved for this purpose by the Office of Personnel Management.

BASIS OF RATING

Competitors for all positions are rated on a scale of 100. Rankings are made:

1. *For competitive appointment at grades 5 and 7*—On the basis of the written test.
2. *For competitive appointments above GS–7*—On the basis of the extent and quality of experience and training relevant to the duties of the position.

SPECIAL PHYSICAL REQUIREMENTS

Ability to read without strain printed material the size of typewritten characters is required, corrective lenses permitted. Ability to speak without impediment may be required for some positions. Ability to hear the conversational voice, with or without a hearing aid, is required for most positions; however, some positions may be suitable for the deaf.

Statistician GS-5
Statistician (appropriate subject-matter specialization) GS-7/15
Survey Statistician GS-7/15

DESCRIPTION OF WORK

Statisticians do professional work or provide professional consultation requiring the application of statistical theory and technique in the collection, compilation, analysis and interpretation of quantitative information in a variety of subject-matter fields, including the biological, social and physical sciences, engineering, agriculture, and administration.

Statisticians (appropriate subject-matter specialization) are primarily concerned with the use of statistical theory, techniques and methods to determine meaningful relationships or to measure the significance of quantified information in a particular subject-matter field, e.g., biology, demography, engineering, economics, etc.

Survey Statisticians are concerned with the application of statistical theory and technique to the planning, organization, and operation of programs for collecting, verifying, adjusting, processing, summarizing, and presenting information expressed numerically.

BASIC REQUIREMENTS FOR ALL GRADES

1. Applicants for all grades must have successfully completed one of the following, A *or* B:

A. A full 4-year course leading to a bachelor's degree in an accredited college or university which has included 15 semester hours in statistics, (or in mathematics and statistics provided at least 6 semester hours are in statistics) and 9 additional hours in one of the following: the physical or biological sciences; medicine; education or engineering; or in the social sciences, including demography, history, economics, social welfare, geography, international relations, social or cultural anthropology, health sociology, political science, public administration, psychology, etc. Credit toward meeting statistical course requirements should be given for courses in which 50 percent of the course content appears to be statistical method.

B. Courses are given in A above, plus additional appropriate experience or education which when combined with these courses will total 4 years of education and experience and give the applicant a technical knowledge comparable to that which would have been acquired through successful completion of a full 4-year course.

2. The experience offered in combination with specified educational courses to meet the requirements specified in paragraph B above should include evidence of professional statistical work such as (a) sampling; (b) collecting, computing and analyzing statistical data; (c) applying known statistical techniques to data such as measurement of central tendency, dispersion, skewness, sampling error, simple and multiple correlation, analysis of variance and tests of significance.

Without other indication of professional statistical experience, work in the processing of numerical or quantified information by other than statistical methods is not considered appropriate qualifying experience.

3. For positions involving highly technical research, development or similar complex scientific functions, selection may be restricted to eligibles who show the successful completion of a full college course in the appropriate field as designated above.

GS-5.—The basic requirements which apply to all grades are fully qualifying for grade GS-5.

ADDITIONAL EXPERIENCE AND TRAINING REQUIREMENTS

Candidates for grades GS-7 and above must have had either professional experience or graduate education (or an equivalent combination of both) in addition to meeting the basic requirements. Such professional experience or graduate education must have been in, or directly related to, statistics or an appropriate subject-matter field. For statistician positions at GS–9 and above in one of the specializations listed below, the experience or education must have provided specialized knowledge of the subject-matter field:

Subject-Matter fields:
1. Agriculture
2. Biology
3. Health
4. Medicine
5. Engineering
6. Social Science
7. Operations and Administration including logistics
8. Economics
9. Demography
10. Education
11. Physical Science

1. EXPERIENCE

In addition to the basic requirements, the following amounts of professional experience are required for grades GS–7 and above:

Minimum amount of professional experience in appropriate subject-matter fields

Grade:	(years)
GS–7	1
GS–9	2
GS–11 and above	3

For grades GS–11 and below, at least 6 months of the required experience must have been at the level of difficulty comparable to that of the next lower grade, or 1 year comparable to the second lower grade, in the Federal service. For grades GS–12 and above, at least 1 year of the required experience must have been at a level of difficulty comparable to that of the next lower grade in the Federal service.

2. EDUCATION

In addition to the basic requirements, the following amounts and levels of education are qualifying for grades GS–7 and above, as shown:

Grade:	*Minimum amount or level of education in appropriate subject-matter fields*
GS–7—	One full academic year of graduate education.
GS–9—	Completion of all requirements for a master's or equivalent degree; *or*
	Two full academic years of graduate education.
GS–11—	Completion of all requirements for a doctoral degree (Ph.D. or equivalent); *or*
	Three full academic years of graduate education.
GS–11 (Analytical positions)—	Completion of all requirements for a master's or an equivalent degree for which at least 2 years of graduate study is required when—
	a. The position involves primarily analytical work of a creative or advanced scientific nature.
	b. The knowledge required for the work is *typically and preferably* acquired through graduate study.
	c. The work is of such character that the academic preparation will equip the candidate to perform fully the professional work at the GS–11 level after a short orientation period.

To be acceptable, the graduate education must have included a course in statistical or related theory for which knowledge of calculus is required.

3. COMBINATIONS OF PROFESSIONAL EXPERIENCE AND GRADUATE EDUCATION

Equivalent combinations of professional experience and graduate education of the types described above are acceptable at each grade.

4. ALTERNATE REQUIREMENTS

Superior academic achievement at the baccalaureate level or 1 year of student trainee experience is qualifying at grade GS–7. A combination of superior academic achievement at the baccalaureate level and 1 year of appropriate professional experience is qualifying at grade GS–9.

BASIS OF RATING

No written test is required. Applicants' qualifications will be rated on a scale of 100, and will be evaluated on the basis of their education, training, and experience as shown in the application, and on corroborative evidence obtained by the Office of Personnel Management.

Librarian
Administrative Librarian
Supervisory Librarian
Library Director
(with specializations as appropriate)
Grades GS–7/15
Librarian Trainee
(Special provision at GS–5)

DESCRIPTION OF WORK

Positions involve work that primarily requires a full professional knowledge of the theories, principles, and techniques of librarianship. An inherent requirement of these positions is a knowledge of literature resources. Such work is concerned with the collection, organization, preservation, and retrieval of recorded knowledge in printed, written, audio-visual, film, wax, near-print methods, magnetic tape, or other media. Typical library functions include one or more of the following: selection, acquisition, cataloging and classification of materials, bibliographic and readers' advisory services, reference and literature searching services, library management and systems planning, or the development and strengthening of library service. Some positions may involve work in connection with the development of information retrieval systems.

SPECIALIZATIONS

Since many libraries are highly specialized, the work often lies chiefly in one subject-matter field, or closely related subject areas. To serve subject specialists who are the principal users of these libraries, some librarians require a knowledge of a specialized subject or field of endeavor. Such subject-matter knowledge typically covers a broad field, rather than a deep subject knowledge and competence related to a specific discipline or a full knowledge of the state of the art. Because materials in libraries are often in foreign languages, some librarians also must have a proficient knowledge of one or more foreign languages.

To provide qualified personnel for librarian positions requiring knowledge of a subject-matter field and/or proficient knowledge of several foreign languages, the following specializations are authorized:

Subject-matter specializations

Biological Sciences	Education
Medical Sciences	Fine Arts
Physical Sciences	Humanities
Social Sciences	Law
Business and Industry	Music
Engineering	

Foreign language specializations

Germanic	Slavic
Oriental	Arabic
Romance	

EXPERIENCE AND EDUCATION REQUIREMENTS

All Librarians must meet the requirements for professional education in library science or possess equivalent experience as shown in IA, IB, IC or IIA, below. The usual way of entering the profession is to qualify at grade GS–9 on the basis of a master's degree in library science. However, it is possible to qualify for entrance at the GS–7 level on other bases as indicated.

For Librarian (appropriate specialization) positions all candidates must also meet requirements which are directly related to the subject matter or language of the specialization. These requirements are in addition to the basic professional library science requirements which apply to all positions. However, these requirements may be included within, or may be supplemental to, those specified for all positions at GS–7 and GS–9.

I. REQUIREMENTS FOR LIBRARIAN POSITIONS, GS–7

To qualify for all Librarian GS–7 positions, the applicant must meet the requirements specified in paragraphs A, B, or C below. (*Note:* Applicants who qualify under provisions of paragraphs A or B will not be required to take a subject-matter test in library science.)

A. Completion of 1 full academic year of graduate study in library science in an accredited college or university, in addition to completion of all work required for a bachelor's degree; *or*

B. Completion of all requirements for a "5th-year" bachelor's degree in library science. *In addition,* the applicant must have had at least 1 year of library experience which included the performance of duties in one or more functional areas of librarianship at the GS–5 or higher grade level; *or*

C. A total, in some combination, of not less than 5 years of college-level education, training, and/or experience. To qualify on this basis, the applicant must establish conclusively that the education, training, and/or experience has provided a knowledge and understanding of the theories, principles, and techniques of professional librarianship; a knowledge of literature re-

sources; and the knowledges and abilities essential for providing effective library services. Under this provision:

(1) Applicants must pass a subject-matter test in library science.

(2) If the applicant qualifies on the basis of a college level education, he must have had at least 1 year of library experience comparable in difficulty and responsibility to that of a GS–5 or higher level) library technician, technical information specialist, or subject-matter specialist performing library services.

(3) If the applicant qualifies on the basis of experience alone, with no college level education or training, he must have had at least 2 years of library experience comparable in difficulty and responsibility to that of a GS–5 (or higher level) library technician.

(4) The applicant may qualify under any time and quality equivalent combinations of the requirements shown in paragraphs (2) and (3).

(5) Specialized training, e.g., training at a school for library technicians or through "in-house" courses, will be allowed appropriate credit depending upon its applicability and extent.

To qualify for Librarian (appropriate specialization) positions GS–7, the applicant must also possess specialized knowledges of a subject-matter field and/or proficiency in one or more foreign languages which are directly related to the positions being filled. When such knowledges *are required by the position,* the applicant's education or experience must have included or been supplemented by the requirements specified in one of the paragraphs below:

(a) A full 4-year course of study in an accredited college or university which meets all academic requirements for a bachelor's degree, and also (1) has included at least 24 semester hour credits in the specialized field for which the applicant is being considered, *or* (2) has included any combination of subjects with at least 15 semester hour credits in a major subject which is especially applicable to the position for which the applicant is being considered; *or*

(b) Completion of at least 24 semester hours

of legal study in an accredited law school for positions primarily concerned with providing library services in law or legislative reference; *or*

(c) Four years of successful and pertinent experience of such nature and level to provide a knowledge of the basic principles, theories, practices, techniques, terminology and expressions of the appropriate discipline or subject-matter field; an understanding of the standard methods, procedures, and techniques of research and analysis in the subject-matter field; ability to acquire additional information about the field and related fields; and some knowledge of literature resources in the field.

(d) Any time equivalent combination of experience as described in item "(c)" with education as described in item "(a)" or "(b)" above.

(e) Demonstrated ability as shown by education or experience to read or translate information from one or more foreign languages into English.

II. REQUIREMENTS FOR LIBRARIAN POSITIONS, GS–9

A. Completion of all requirements for a master's degree or 2 full academic years of graduate study in library science, in an accredited college or university, meets all requirements for Librarian positions, GS–9.

B. In addition to meeting one of the requirements for GS–7 (A, B, or C above) must have had professional *or* advanced experience *or* graduate study as follows:

(1) One year of professional experience in librarianship which included the performance, supervision, or administration of one or more major functional areas of librarianship.

   Some positions are highly specialized in one functional area, and may require that the advanced experience be in the appropriate function to qualify at these higher grade levels.

(2) One year of professional or advanced experience in the subject matter or language which has provided the applicant with the professional, technical, language, or other specialized knowledges and abilities required by the particular position for which he is being considered.

   Graduate education in a subject-matter field which is especially applicable to the position, and provides the knowledges required to perform the duties of the position, as follows:

   (a) Completion of all requirements for a master's degree; *or*

   (b) Two full academic years of graduate education.

III. REQUIREMENTS FOR LIBRARIAN POSITIONS, GS–11 AND ABOVE

A. In addition to meeting the requirements for GS–9 (either A or B) candidates must have had either:

(1) One year of professional experience in librarianship; *or*

(2) One year of professional or advanced experience in a subject-matter or language area appropriate to the position.

B. Completion of all the requirements for a doctoral degree (or equivalent) or 3 full academic years of graduate education in library science.

C. In addition to possessing professional education in library science (or equivalent experience) as required for entrance at grades GS–7 or GS–9, candidates must have completed graduate study in a subject matter or language area appropriate to the position as follows:

(1) All requirements for a doctoral degree (Ph.D. or equivalent); *or*

(2) Three full academic years of graduate education.

IV. COMBINATIONS OF PROFESSIONAL EXPERIENCE AND GRADUATE EDUCATION

Equivalent combinations of professional experience and graduate education of the types described above are acceptable at each grade.

QUALITY OF EXPERIENCE

For grades GS–11 and below, at least 6 months of the required experience must have been at the level of difficulty comparable to that of the next lower grade, or 1 year comparable to the second lower grade, in the Federal service. For grades GS–12 and above, at least 1 year of the required experience must have been at a level of difficulty comparable to that of the next lower grade in the Federal service.

SUPERVISORY AND ADMINISTRATIVE POSITIONS

For positions concerned with administration, management, or direction of library programs, candidates must meet all other requirements for the particular grade and also show that they possess the required administrative and/or managerial ability to perform successfully the duties of such positions. Education, training, or experience of the candidate should demonstrate, e.g., ability to manage or direct a library, group of libraries, or library system; ability to plan, organize, and direct the development and execution of library programs, policies, and procedures; ability to plan or conduct management studies, public relations and educational activities; ability to plan, develop and carry out administrative activities of the library or library system concerned with budget and finance, personnel, plant and equipment, etc.

BASIS OF RATING

All competitors who meet the education and experience requirements for GS–7 and above, who pass the written test in library science when required, will be rated based upon an evaluation of their experience and training in library work. The library science written test, when required, will be used for qualification purposes only.

EVALUATING EXPERIENCE AND TRAINING

In evaluating experience and training, consideration will be given to the type, level, and scope of experience relating directly to the particular position or positions under consideration, as indicated in the application, and to any additional pertinent information obtained from references, employees, associates and colleagues.

NONQUALIFYING EXPERIENCE AND TRAINING

No credit will be given toward meeting the experience requirements for positions in this series for work in the following situations:

1. Work with collections of fiction, recreational or other reading material where no formal cataloging or classification of material is performed.
2. Experience in wholesale or retail bookstores, circulating fiction and club libraries, or hospital record departments.
3. Experience as a library page, as a library attendant or as a clerical worker, even though the duties included such work as charging and discharging books or typing catalog cards or orders for books and materials.
4. Nonprofessional work in a library on a part-time basis or on a volunteer basis.
5. No credit will be given for training in the particular use of libraries and library facilities such as is given in orientation courses to college freshmen.

WRITTEN TESTS

Applicants for all grades who (1) have a master's degree or the required education in library science, or (2) have a 5th-year bachelor's degree in library science, will *not* be required to take a written test.

Applicants for *all grades* who qualify on the basis of experience alone or a combination of experience and education *must pass a subject-matter test* in library science. This written test is designed to measure the candidate's knowledge of the fundamentals underlying professional library science and his understanding of its methods and techniques and their applications to effective library science. Questions will be asked on facts, principles, applications, tools, practices, and theory of professional librarianship as found in a variety of libraries.

SPECIAL PROVISIONS

A. *For all librarian positions*

At GS–9 and above, Librarian positions concerned with acquisition, cataloging, or reference work are sometimes highly specialized. In filling such positions, consideration may be limited to those eligibles who have had experience in the appropriate specialization at a qualifying level of difficulty.

SPECIAL PROVISION FOR FILLING POSITIONS OF LIBRARIAN (TRAINEE), GS–5

This is a special provision which may be used when there is a shortage of candidates who are fully qualified for GS–7 level Librarian or Librarian (appropriate specialization) positions. This provision is included because of the reported dearth of fully-qualified librarians. It is intended for use in those situations where the Librarian (Trainee) can be expected to complete his/her education or training in library science within a reasonable period of time, and thus meet requirements for librarian positions at the GS–7 level.

Under this provision, applicants for positions of Librarian (Trainee), GS–5 must meet the following requirements: completion of a full 4-year course of study in an accredited college or university which meets all academic requirements for a bachelor's degree, or equivalent experience.

—Qualification of candidates under this provision is demonstrated by eligibility on a civil service register, or an appropriate subject-matter register. Appointing officers may request certification of eligible candidates with major study in a subject-matter field which is considered appropriate for the position being filled.

Individuals hired as Librarian (Trainee), GS–5, *may not* be employed or promoted to a position of Librarian GS–7 until they fully meet the requirement specified for GS–7 Librarian positions.

Social Worker GS– 7/15
Social Work Program Specialist GS–9/15

DESCRIPTION OF WORK

Social Workers perform professional social work involved in carrying out agency programs of service to people with whom they are concerned, such as patients in agency-operated hospitals and clinics, wards of child welfare agencies and their families, inmates of correctional institutions, etc.

Most positions involve direct professional services to individuals. Some positions also include working with clients in groups when appropriate, and/or working with and advising members of the community in the development of local resources to prevent or alleviate social problems. There are positions which are primarily concerned with supervision of social work staff and/or students, with directing programs of social work, or with research to improve social work practice.

Social Work Program Specialists advise on, develop, evaluate, and promote social welfare programs and services administered by State agencies and other public and nonprofit organizations and institutions. More specifically, they develop and issue material on new knowledge, set minimum standards for administration and operation of programs; evaluate the soundness and effectiveness of program administration and operation; and work with State, community, and professional leaders who are interested in strengthening service programs, etc.

MINIMUM EDUCATION REQUIREMENT

Applicants must have successfully completed a course of study in an accredited school of social work which has fulfilled all of the requirements for the master's degree in social work. The recognized accrediting association in the field is the Council on Social Work Education.

ADDITIONAL TRAINING AND EXPERIENCE REQUIREMENTS

For GS–7: No additional training or experience needed.

For GS–9: In addition to meeting the requirements for grade GS–7, applicants must have successfully completed one of the following:

A. Related practice training in professional social work during field placement as part of the graduate study.

B. At least 1 year of professional social work experience under professional supervision.

For GS–11: In addition to meeting the requirements for grade GS–9, applicants must have had a minimum of → 1 year ← of professional social work experience under professional supervision. Experience must have demonstrated the ability to perform advanced assignments independently.

For GS–12/15: In addition to meeting the requirements for GS–11, applicants must have had a minimum of 1 additional year of professional social work experience which has demonstrated broad knowledge of the field of social work and superior skill and judgment in professional practice.

For program specialist positions, the experience must have included one or, in some cases, a combination of two or more functions, such as program planning, program development, program evaluation, consultation, and cooperative community relationships in an agency providing social work service to families, children, or adults; *or*

Supervisory, administrative, or consultative work in a public or voluntary welfare or health agency with an organized social work program. For positions with staff development responsibilities, the required experience must have included experience in planning or conducting a social work education or staff development program in a health or welfare agency, or teaching in an accredited school of social work.

QUALITY OF EXPERIENCE AND TRAINING

The number of years of experience required for any grade level represents the minimum amount of time necessary to qualify for the appropriate position, but length of time is not of itself qualifying. The applicant's work experience must also have been of a quality and scope sufficient to enable him to perform satisfactorily assignments typical of the grade level for which he is being considered. The evaluation of the applicant's performance and potentialities will be based upon information acquired through confidential inquiry of his supervisors and others familiar with the nature and quality of his work.

For positions at grade GS–9, at least 1 year of experience must have been at a level comparable in scope and difficulty to that of grade GS–7 in the Federal service; for grade GS–11, at least → 1 year ← of the required experience must have been comparable in scope and difficulty to that of GS–9; and for GS–12 and above, at least 1 year must have been comparable in scope and difficulty to that of the next lower grade.

NONQUALIFYING EXPERIENCE

Except for the substitution of supervised field training completed as part of an educational curriculum (see above), experience acquired prior to completion of all requirements for the master's degree is not considered as qualifying.

An applicant who has been out of social work practice for 10 or more years may be asked to provide additional evidence that his qualifications fully meet the requirements of competence to practice in terms of current professional knowledge and standards of practice.

QUALIFICATION INQUIRIES

For all grades of these positions, confidential inquiries, including contacts with the applicant's supervisors and associates, or with other persons familiar with his qualifications, may be made to obtain further information about qualifications, character, and suitability for these positions.

SELECTIVE PLACEMENT

Some positions will require the background and approach of a particular method of practice. For such positions, consideration may be restricted to eligibles who possess the pertinent experience and knowledge required to perform the duties of the positions covered in this occupation. At grade GS–11 and above there are some positions that require experience specifically related to such fields of practice as programs of service to medical and psychiatric patients in hospitals and clinics, programs of rehabilitation for inmates of correctional institutions, or programs for the protection of children.

For some program specialist positions, some of the qualifying experience must have provided a knowledge of specific aspects of an agency program such as foster care, work with the ag-

ing, services to unmarried mothers, community planning, volunteer services, etc.

Other positions may require experience which has provided a knowledge of one or more specific areas of child welfare, such as adoptions, foster family care, group care, day care, services to children in their own homes, homemaker service, services for mentally retarded and emotionally disturbed children, etc.

Some positions in *Medical Programs* require experience which has provided a knowledge of health and medical care social services for mothers and children.

Agencies requesting selective referrals must show the connection between the kind of training or experience on which they wish to base selective consideration and the duties of the position to be filled.

DRIVER'S LICENSE

For certain positions, applicants may be required to have a driver's license.

WRITTEN TEST

No written test is required. Applicants will be rated on a scale of 100 on the basis of education, experience, training, and personal qualifications in relation to the requirements of the specific position for which they are being considered. Ratings will be based upon competitors' statements in their applications and upon any additional evidence which may be secured through qualification inquiries or similar means.

SPECIAL PHYSICAL REQUIREMENTS

There may be a few positions in larger offices where the casework load would permit the employment of a blind person in a restricted area of activity.

HEALTH CARE POSITIONS

Physician's Assistant GS–7/11

DESCRIPTION OF WORK

Physician's Assistants help physicians by providing diagnostic and therapeutic medical care and services under the physician's supervision. The work requires knowledge of specific observation and examination procedures, and ability to perform designated diagnostic and therapeutic tasks. The work does not include the full scope of interpretation of medical findings requiring the professional background of the licensed physician.

In clinics or during hospital rounds, physician's assistants assist in the observation and evaluation of patients by performing such duties as taking case histories, conducting physical examinations, and ordering laboratory studies. As directed by a physician, physician's assistants carry out special procedures such as applying and removing casts, performing lumbar punctures, or suturing minor lacerations.

EXPERIENCE, TRAINING, AND RELATED REQUIREMENTS

REQUIREMENTS FOR GS–7

Candidates for positions at GS–7 must meet requirements (1) and (2) below:
(1) A broad background of knowledge of the medical environment, practices, and procedures such as would be acquired by a bachelor's degree in a health care occupation such as nursing, medical technology, or physical therapy or by 3 years of responsible and progressive health care experience such as medical corpsman, nursing assistant, or medical technician, *and*
(2) Successful completion of a course of study of at least 12 months, including clinical training or preceptorship, specifically designed for professional-caliber physician's assistants.

The course of study or training must be approved by a nationally-recognized professional medical body such as the American Medical Association or the Association of American Medical Colleges, or by a panel of physicians established by a Federal agency for this purpose.

REQUIREMENTS FOR GS–9 AND GS–11

In addition to the requirements for GS–7, the following amounts of pertinent professional-caliber experience comparable to the work of a physician's assistant are required for grades GS–9 and GS–11:

Grade	*Minimum amount of experience (years)*
GS–9	1
GS–11	2

The required education, training, and experience must have demonstrated the ability to perform professional-caliber medical work as a physician's assistant with minimal supervision, including the exercise of a degree of judgment in integrating and interpreting diagnostic findings and in determining the need for referral to a physician.

For all grades, at least 6 months of the required experience must have been at the level of difficulty comparable to that of the next lower grade, or 1 year comparable to the second lower grade, in the Federal service.

ACCEPTANCE OF PROFESSIONAL MEDICAL EDUCATION

Candidates who have completed 3 full years of a curriculum in an accredited medical school leading to the doctor of medicine or doctor of osteopathy degree may be rated eligible at GS–9.

Candidates who have completed the requirements for the degree of doctor of medicine or osteopathy but who lack licensure to practice medicine in the United States, may be rated eligible at GS–11.

SELECTIVE PLACEMENT

Some positions demand specific competence in a particular specialty. For such positions, consideration may be limited to those candidates whose records show evidence of the required knowledges, abilities, skills, and personal characteristics.

BASIS OF RATING

Ratings will be based upon candidates' statements in their applications and all available evidence concerning the quality and scope of their knowledge and ability including the candidate's education, experience, training, avocations, and personal characteristics.

REQUIRED KNOWLEDGES AND ABILITIES

Candidates will be rated on the degree to which they possess the knowledges and abilities of the kinds listed below, as appropriate to the grade level:

1. Ability to identify a medical problem and determine appropriate action to meet the problem, including referral to a physician.
2. Knowledge and understanding of the environment, principles, ethics, and special human relationships in the field of medicine.
3. Knowledge of the medical, biological, and physical sciences related to the applicable area of medicine.
4. Knowledge of and ability to perform specified diagnostic and therapeutic practices and procedures.
5. Ability to work responsibly with physicians and other members of the medical team, and to deal effectively with patients.
6. Ability to communicate effectively, both orally and in writing.

Nonsupervisory Nonprofessional Nursing Care Positions GS–1/6
Nursing Aid
Nursing Assistant
Operating Room Nursing Assistant
Psychiatric Nursing Assistant

DESCRIPTION OF WORK

Nursing Aids, under close supervision, perform simple and repetitive personal and nursing care procedures. Nursing aid positions are normally established for training purposes.

Nursing Assistants receive on-the-job training in nursing care which requires some knowledge of human body functions and behavior for the purpose of providing personal nursing care, sup-

port duties for diagnostic procedures, technical treatment procedures, patient charting, and patient teaching.

Operating Room Nursing Assistants assist registered nurses and surgeons in a variety of operating room and delivery room activities. They position and drape patients, ensure proper lighting, pass instruments and materials, maintain sterile conditions, assist in sponge and needle counts, and dispose of contaminated materials.

Psychiatric Nursing Assistants give general nursing care, observe and report changes in behavior, and provide reassurance and technical support to mentally ill patients.

EXPERIENCE, TRAINING, AND RELATED REQUIREMENTS

Except for the substitutions provided for below, candidates must have had qualifying experience in the amounts shown in the following table:

Minimum Amounts of Experience

Grade	General experience (years)	Specialized experience (years)	Total experience (years)
GS–1	none	none	*none
GS–2	½	none	½
GS–3	1	none	1
GS–4	1½	½	2
GS–5	2	1	3
GS–6	2	2	4

*It should be noted that for grade GS–1, no experience, training or education is required. No written test is required. Candidates must be willing to do personal and nursing care work and show evidence of likelihood of success in assignments.

GENERAL EXPERIENCE

This is experience which has demonstrated the ability:
(1) to learn and perform nursing care duties;
(2) to deal successfully with people; and
(3) to be adaptable to the work situation.

SPECIALIZED EXPERIENCE

This is experience in nonprofessional nursing care work in a hospital, outpatient clinic, nursing home, or other supervised medical, nursing, or patient care facility. Illustrative examples of nursing care work follow:
(1) Caring for mentally ill patients, including observing, recording, and reporting changes in their behavior;
(2) Providing reassurance and encouragement to mentally ill patients;
(3) Assisting surgeons and registered nurses in operating room activities, including passing instruments, maintaining sterile conditions, and draping and positioning patients;
(4) Providing pre- and post-operative care; and
(5) Setting up and operating special medical equipment and apparatus.
Candidates are not required to be proficient in all tasks listed above. However, their experience, education, and training must clearly show that they possess the skills and knowledges required to perform the work of the job at the grade level for which application is made. As a minimum, the candidate must show:
(*1*) A practical knowledge of:
  (a) human body structure,
  (b) sterile techniques and procedures, and
  (c) how to meet, deal, and work with medical, surgical, and psychiatric patients; and
(*2*) Knowledge of, and skill in, the performance of personal and nursing care procedures and techniques pertinent to the specialized area and grade for which application is made.

QUALITY AND LEVEL OF EXPERIENCE

Applicants must demonstrate progressively responsible experience of a scope, quality, and degree such as to have equipped them with the ability to perform duties at the grade level of the position for which application is made. Typically, this is demonstrated by accomplishment of assignments of the difficulty and responsibility described in the position classification standard used to evaluate positions at the next lower grade in the normal line of promotion to the position being filled.

SUBSTITUTION OF EDUCATION AND TRAINING FOR EXPERIENCE

Successfully completed education and training of acceptable type and quality may be substituted for experience requirements as specified below:

(*1*) Graduation from a high school or its equivalent may be substituted in full for the experience requirements at the GS–2 level. (High school education or its equivalent may not be substituted for any part of the experience requirements for GS–3 and above.)

(*2*) Successful completion of a 2-year associate degree program in an accredited community college, junior college, or college or university in a field of study appropriate to the specialization of the position being filled, psychiatric technician, or operating room technician may be substituted for the 2 years of experience required for GS–4.

(*3*) Partial completion of professional or practical nurse training in a school approved by the State-approving body may be substituted on a month-for-month basis up to 1 year of specialized experience when the following provisions are met. The candidate must have been in good standing when the training was interrupted. In order to substitute the training for specialized experience, the applicant must have satisfactorily completed courses which involved clinical practice in medical and surgical nursing and infant and child care. Candidates lacking clinical practice in infant and child care may substitute clinical practice in psychiatric or another specialized field of nursing. Any excess specialized training may be credited as general experience.

(*4*) Education and training other than that outlined above will be allowed appropriate credit for either general or specialized experience, depending upon its applicability and extent.

The maximum amount of experience for which education or training of any kind may be substituted is 3 years (2 years of general and 1 year of specialized experience).

WRITTEN TEST

Candidates for positions at GS–2 and GS–3 must pass a written test of abilities necessary to learn and perform the duties of these positions. The written test should be waived for candidates who qualify on the basis of successful completion of specialized education or training that is substitutable for specialized experience.

BASIS OF RATING

Applicants who meet the minimum qualification requirements, including a passing score on the written test, when required, will be rated on a scale of 70 to 100 based on:

For positions at grade GS–1—an evaluation of the applicant's willingness to do simple and repetitive work of the occupation, dependability, and ability to work safely;

For positions at grades GS–2/3—the applicant's score on the written test or for those competitors not required to pass the written test (see Written Test section above), an evaluation of education, training, and/or experience; and

For positions at grade GS–4 and above—an evaluation of the quality and extent of the applicant's experience, education, training, or other achievements pertinent to the duties of the position to be filled.

For Positions in the Public Health Nurse Occupation, Grades GS–5/15

Public Health Nurse
Consulting Public Health Nurse
Public Health Nurse (Training)
Research Public Health Nurse

DESCRIPTION OF WORK

Public health nurses supervise or give public health nursing care, health teaching, and guidance to individuals and families in homes and schools. Such positions typically are found in public health nursing services which emphasize comprehensive care for mothers and children, and services to patients having communicable diseases and chronic illnesses.

A few public health nurse positions primarily involve advice and consultation on public health nursing programs, teaching or training in public health nursing programs, teaching or training in public health nursing, or research in public health nursing.

EDUCATION, EXPERIENCE, AND OTHER REQUIREMENTS

I. BASIC EDUCATIONAL REQUIREMENTS

Candidates for all positions must meet one of the following requirements:

A. Graduation from a baccalaureate or higher degree program in nursing approved by the legally-designated State approving body. To be acceptable the program must have been accredited by the nationally recognized accrediting agency (or else must have included course content and field practice in public health nursing equivalent to that of programs that are accredited).

B. Graduation from either a diploma or associate degree program in professional nursing approved by the legally-designated State approving body and at least 1 academic year in a university public health nursing program accredited by the nationally recognized accrediting agency.

C. Graduation from a foreign school of professional nursing, provided that the nursing education and the nursing knowledge acquired therefrom are substantially comparable and equivalent to that of graduates of nursing schools as described in paragraph A above. Such equivalence must have been evaluated by a school of nursing accredited by the nationally recognized accrediting agency as equivalent to that of its program.

Candidates for positions which involve highly technical research or development or comparable highly technical and scientific functional areas of nursing work must meet the requirements described in paragraph A above.

II. REGISTRATION REQUIREMENTS

Applicants for all positions must have active, current registration as a professional nurse in a State, District of Columbia, the Commonwealth of Puerto Rico, or a Territory of the United States.

An applicant who has, within the past 12 months, graduated from a baccalaureate or higher degree program in nursing approved by the legally-designated State approving body, with qualifying preparation in public health nursing, may be appointed at the entrance grade level for which qualified pending attaining State registration as a professional nurse within 6 months after appointment. No person appointed pending registration may be retained beyond 6 months or promoted if registration has not been attained.

GS–5.—The basic requirements which apply to all grades are fully qualifying for grade GS–5.

ADDITIONAL EXPERIENCE AND TRAINING REQUIREMENTS

Candidates for grades GS–7 and above must have had either professional experience or graduate education (or an equivalent combination of both) in addition to meeting the basic educational requirements. Such professional experience must have been in public health nursing, general nursing, or another specialty area of nursing that is directly applicable to the position to be filled. For GS–9 at least 1 year, and for GS–11 and above at least 2 years of the required professional nursing experience must have been in the public health nursing field.

Such graduate education must have been in nursing in a field that is directly applicable to the position to be filled. An exception to this requirement is that 1 year of the graduate education may have been in directly related fields. Graduate education in the "directly related fields" is qualifying for grade GS–7 only.

1. EXPERIENCE

In addition to the basic educational requirements, the following amounts of professional experience are required for grades GS–7 and above:

Grade:	Minimum amount of professional experience in appropriate subject-matter fields (years)
GS–7	1
GS–9	2
GS–11 and above	3

For grades GS–11 and below, at least 6 months of the required experience must have been at the level of difficulty comparable to that of the next lower grade, or 1 year comparable to the second lower grade, in the Federal service. For grades GS–12 and above, at least 1 year of the required experience must have been at a level of difficulty comparable to that of the next lower grade in the Federal service.

2. EDUCATION

In addition to the basic educational requirements, the following amounts and levels of education are qualifying for grades GS–7 and above, as shown:

Grade	Minimum amount or level of education in appropriate subject-matter fields
GS–7	One full academic year of graduate education.
GS–9	Completion of all requirements for a master's or equivalent degree; *or* Two full academic years of graduate education.
GS–11	Completion of all requirements for a doctoral degree (Ph.D. or equivalent); *or* Three full academic years of graduate education.

3. COMBINATIONS OF PROFESSIONAL EXPERIENCE AND GRADUATE EDUCATION

Equivalent combinations of professional experience and graduate education of the types described above are acceptable at each grade.

4. ALTERNATE REQUIREMENTS

Superior academic achievement at the baccalaureate level or 1 year of student trainee experience is qualifying at grade GS–7. A combination of superior academic achievement at the baccalaureate level and 1 year of appropriate professional experience is qualifying at grade GS–9.

SELECTIVE PLACEMENT

Some public health nurse positions demand specific competence in a particular specialty and/or in special functional areas such as giving advice and consultation, teaching, research. For such positions, consideration may be limited to those candidates whose records show evidence of the required knowledges, abilities, skills, and personal characteristics.

PERSONAL CHARACTERISTICS REQUIRED

Public health nurse positions require the ability (a) to work harmoniously and effectively with others in the organization and (b) to establish and maintain satisfactory working relationships with others in hospitals, clinics, the school, social agencies, etc. Public health nurses must have the ability to inspire confidence and motivate patients and the patient's family to follow the treatment program and to use the available health facilities.

Many public health nurses perform their work in homes and schools in which direction and supervision may not be immediately available. In these situations the work requires an extra measure of personal traits such as maturity, objectivity, resourcefulness, and sound judgment.

Some public health nurses require the knowledges, abilities, and skills to give advice and leadership to States and/or localities on the nursing aspects of health services in a specialty area such as maternal and child health, psychiatry, tuberculosis, etc.

These factors should be considered in evaluating candidates in relationship to the requirements of the specific position to be filled.

INTERVIEW

Applicants who meet the education, experience, and other requirements may be requested to appear for an employment interview.

QUALIFICATION INQUIRIES

Reference inquiries, including contacts with candidate's teachers, supervisors, or other persons familiar with the candidate's qualifications, may be made to obtain further information about the candidate's professional and personal qualifications for these positions.

BASIS OF RATING

No written test is required. Applicants will be rated on the extent and quality of their education and experience.

Nurse GS–4/15

Occupational Coverage: Nurse, Clinical Nurse, Community Health Nurse, Occupational Health Nurse, Operating Room Nurse, Psychiatric Nurse, Nurse Anesthetist, Nurse Consultant, Nurse Educator, Nurse Midwife, Nurse Practitioner, Nurse Specialist, Research Nurse.

DESCRIPTION OF WORK

Nurses apply a professional knowledge of nursing to advise on, administer, supervise, or perform direct or indirect care of patients in hospitals, clinics, health units, homes, schools, and communities; they administer anesthetic agents and supportive treatments to patients undergoing surgery or other medical procedures; promote better health practices; teach;

perform research; act as nurse midwives or consult with and advise nurses who provide direct care to patients.

Professional nursing includes a wide variety of categories of work, many of which are highly specialized. For example:

Clinical Nurses provide direct nursing service in the assessment, planning, implementation and evaluation of patient care in hospitals, clinics or other patient care facilities. They frequently work in a specialized clinical area, e.g., surgical ward, ambulatory care, emergency room.

Community Health Nurses provide therapeutic services and coordinate patient and family health information and services to, between, or in homes, hospitals, clinics, schools and communities. They function as client advocates and promote the health maintenance activities of early detection and prevention.

Occupational Health Nurses provide nursing and health services to employees in relation to their occupations and working environments. This entails both the nursing care and treatment of injuries and illnesses of employees, and participation in preventive health programs, health education, and counseling aimed at prevention of disease and health maintenance, and environmental surveys.

Operating Room Nurses provide specialized nursing care to meet the needs of patients undergoing surgical procedures, providing for patient counseling and continuity of care. This involves responsibility for and supervision of the preparation of the operating room and necessary equipment, and for the scheduling of facilities and personnel.

Psychiatric Nurses provide direct nursing service to patients in psychiatric hospitals, psychiatric units in general medical and surgical hospitals, or mental health clinics. This work requires advanced knowledges, skills, and experience in counseling and guidance, and communicative skills which contribute to the redirection of behavior of patients or their families.

Nurse Anesthetists administer anesthetic agents and provide supportive treatment to patients undergoing surgery or other medical procedures.

Nurse Consultants provide consultative and advisory service with respect to one or more facets of the nursing field. They work independently, and the services cover a broad range of activities involving assessing, planning, implementing, coordinating and evaluating nursing programs both within and outside the employing agency.

Nurse Educators develop, provide and administer educational programs and activities for nurses. They teach courses, develop technical phases of educational programs, plan curriculum content and methods of teaching, and advise on the application of approved educational methods for individual schools and communities.

Nurse Midwives provide care for mothers and babies throughout an essentially normal maternity cycle within the framework of a medically directed health service, and are responsible for management, counseling and teaching.

Nurse Practitioners, through advanced competence in primary health care, provide direct, comprehensive nursing, preventive and therapeutic health services to individuals, families or groups. This includes assessing the health status of individuals, managing the care of selected patients, and providing treatment, health teaching, counseling, guidance, and instructions to individuals/families so that they participate in a plan of care.

Nurse Specialists have an advanced level of competence in the special field for which applying, with experience in clinical practice that demonstrates ability to develop innovative techniques, practices and approaches for patient care.

Research Nurses perform, participate in and/or direct research activities toward development of new or expanded knowledge of the field of nursing or health systems which improve patient care and enhance the clinical practice of nursing.

BASIC REGISTRATION REQUIREMENTS FOR ALL NURSE POSITIONS

Applicants for nurse positions must have active, current registration as a professional nurse in a State, District of Columbia, the Commonwealth of Puerto Rico, or a Territory of the United States.

An applicant who has within the past 12 months, graduated from a school of professional nursing approved by a legally designated State approving agency at the time of graduation, may be appointed at the entrance grade level for which qualified pending attaining State registration as a professional nurse within 6 months after appointment. No person appointed pending registration may be retained beyond 6 months or promoted if registration has not been attained.

BASIC EDUCATIONAL REQUIREMENTS FOR ALL NURSE POSITIONS

Candidates for positions at all grades must meet one of the following requirements:

A. Graduation with a bachelor's or higher degree in nursing from a school of professional nursing, approved by the legally designated State accrediting agency at the time the program was completed by the candidate.

B. Graduation from a 3-year (at least 30 months) diploma program of professional nursing approved by the legally designated State accrediting agency at the time the program was completed by the candidate.

C. Graduation from an associate degree program or other program of at least 2 years, in a school of professional nursing approved by the legally designated State accrediting agency at the time the program was completed by the candidate.

D. Graduation from a school of professional nursing (including foreign schools), of at least 2 years in length other than one covered by A, B, or C above, provided that the professional nurse training and the nursing knowledge acquired therefrom are substantially comparable and equivalent to that of graduates of an approved school as described above. Comparability should be evaluated by a State Board of Nursing. Registration as defined above meets this requirement.

NOTE.—Successfully completed college level course work in nursing, the behavioral, physical or biological sciences related to nursing; nutrition; public health; and maternal and child health in excess of the minimum basic education requirement may be substituted for professional nursing experience at the rate of 1 academic year of appropriate education for 9 months of professional nursing experience in establishing eligibility for the GS-5 level. Tutorial or remedial work cannot be substituted.

BASIC EDUCATIONAL REQUIREMENTS FOR CERTAIN SPECIALIZED POSITIONS

In addition to meeting the basic requirements for all nurse positions:

Community Health Nurse.—Candidates for these positions at GS-5 and above must have graduated from a baccalaureate or higher degree program in nursing approved by the legally designated State approving body.

Nurse Anesthetist.—Candidates for nurse anesthetist positions at GS-9 and above must have graduated from at least an 18 month course in a school of anesthesia for nurses accredited by the American Association of Nurse Anesthetists for the year of the applicant's graduation.

Nurse Midwife.—Candidates for nurse midwife positions must have completed an organized program of study and clinical experience recognized by the American College of Nurse Midwives.

ENTRY LEVEL CREDIT FOR MILITARY EXPERIENCE

Nurse experience gained while in the military as a military corpsman will be accepted for initial appointment at grade GS-4 to the extent that it is accepted by a State licensing body.

EDUCATION AND EXPERIENCE ABOVE THE ENTRY LEVELS

Candidates for grades GS-7 and above must have had either professional experience or graduate education (or an equivalent combination of both) in addition to meeting the basic educational requirements for all nurse positions. Such professional experience must have been in nursing. Such graduate education must have been in nursing with a concentration in a field of nursing or closely related non-nursing fields directly applicable to the requirements for the position to be filled.

1. EXPERIENCE

The required amounts of professional experience are:

	Associate degree program or diploma program of less than 30 months (years)	Diploma program of 30 months or more (years)	Baccalaureate degree program (years)
GS–4	0	0	0
GS–5	1	0	0
GS–7	2	1	1
GS–9	3	2	2
GS–11 and above	4	3	3

For positions at GS–5: graduates of an associate degree or diploma nursing program of less than 30 months' duration may have experience as a practical nurse or nursing assistant (either voluntary or paid) credited for grade GS–5 on a month-for-month basis to a maximum of 12 months. The practical nurse or nursing experience must have been:

(a) gained under the supervision of a professional nurse;

(b) equivalent to GS–4 or higher; and

(c) relevant to the position to be filled.

For grades GS–7 through 11 at least 6 months of the professional nursing experience must have been at the level of difficulty comparable to that of the next lower grade in the Federal service, or 1 year comparable to the second lower grade.

For specialized positions at GS–9 and above, 1 year of professional nursing experience must be sufficiently related to the specialty in both subject-matter and grade-level, to demonstrate the candidate's ability to perform the major duties of the position being filled.

Candidates for positions at GS–12 and above must have at least 1 year of experience at the next lower grade, and must demonstrate a record of accomplishment, professional competence, leadership, and recognition in the profession as in the planning, organizing, directing, and coordinating of nursing projects, or in well-established service as an expert and consultant.

2. EDUCATION

In addition to the basic requirements, the following amounts and levels of education are qualifying for grades GS–7 and above, as shown:

Grade:	Minimum amount or level of education in appropriate subject-matter fields
GS–7	One full academic year of graduate education.
GS–9	Completion of all requirements for a master's or equivalent degree *or* Two full academic years of graduate education.
GS–11	Completion of all requirements for a doctoral degree (Ph. D. or equivalent) *or* Three full academic years of graduate education.

Currency of Knowledges and Skills

At all grade levels, greater credit may be given to applicants who have knowledges of and skills in current nursing practices.

Alternate Requirements

Superior academic achievement at the baccalaureate level is qualifying at grade GS–7. A combination of superior academic achievement at the baccalaureate level and 1 year of appropriate professional experience is qualifying at grade GS–9.

3. COMBINATIONS OF PROFESSIONAL EXPERIENCE AND GRADUATE EDUCATION

Equivalent combinations of professional experience and graduate education of the types described above are acceptable at each grade. Specialized areas of nursing (see Description of Work) may require particular specialized education and experience.

POSSIBLE SELECTIVE FACTORS

Many nursing positions GS–9 and above demand competence in a particular area, gained through specialized experience and/or training. Selective factors for these positions should be reflected in the knowledges, skills and abilities described in the position description.

INTERVIEW

Applicants who meet the education, experience, and other requirements may be required to appear for an employment interview.

QUALIFICATION INQUIRIES

Reference inquiries, including contacts with candidate's teachers, supervisors, or other persons familiar with the candidate's qualifications may be made to obtain further information about the candidate's professional and personal qualifications for these positions.

BASIS FOR RATING

No written test is required. Applicants will be rated on the extent and quality of their education and experience. Such ratings will be based upon the applicant's statements in the application and upon any additional information that may be secured, including that secured by inquiries made to supervisors, schools and other references.

Dietitian GS–5/15
Nutritionist GS–5/15
Public Health Nutritionist GS–9/15

DESCRIPTION OF WORK

Dietitians and nutritionists advise on, administer, supervise, or perform work which requires the application of a professional knowledge of the science of nutrition. Dietitians and nutritionists are both concerned with human nutrition needs and are responsible for the development of diet plans or programs for individuals or groups, for instructing others in nutrition matters, and for applying a knowledge of socioeconomic conditions which affect the eating habits of individuals and groups. Dietitians usually perform work which is associated with institutional health care, such as hospitals, domiciliaries, or privately operated group care facilities in the community, and involves responsibility for individual diet plans and for the management of the food service system. Public Health Nutritionists perform work associated with public health services and programs designed to meet the health needs of target groups within the population, such as maternal and child health, geriatrics, and American Indians. Nutritionists perform in nontreatment food assistance programs designed to help target groups within the population, or in research. Major specialties and subspecialties are summarized as follows:

Dietitians are responsible for nutritional care in managing individual or group feeding, in imparting knowledge concerning food and nutrition, and in applying knowledge to developing and implementing plans for health maintenance and/or improvement.

Administrative Dietitians are members of the management team, responsible for planning and evaluating the food service system, directing and managing food service personnel, planning budgets and managing resources, establishing standards of safety and sanitation, developing specifications for the procurement of equipment and supplies, and developing menu patterns and evaluating client acceptance.

Clinical Dietitians are members of the health care team concerned with continuously providing for the nutritional needs of individuals and groups in acute, intermediate, long-term care and hospital based community care facilities generally involving a specialized program. They are primarily concerned with assessing nutritional needs, developing therapeutic diets, recording progress in the medical records, providing nutritional education to the patient and family, and recommending changes to the physician. A dietitian may be responsible for one or more wards in a hospital involving patients with general or specialized problems, or for a nutrition or an outpatient clinic which provides similar care for ambulatory or outpatients.

Community Dietitians serve as members of the community health team, responsible for assessing the nutritional needs of individuals and groups located in nursing homes, private homes, or other group care facilities, and for evaluating and advising on the nutritional services provided by the institution to the individual.

Research Dietitians assist physicians or research scientists by planning the diet for the proposed study, by developing precise and complete data on patient nutrient intake and output, and by stimulating participation by patients or volunteer subjects.

Consultant Dietitians provide advice or services in nutritional care which affect the management of resources, such as the evaluating of food service systems, developing budgets and records systems, developing educational materials, recommending layout designs and equipment needs, or counseling clients and consulting with health care teams.

Teaching Dietitians plan, schedule or conduct educational programs for professional staff development, inservice training of nonprofessional staff, and may include training for medical interns, nurses, volunteers, patients, or dietetic interns or students.

Nutritionists are specialists in human nutrition concerned with nutritional or food assistance services provided by social, agricultural, or educational agencies to target populations. They perform such duties as assessing nutritional needs of groups, evaluating the nutrition component of programs, interpreting nutrition research or legislation, provide consultation and training, or participating in research.

Public Health Nutritionists serve as members of the health team, and are responsible for planning and administering the community nutrition program for a geographical area or specialty area. This involves such duties as assessing the nutritive quality of food eaten by people in the community; providing consultation and training to administrators, health professionals, and food service personnel in a variety of programs with a food service, nutrition education, and/or health component; conducting dietary studies and providing patient education to groups or individuals in normal and therapeutic nutrition; and consult-

ing on the development and improvement of standards or services provided.

Nutritionists in specialized areas. Current major specializations include maternal and child health, school nutrition and health, group feeding, gerontology, chronic disease, rehabilitation, clinical dietetics, group food service, research, education, and training. The nutritionist plans, develops, implements, evaluates, and promotes the nutrition component of the specialty area to serve the needs of the target population.

Community Nutritionists function as members of the community health team assessing nutrition needs of individuals and groups in the community and providing education and information through individual and group counseling, and through displays, newspapers, radios, and other informational devices.

Nutritionists in Administration plan policy and action related to changing health, service or program needs as influenced by nutrition practices and socioeconomic forces, determine program priorities through the projection of anticipated benefits and expected costs, and evaluate the effectiveness of program services provided.

EXPERIENCE AND TRAINING REQUIREMENTS

1. BASIC REQUIREMENTS FOR ALL GRADES

Successful completion of a full 4-year course of study in an accredited college or university creditable toward a baccalaureate or higher degree in dietetics, food, nutrition, food service management, institution management, or closely related science.

Dietitian: For positions of dietitian the curriculum must have been in accordance with the qualifying requirements established by The American Dietetic Association (ADA) in effect at the time of graduation. (Professional registration as a registered dietitian (R.D.) is evidence of meeting ADA requirements.)

GS–5—For dietitians and nutritionists, completion of the basic requirement is qualifying for GS–5.

Public Health Nutritionist: Successful completion of a master's degree in public health nutrition, community nutrition, or in nutrition supplemented by public health courses from an accredited college or university.

GS−9—For public health nutritionists, completion of the basic requirement is qualifying for GS−9.

2. ADDITIONAL EXPERIENCE AND TRAINING REQUIREMENTS

Candidates for grades GS−7 and above must have had either professional experience or graduate education, or an equivalent combination of both, in addition to meeting the basic requirements. This professional experience or graduate education must have been in or directly related to dietetics or nutrition, or in a field closely related to the position to be filled.

a. Experience

In addition to the basic requirements, the following amounts of professional experience are required for grades GS−7 and above:

Grade:	Years
GS−7	1
GS−9	2
GS−11 and above	3

Completion of a coordinated undergraduate program, internship, or other clinical component approved by The American Dietetic Association, which was conducted as part of the undergraduate program, or after completion of the basic requirements for a baccalaureate degree, is qualifying at grade GS−7 for dietitians or nutritionists.

Candidates possessing professional registration as a Registered Dietitian meet the full requirements for eligibility at GS−7.

For grades GS−11 and below at least 6 months of the required experience must have been at a level of difficulty comparable to that of the next lower grade or 1 year comparable to the second lower grade in the Federal service. For grades GS−12 and above at least 1 year of the required experience must have been at a level of difficulty comparable to that of the next lower grade in the Federal service.

For any grade, the required amount of experience will not, in itself, be accepted as proof of qualification for a position. The quality of experience, rather than its length, will be given primary consideration. The applicant's total education and experience must give positive evidence of ability to perform all of the duties of the position.

b. Substitution of Education for Experience

In addition to the basic requirements, the following amounts and levels of education are qualifying for grades GS−7 and above. This education must have been either in dietetics or nutrition, or in directly related fields such as public health nutrition.

GS−7 .... One full academic year of graduate education.

GS−9 .... Completion of all requirements for a master's or equivalent degree; or two full academic years of graduate education.

GS−11 ... Completion of all requirements for a doctoral degree (Ph.D. or equivalent); or,

Three full academic years of graduate education.

c. Combinations of professional experience and graduate education.

Equivalent combinations of professional experience and graduate education of the type described above are acceptable at each grade.

Professional experience is defined as nonroutine work that required and was characterized by (1) a knowledge of the principles, theories, and methods of dietetics or nutrition; (2) ability to apply such knowledge in the work situation; and (3) positive and continuing development of knowledge and ability, to keep abreast of the advancing and changing discipline.

d. Superior academic achievement

Superior academic achievement cannot be substituted for experience requirements of positions in this series.

EMPLOYMENT INTERVIEW

Applicants who meet the education, experience, and other requirements may be requested to appear for an employment interview.

BASIS OF RATING

No written test is required. Candidates will be rated on the extent, quality and recency of their experience and training, since a professional must keep abreast of constant changes in technology and trends. Ratings will be based upon candidates' statements in their applications and upon any additional information that may be secured, including that secured by inquiries made to supervisors, schools, and other references.

SELECTIVE FACTORS

For some specialized positions, only candidates who possess specific job-related knowledges, skills, and/or abilities may be qualified. For example, if a position requires highly developed skill in research techniques or in maternal and child care, that skill or knowledge may be used as an "in-or-out" selective placement factor. Justification for selective placement factors must show: (a) how the selective factor is directly related to the duties and responsibilities of the position; and (b) why possession of the knowledges, skills, and/or abilities identified as selective factors are necessary for successful performance in the position.

Specialized requirements, for example, are most commonly found in the following areas:

—Research positions, some of which require advanced preparation in dietetics or nutrition as well as in research techniques, to plan, investigate, interpret, evaluate, apply, and expand knowledge in one or more phases of dietetics or nutrition, and to communicate findings through reports and publications.

—Teaching positions, some of which require advanced preparation in dietetics, nutrition, and/or education, to plan, conduct, and evaluate educational programs in one or more dietetic or nutrition subject matter areas.

—Professional registration, (or other acceptable evidence of demonstrated ability to perform at the required level), is required for many positions of director of a dietetic or public health nutrition program in a hospital or other health care facility.

GUIDE FOR EVALUATION OF CANDIDATES

CANDIDATES FOR POSITIONS AT GS-5/7

Evaluation of candidates for these grades is based largely on their academic career, with consideration also being given to any experience they may have had.

1. Education: When evaluating a candidate's academic record, consideration should be given to the extent to which the courses successfully completed contribute to the basic knowledge required in the particular position to be filled.

2. Internship: In evaluating experience gained through an internship, the experience should be related to the duties to be performed.

3. Registration: A Registered Dietitian is a person who meets the qualifications established by the Commission on Dietetic Registration of The American Dietetic Association. Among the requirements for registration are successful completion of the examination for professional registration and the maintaining of continuing education requirements. Since the purpose of the examination and the continuing education requirements is to assure that the dietitian possesses and maintains the common core of knowledge of the profession, registration may be considered in the evaluation of the candidates.

CANDIDATES FOR POSITIONS AT GS-9 AND ABOVE

For positions at these levels, evaluation of undergraduate college training is less important than the consideration of graduate education and professional work experience. The same factors that are used to evaluate the undergraduate academic record may also be used to evaluate the graduate record.

1. The evaluation of a candidate's work experience should consider its nature and significance, its relationship to the requirements of the position, and whether it has involved the performance of professional work of increasing difficulty and complexity, and the assumption of more responsibility.

2. Candidates qualifying on the basis of a master's degree or Ph.D. may be evaluated for completion of a clinical component.

3. Registration by the Commission on Dietetic Registration of The American Dietetic Association may be considered in the evaluation of candidates for positions of dietitian or public health nutritionist.

4. Candidates may also be evaluated for active membership in and presentations before professional organizations, technical publications, participation in seminars and study groups, patents, awards, etc. Technical publications should be evaluated for their contribution to advancing knowledge in dietetics and nutrition, rather than on their quantity alone.

5. Recency of education and experience, and evidence of continuing education in dietetics and nutrition and in related fields, are important elements of full professional competence and may be considered in the evaluation of candidates.

6. Candidates for positions at GS–9 and above should also be evaluated for such skills and abilities as:
—Ability to plan work and evaluate results;
—Skill in analyzing, adapting, or developing materials, such as criteria, specifications, menus, and patient's needs and progress;
—Skill in interpersonal relationships, such as leadership, flexibility, and persuasiveness;
—Skill in oral communications for explaining nutrition to individuals or groups having a wide range of backgrounds, and for teaching students, other professionals, and communicating with groups;
—Skill in written communications for developing technical reports, informational materials, specifications, procedures, and similar tools;
—Ability to stay abreast of changes and new developments within the discipline and closely related areas;
—Ability to work independently, including originating workable solutions.

SPECIAL PHYSICAL REQUIREMENTS

Most positions involve moderate physical exertion, including moving substantial distances, within hospitals or similar facilities, standing, bending, and lifting of light objects, such as medical or procurement records. Ability to read printed material and handwriting, is required in most positions, as well as the ability to communicate effectively and efficiently with patients and others. Many positions involve some amount of exposure to contagious diseases, noise and hazards of kitchen equipment. Protective clothing is required in some situations. A few positions require travel to remote parts of the country.

Dental Aid, GS–1
Dental Assistant, GS–2/5
Dental Assistant (Expanded Function), GS–5/6

DESCRIPTION OF WORK

Dental Assistants provide assistance to the dentist by receiving and preparing patients for dental treatment, preparing materials and equipment for use by the dentist, assisting the dentist at chairside or bedside in the treatment of patients, taking dental radiographs, and maintaining records related to appointments, examinations, treatment and supplies. Dental Assistants may work in general dentistry or in a specialized field of dentistry such as prosthodontics or oral surgery.

Dental Assistants (Expanded Function) are primarily concerned with the performance of reversible intra-oral procedures, such as placing and finishing restorations in teeth prepared by a dentist. Dental Assistants (Expanded Function) also perform chairside assistance and other services typically provided by dental assistants.

MINIMUM QUALIFYING EXPERIENCE

For positions at GS–1, no written test, experience, training, or education is required. Candidates must be willing to perform simple dental aid work and show ability to follow specific instructions. Evidence of this ability may be obtained from personal references, interviews, etc.

For positions at GS–2, six months of experience is required which has provided a knowledge of simple clinic maintenance procedures such as clearing work areas of used materials; replacing soiled linens; storing medical and dental supplies; and filing records in alphabetic or numeric order.

For positions at GS–3, one year of experience is required which has provided all of the following knowledges:

— knowledge of clinical routines and procedures such as receiving, routing, and scheduling patients, ordering supplies, requesting medical or dental laboratory work;
— knowledge of the use, care and storage of dental, medical, or laboratory instruments, materials and equipment;
— knowledge of sterilization techniques sufficient to sterilize dental instruments and materials; and
— knowledge of dental or medical terminology to maintain records related to patients, supplies and recurring medical or dental activities.

For positions at GS–4 and above, candidates must have had 1 year of qualifying experience at the next lower grade in the General Schedule or equivalent experience outside the General Schedule. Qualifying experience at this level is experience in dental assistance to general or specialized dentistry, dental assistant (expanded function) work or any combination of these appropriate to the position being filled.

SUBSTITUTIONS OF EDUCATION AND TRAINING FOR EXPERIENCE

1. For positions at GS–2, completion of a full four-year high school curriculum or high school equivalency is qualifying.

2. For positions at GS–3, the following education and training may be substituted for experience requirements:
— successful completion of a one-year dental assistant program or completion of one year of a dental hygiene program accredited by the American Dental Association's Com-

mission on Accreditation is fully qualifying;
— successful completion of practical nurse training approved by the appropriate State or District of Columbia accrediting body is qualifying;
— completion of education and training other than that outlined above, which is directly related to the routines, procedures, and terminology used in a medical or dental treatment situation may be substituted on a month-for-month basis for the experience requirements. Examples of this training may include, but are not limited to, the U.S. Armed Forces, manpower development, or inservice training programs.

3. For positions at GS–4, the following may be substituted:
— successful completion of a two-year dental assistant program or completion of a two-year dental hygiene program accredited by the American Dental Association's Commission on Accreditation is fully qualifying;
— other training and education which is directly applicable to the performance of dental assistant work may be substituted on a month-for-month basis for the experience requirements. Examples of this training include, the U.S. Armed Forces, manpower development, or inservice training programs.

4. Special Requirements for Dental Assistant (Expanded Function) positions, GS–5 and above.

Candidates for Dental Assistant (Expanded Function) positions must have completed one year of acceptable coursework, preceptorship, or other formal training and/or work assignments specifically designed to equip the candidate with the knowledges and skills required to perform intra-oral procedures involved in the position to be filled, including:
— knowledge of the methods and techniques used in dentistry to perform intra-oral procedures;
— knowledge of the characteristics of a variety of materials and instruments used in performing intra-oral procedures; and
— ability to recognize common dental disorders and conditions such as caries, formations of plaque and calculus, and inflammation of gums.

Examples of acceptable training are:
— courses in a dental hygiene or dental assist-

ant program accredited by the American Dental Association's Commission on Accreditation which are directly related to intra-oral procedures (also referred to as expanded functions) to be performed in the position to be filled;

—U.S. Army's Dental Therapy Assistant Training Program;

—continuing education courses in expanded functions for dental assistants offered by the Indian Health Service of Department of Health, Education, and Welfare;

—other training comparable to the above in private or governmental hospitals, clinics or schools which include formal classroom instruction and clinical training in the knowledges and skills required to perform intra-oral procedures in the position to be filled.

Training may be credited on a month-for-month basis for the experience requirements. Dental Assistant (Expanded Function) positions at GS−6 require one year experience comparable to that of GS−5 level Dental Assistant (Expanded Function).

A written test is required at grade GS−2 and is not to be waived for appointment outside the register, unless authorized by the Office of Personnel Management.

BASIS OF RATING AND RANKING CANDIDATES

Candidates who meet the minimum qualification requirements, including a passing score on the written test, when required, will be rated on a scale of 70 to 100 based on:

For positions at grade GS−1—an evaluation of the candidate's willingness to do simple and repetitive dental aid work, dependability, and ability to work safely.

For positions at grade GS−2—the candidate's score on the written test.

For positions at grades GS−3 and above—an evaluation of the quality and extent of the candidate's experience, education, training or other achievements pertinent to the duties of the position being filled.

In ranking candidates who have met the minimum experience requirements, candidates with dental assistant training should be ranked higher based on the recognition that dental assistant training is more specifically focused on the knowledge, skills, and abilities required by dental assisting work.

PERSONAL CHARACTERISTICS

Dental Assistant and Dental Assistant (Expanded Function) positions involve significant contacts with patients. Candidates must demonstrate the ability to work with patients in a tactful and courteous manner, and relieve fears, and comfort their patients.

SPECIAL PHYSICAL REQUIREMENTS

Usable vision is required and, depending on the essential duties of a specific position, usable hearing and speech may be required.

Dental Hygienist, GS−4/8
Community Health Dental Hygienist, GS−5 and Above

DESCRIPTION OF WORK

Dental Hygienists work in hospitals and outpatient clinics performing oral prophylaxis; applying topical fluorides and desensitizing agents to the teeth; performing examinations of the teeth and surrounding tissues involving the use of diagnostic tests and X-rays; preparing treatment plans for plaque control; instructing individual patients, patient groups, nurses and nursing assistants or other dental hygienists and dental assistants in the techniques and practice of maintaining oral health.

Community Health Dental Hygienists work primarily in nonclinical settings on military installations or in public health program areas planning and carrying out dental health programs to promote public awareness, acceptance, and practice of oral health measures for groups of individuals and communities. Typically, they plan and conduct oral health instructional programs directed toward the needs of various community groups, provide technical advice and assistance to dental personnel on public health matters relating to oral health, make onsite visits to provide policy guidance and insure consistency among areas in accomplishing the objectives of the dental program, conduct surveys and special studies to evaluate the effectiveness of the oral health program and to recommend new or improved methods of oral hygiene, plan and conduct dental inspection programs, develop teaching aids and materials used to improve the oral health of the community, present lectures and demonstrations in new or improved dental techniques and developments, and prepare and compile a variety of records and reports pertaining to the administration of the oral health program.

LICENSURE REQUIREMENTS

Applicants for all grades and specifications must be currently licensed to practice as dental hygienists in a State or territory of the United States or the District of Columbia.

EXPERIENCE REQUIREMENTS FOR CLINICAL DENTAL HYGIENE POSITIONS

For positions at GS–4, no experience is required.

For positions at GS–5, one year of experience as a licensed dental hygienist. This is experience in performing routine oral prophylactic care such as: scaling and polishing the teeth, applying topical flourides and desensitizing agents to the teeth, taking X-rays, sterilizing instruments and instructing patients at chairside in brushing and flossing techniques.

For positions at GS–6, two years of experience as a licensed dental hygienist of which at least one year included duties such as: examining the patient's teeth and surrounding tissues; cleaning, polishing, and applying topical fluorides and other anticariogenic agents to the teeth; treating common abnormalities such as inflammations of the gums; taking and interpreting X-rays for presence of caries and providing oral health care instructions to individuals and groups of patients.

For positions at GS–7, three years of experience as a licensed dental hygienist of which at least one year included duties such as: performing oral prophylaxis in cases of acute gingivitis and periodontal diseases requiring the use of a variety of scalers and ultrasound equipment; performing deep scaling, root planing, and subgingival curettage; taking intraoral impressions, placing temporary fillings; placing and removing rubber dams; planning dental hygiene treatment and series of appointments needed to complete treatment; providing oral hygiene instructions to patients with special problems, and training other hygienists and dental personnel in dental hygiene techniques and procedures.

For positions at GS–8, four years of experience as a licensed dental hygienist of which at least one year included advanced prophylactic and therapeutic hygiene procedures in the treatment of patients with related medical and dental problems. This includes duties such as: performing oral prophylaxis on ambulatory and nonambulatory patients requiring specialized procedures for bedridden patients; preparing dental hygiene treatment plans for patients including assessment of the oral problem, type of oral hygiene care required, and the sequence of appointments needed to complete treatment; presenting lectures and demonstrations to various patient groups such as diabetics and oral cancer patients requiring the use of motivation techniques, dental aids, and educational materials; performing advanced dental hygiene procedures such as root planing and curettage under local anesthesia, polishing and finishing amalgam restorations and inserting temporary fillings in teeth.

EDUCATION AND EXPERIENCE REQUIREMENTS FOR COMMUNITY HEALTH DENTAL HYGIENE POSITIONS

For positions at all grades applicants must meet the basic requirements specified under paragraph A or B below:

A. Successful completion of a full four-year course of study in an accredited college or university leading to a bachelor's degree which must have included or been supplemented by successful completion of a full academic curriculum in dental hygiene accredited by the American Dental Association's Commission on Dental Accreditation.

B. Experience in an amount which, in combination with successful completion of a full academic curriculum in dental hygiene accredited by the American Dental Association's Commission on Dental Accreditation, is sufficient to total at least four years of experience and education. Appropriate experience may be equated to education on a year-for-year basis. To be appropriate, this experience must have demonstrated that the applicant possesses the following:

—ability to plan and direct group activities.

—ability to organize, analyze, and evaluate data; to draw conclusions; and to make decisions or recommendations.

—ability to express ideas and communicate information orally and in writing in a clear, logical, and motivating manner.

—ability to demonstrate and/or present new ideas, techniques, and procedures.

—ability to conduct meetings and present lectures.

—ability to deal effectively with individuals and with groups.

For positions at GS–5, the basic requirements which apply to all grades are fully qualifying.

For positions at GS–7 and above, in addition to the basic requirements, the following amounts of specialized experience are required:

Grade:	*Specialized experience (years)*
GS–7	1
GS–9	2
GS–11 and above	3

Specialized experience is experience in dental hygiene or in a directly related kind of work. Examples of work which are considered specialized experience include:

—Experience in preparing and conducting educational lectures and demonstrations on dental hygiene.

—Experience in planning and developing public health type programs of broad scope, e.g., for varying age groups and types of audiences.

—Experience in supervising or instructing groups of dental hygienists in the performance of dental hygiene duties.

—Other experience in performing the duties of a community health dental hygienist as described in the "Description of Work" above.

SUBSTITUTION OF EDUCATION FOR EXPERIENCE

For Clinical Dental Hygiene Positions successful completion of a full four-year course of study in an accredited college or university leading to a bachelor's degree in Dental Hygiene or in a directly related field of study such as public health, health education, or education may be substituted in full for the experience required at grade GS–5.

For Community Health Dental Hygiene Positions successful completion of one full academic year of graduate education in dental hygiene or in a directly related field of study such as public health, health education, or education may be substituted in full for the specialized experience required at grade GS–7.

Successful completion of all requirements for a master's or equivalent degree in dental hygiene or in a directly related field of study may be substituted in full for the specialized experience requirements at grade GS–9.

Education may not be substituted for the full experience requirements above the grade GS–9.

QUALITY OF EXPERIENCE

Applicants must demonstrate progressively responsible experience of a scope, quality, and degree such as to have equipped them with the ability to perform duties at the grade level of the position for which the application is made. Typically, this is demonstrated by accomplishment of assignments of the difficulty and responsibility described in the position classification standard used to evaluate positions at the next lower grade in the normal line of promotion to the position being filled.

BASIS OF RATING

No written test is required. Applicants will be rated on a scale of 70 to 100 based on an evaluation of the quality and extent of their experience, education, and training or other achievements pertinent to the duties of the positions to be filled. Such ratings will be based upon statements of candidates in their applications, upon qualification inquiries, and upon additional information that may be secured by the examining office.

For all positions, the rating of experience and education may take into account the recency of the experience and education. Extra credit may be given to applicants who show evidence of efforts to keep current in their field.

EMPLOYMENT INTERVIEW

Applicants who meet the minimum experience, training, and other requirements may be requested to appear for an employment interview.

ACCREDITED SCHOOLS

A listing of accredited schools of dental hygiene may be secured from the American Dental Association, Commission on Dental Accreditation, 211 East Chicago Avenue, Chicago, Illinois 60611.

Pharmacy Aid GS—1/3
Pharmacy Technician GS—4/7

DESCRIPTION OF WORK

Pharmacy technicians perform, under the supervision of a registered pharmacist, a variety of technical support functions in a pharmacy. Pharmacy technicians receive, care for, store, distribute, and bulk compound pharmaceuticals, prepare sterile solutions, and set up prescriptions for a final check by a pharmacist.

EXPERIENCE, EDUCATION, AND TRAINING REQUIREMENTS

GRADE GS—1

For grade GS—1, no written test, experience, training, or education is required. Candidates must be willing to perform simple routine pharmacy aid work and show evidence of likelihood of success on the job.

Experience requirements
Candidates must have had experience as described below. (Education may be substituted for experience.)

Grade	General experience (years)	Specialized experience (years)	Total experience (years)
GS—1	0	0	0
GS—2	½	0	½
GS—3	1	0	1
GS—4	1½	½	2
GS—5	2	1	3
GS—6	2	2	4
GS—7	2	3	5

General experience

General experience is that which has provided (*a*) a basic knowledge of laboratory procedures and equipment in chemical, biological, or medical laboratories, or (*b*) a background knowledge of the medical environment or hospital or pharmacy procedures.

Specialized experience

This is experience which has provided the knowledges and skills needed to perform pharmacy technician work. The specialized experience must have provided the candidate with a basic knowledge of pharmaceutical nomenclature; characteristics, strengths, and dosage forms of pharmaceuticals; pharmaceutical systems of weights and measures, operation and care of a variety of pharmaceutical equipment; and a variety of procedures and techniques involved in the care, storage, repackaging, bulk compounding, and distribution of pharmaceuticals.

OTHER GRADES

For GS−2 and GS−3, the general experience requirements are broad in intent and do not require any specialized knowledge or skill in pharmacy work.

For GS−4, the six months of specialized experience must have been comparable in difficulty and responsibility to the GS−3 level.

For GS−5, at least one year of the required experience must have been comparable in difficulty and responsibility to the GS−4 level. At least six months of this experience at the GS−4 level must have been specialized experience that included duties such as the care, storage, repackaging, bulk compounding, and distribution of pharmaceuticals.

For GS−6 and GS−7, at least one year of the required specialized experience must have been comparable in difficulty and responsibility to the next lower grade in the Federal service, or two years comparable to the second lower grade in the Federal service.

SUBSTITUTION OF EDUCATION FOR EXPERIENCE

Successfully completed education of acceptable type and quality may be substituted for the experience requirements at the various grade levels, as specified below:

1. Graduation from a full 4-year or senior high school, or possession of a General Education Development High School Equivalency Certificate, may be substituted in full for the experience requirements at the GS−2 level. (High school education, or the General Educational Development High School Equivalency Certificate, may not be substituted for any part of the experience requirements for GS−3 and above.)

2. Successful completion of one academic year of post-high school education that included a course in biology, chemistry, or physics may be substituted for one year of experience and meets in full the experience requirements for GS−3.

3. Successful completion of a course for (*a*) medical technicians, (*b*) hospital corpsmen, (*c*) medical service specialists, or (*d*) hospital training, obtained in a training program given by the Armed Forces or the U.S. Maritime Service under close medical and professional supervision, may be substituted on a month-for-month basis for general experience.

4. Successful completion of pertinent specialized training courses in pharmaceuticals and pharmacy practices while serving in the Armed Forces or in post-high school study may be substituted on a month-for-month basis for up to a total of one year of specialized experience.

5. Successful completion of two academic years of post-high school study in a resident school or institution of pharmacy or pharmacy technology which included course work in the care, storage, distribution, and preparation of pharmaceuticals, and appropriate laboratory work, may be substituted in full for two years of experience required at the GS−4 level (one and one-half years general and one-half year specialized).

6. Successful completion of four years of academic study in pharmacy may be substituted for three years of experience, including one year specialized experience. This meets in full the experience requirements at the GS−5 level.

Appropriate education and training other than that outlined above, such as in "new careers" training programs, manpower development programs, and inservice training programs will be granted credit depending upon its applicability and extent.

Post-high school education or training which is acceptable under these standards may be substituted for part of the required experience on a pro rata basis.

WRITTEN TEST

Candidates for positions at GS–2 and GS–3 must pass the written test of abilities necessary to learn and perform the duties of these positions. The written test may be waived for candidates, who have successfully completed the equivalent of a specialized training program in pharmacy of at least six months.

BASIS OF RATING

Competitors for all positions will be rated on the quality and extent of experience, education, or training in relationship to the duties of the positions. Ranking will be made on the following basis:

For GS–1: An evaluation of the applicant's willingness to do simple and repetitive pharmacy aid work; his dependability; and his ability to work safely.

For GS–2 and GS–3: Written test scores, or an evaluation of experience, education, and training of candidates who attained a passing score on the written test.

For GS–4 and above: An evaluation of experience, education, and training in relationship to the duties of the position.

The information for evaluating experience, education, and training will be taken from the application form and any additional information which may be obtained through reference inquiries to supervisors, teachers, and others.

SELECTIVE PLACEMENT

Some positions may require particular knowledges and skills. For these positions, consideration may be limited to those candidates whose records show that they have the required knowledges and skills.

BASIC SKILLS POSITIONS

Housekeeping Aid, GS–1
Housekeeper, GS–2, 3, 4, 5, 6, 7
Housemother, Matron, Hostess, Cadet Hostess, GS–2, 3, 4, 5, 6, 7

Applicants must have had progressively responsible experience in general housekeeping duties such as dusting, window washing, cleaning, making beds, waxing or polishing floors, or any experience such as work involved in the care, cleaning, maintenance, and servicing of living quarters in homes, lodging houses, hospitals, or other Government establishments; or, being responsible for the discipline and well-being of members of a domiciliary unit, including checking leaves and passes, receiving guests, assisting in recreational activities, orienting new members and giving attention to members of the unit who are sick, answering the telephone and relaying messages. The total experience must have equipped the applicant with a knowledge of cleaning methods, tools, supplies, and equipment used in general housekeeping operations. For positions in grade GS–4 and below with supervisory duties, the applicant's experience must indicate that she possesses supervisory qualifications, preferably demonstrated by supervisory experience. Grades GS–5, 6, and 7 require supervisory experience.

Grade	Total (years)	Supervisory (years)
GS–1	½	None
GS–2	1	None
GS–3	1½	None
GS–4	2	None
GS–5	2½	½
GS–6	3	¾
GS–7	3½	1

Appointment to Housekeeping Aid and to most Housekeeper positions is restricted by law to persons who are entitled to veteran preference, as long as such persons are available. There are, however, Housekeeper positions which are noncustodial in nature and for these positions appointment is not restricted to persons who are entitled to veteran preference.

Messenger, GS–1/3
Messenger (Motor Vehicle Operator), GS–1/3

Appointment is restricted to persons entitled to veterans' preference as long as such persons are available.

DESCRIPTION OF WORK

Messenger work involves the receipt, individual-route sorting, collection or pick-up, and delivery of mail and a variety of other papers, documents, and administrative material processed in a mail unit or messenger room. Messenger positions may also include the performance, as required, of miscellaneous tasks such as operating simple duplicating equipment in an office situation; light manual work such as lifting and emptying mail sacks, moving office machines and equipment, etc.; simple office duties such as checking outgoing material for complete address, noting changes on messenger route, filing alphabetically, date stamping material, etc.; and/or the operation of automotive equipment to facilitate the performance of messenger work.

REQUIREMENTS

For grade GS–1, no written test, experience, training, or education is required. Candidates must be interested in, and willing to perform, routine messenger work, and to show likelihood of success on the job.

Experience which meets the requirements as shown below for grades GS–2 and GS–3 must have been in messenger or general clerical work.

Grade:	*Total years*
GS–1	None
GS–2	½
GS–3	1

SUBSTITUTION

The successful completion of a full 4-year senior high school curriculum may be substituted for 6 months of the required experience.

WRITTEN TEST

For grade GS–1, no written test is required. All candidates for competitive appointment at grades GS–2 and GS–3 are required to pass the appropriate written test.

BASIS OF RATING

For GS–1: An evaluation of the candidate's interest in and willingness to perform routine and repetitive messenger work, dependability, and the ability to perform work safely.

For GS–2 and 3: The score on the written test and an evaluation of the extent and quality of experience and education.

REQUIREMENTS FOR MOTOR VEHICLE OPERATION

For those positions requiring the operation of Government-owned automotive vehicles, applicants must either hold or obtain within 30 days of employment, appropriate state permit and U.S. Government motor vehicle operators' identification card.

Park Aid GS–1/3
Park Technician GS–4/9

DESCRIPTION OF WORK

Park Aids and Park Technicians perform technical and practical work supporting the management, conservation, interpretation, development, and use of park areas and resources. Park Aids and Park Technicians carry out various operating tasks involved in law enforcement, traffic control, recreation program operation, campground and picnic area operation, accident prevention, fire control, plant disease and insect control, fish and wildlife surveys, soil and water conservation, preservation of historical structures and objects, and comparable aspects of park operations. The mix of duties depends on the particular needs of areas served.

EXPERIENCE AND TRAINING REQUIRED

Candidates must have had experience as described as follows. (Education may be substituted for experience.)

Grade	General experience (years)	Specialized experience (years)	Total experience (years)
GS–1	None	None	None
GS–2	½	None	½
GS–3	1	None	1
GS–4	1½	½	2
GS–5	2	1	3
GS–6	2	2	4
GS–7	2	3	5
GS–8 and above	2	4	6

General experience

This is experience in park operations or in related fields which provided basic knowledges and skills applicable to general park operations and conservation work.

Specialized experience

This is technical experience gained in actual park operations, or in activities which directly support park, fish and wildlife, recreation management, historic preservation, conservation or park-related work.

QUALITY AND LEVEL OF EXPERIENCE

For eligibility at grade GS–4, the required 6 months of specialized experience must have been comparable in difficulty and responsibility to the GS–3 level in the Federal service.

For eligibility at grade GS–5, at least 1 year of required experience, including 6 months of specialized experience, must have been comparable in difficulty and responsibility to the GS–4 level.

For eligibility at grades GS–6 and above, at least 1 year of the required specialized experience must have been comparable in difficulty and responsibility to the next lower grade in the Federal service; or 2 years must have been comparable to the second lower grade in the Federal service.

For positions at GS–9, at least 1 year of the specialized experience must be directly related to the duties of the specific position to be filled. Placement of technicians in positions at GS–9 must be predicated upon (1) a detailed analysis of the knowledges, abilities, and skills required for the work, and (2) a sound matching of the candidate's knowledges, abilities, and skills to the requirements.

WRITTEN TEST

Candidates for positions at GS–2 and GS–3 must pass a written test of abilities necessary to learn and perform the duties of the positions.

SUBSTITUTION OF EDUCATION FOR EXPERIENCE

Successfully completed education at the high school or higher levels may be substituted for the required experience, as indicated below:

GS–2: Completion of a senior high school curriculum or General Educational Development (GED) high school equivalency certificate may be substituted for the general experience requirement at the GS–2 level. High school education or GED equivalency certificate may not be substituted for any part of the experience requirements at GS–3 and above.

GS–3: Successful completion of at least 1 academic year of post high school education that included at least 12 semester hours credit in any combination of courses listed below may be substituted for 1 year of experience and meets in full the experience requirements at the GS–3 level. Acceptable course work includes any field-oriented natural science, history, archeology, police science, and park and recreation management.

GS–4: Two years of academic study as described for GS–3 above which included or was supplemented by at least 18 semester hours in any combination of the subjects shown for GS–3 above, may be substituted for 2 years of experience including ½ year of specialized experience, and meets in full the experience requirements at the GS–4 level.

GS–5: A full 4-year course of study in an accredited college or university leading to a bachelor's or higher degree which includes at least 24 semester hours in any combination of the subjects described for GS–3 above may be substituted for 3 years of experience. Such substitution meets in full the experience requirements at the GS–5 level, including the 1 year of required specialized experience.

Appropriate education and training other than that outlined above, such as in manpower development programs or military training programs, will be credited depending upon their applicability and extent, generally on a month-for-month basis. Maximum substitution of education for experience is 3 years.

BASIS OF RATING

Competitors for all positions will be rated on a scale of 100. The basis for rating will be as follows:

For grade GS–1: An evaluation of the candidate's willingness to do simple park aid work, his dependability, and his ability to work safely.

For grades GS–2 and GS–3: Written test score.

For grades GS–4 and above: An evaluation of training and experience.

ABILITY IN WORKING WITH THE PUBLIC

Most of these positions require contact with the public to explain programs and procedures, to give general assistance, to interpret the natural, historic, scientific, and/or recreational features of park areas, and to enlist the public's cooperation and support. For such positions candidates must demonstrate that they have the required ability.

ADDITIONAL TECHNICIAN KNOWLEDGES AND SKILLS

Some park technician positions may require specialized technical knowledges and skills in particular phases or types of park work. These include skills in: use of complex audiovisual equipment, fire control practices, wildlife management practices, driving or piloting custom-built land and water conveyances, techniques for mountain or water rescue, use of special recreation equipment, equestrian patrolling, saddling horses and packing supplies and equipment, and comparable activities. For such positions, candidates must show that their experience and training has given them the specific technical knowledges and skills needed to perform the duties of the position for which they are being considered.

INTERVIEW REQUIREMENTS

Candidates may, at the option of the agency, be required to appear for a preemployment interview to evaluate skill in personal relationships for the public contact aspects of park technician work.

REQUIREMENTS FOR MOTOR VEHICLE OPERATION

The duties of these positions normally include driving an automobile or truck. The applicant must, therefore, be a capable driver, and must possess at the time of appointment, or obtain within 30 days, a valid driver's permit for the State or territory in which he lives, or in which he will be principally employed, and a valid U.S. Government operator's permit.

SELECTIVE PLACEMENT

For positions at grades GS–4 and above that require particular knowledges and skills, consideration may be restricted to those candidates whose background indicates that they possess the required knowledges and skills.

GUIDE FOR EVALUATION OF CANDIDATES IN RELATION TO JOB REQUIREMENTS

In evaluating each applicant's experience and training, attention should be given to the following factors:

1. Knowledge of general park operations, conservation, or outdoor recreation programs applicable to parks.
2. Knowledge of history or scientific fields applicable to park work.
3. Specialized technical knowledges and skills of the types described under *Additional Technical Knowledges and Skills* (primarily for GS–5 and above).
4. Ability to make constructive suggestions for modification or improvement of methods, procedures, plans, techniques, equipment or programs.
5. Ability to work independently and plan day-to-day activities.
6. Ability to meet and deal effectively with the park visitors.

The information for evaluating experience and training will be obtained from the application form. Confidential reference inquiries may be sent to supervisors, teachers, and others who can furnish useful information about the candidate's qualifications.

SPECIAL PHYSICAL REQUIREMENTS

Applicants must be physically able to perform efficiently the duties of the positions. Some of the positions require arduous physical exertion under rigorous and unusual environmental conditions, such as travel over rugged, precipitous, slippery, and extremely hazardous terrain at high elevations, carrying packs of heavy equipment. Applicants must be proportioned as to height and weight, and gross disproportion will be cause for rejection. Amputation or serious disabilities of arm, hand, leg, or foot will disqualify an applicant for appointment; however, there may be a few positions suitable for persons with minor handicaps. Vision, with or without glasses, must test at least 20/30 (Snellen) each eye. However, applicants with vision less than 20/30 (Snellen) in one eye will receive consideration if the other eye tests 20/20 (Snellen) with or without glasses. Applicants must be able to distinguish basic colors and must be able to hear the conversational voice, each ear, with or without the use of a hearing aid. Since the duties of the position are exacting, responsible, and require extensive oral communication with the public, applicants must possess emotional and mental stability and unimpaired speech.

THE U.S. POSTAL SERVICE POSITIONS

The United States Postal Service is an independent agency of the Federal Government. As such, employees of the Postal Service are federal employees who enjoy the very generous benefits offered by the government. These benefits include an automatic raise at least once a year, regular cost of living adjustments, liberal paid vacation and sick leave, life insurance, hospitalization, and the opportunity to join a credit union. At the same time, the operation of the Postal Service is businesslike and independent of politics. A postal worker's job is secure even though administrations may change. An examination system is used to fill vacancies. The examination system provides opportunities for those who are able and motivated to enter the Postal Service and to move within it.

Since postal employment is so popular, entry is very competitive. In most areas the Distribution Clerk, Machine, Exam is administered only once every three years. The resulting list is used to fill vacancies as they occur in the next three years. An individual who is already employed by the Postal Service, however, may request to take an exam during those intervening years. Any person who has satisfactorily filled a position for a year or more may ask to take the exam for any other position and, if properly qualified, may fill a vacancy ahead of a person whose name is on the regular list. It is even possible to change careers within the Postal Service. If the exam for the precise position that you want will not be administered for some time, it might be worthwhile to take the exam for another position in hopes of entering the Postal Service and then moving from within.

One very common "instant progression" within the Postal Service is that from clerk-carrier, a salary level 5 position, to distribution clerk, machine (also known as letter sorting machine operator), a level 6 position. Anyone who qualifies as a clerk-carrier is automatically offered the opportunity to take the machine exam. The advantages of becoming a letter sorting machine operator include not only higher salary, but also increased employment possibilities. Mechanization is the wave of the future. The field is expanding, and there are far more openings for machine operators than there are for clerks or carriers. Of course, the desirability of the job leads to a greater number of applicants and a still more competitive position for you. This fact should further motivate you to study hard for your exam.

Salaries, hours, and some other working conditions as well are subject to frequent change. The postal workers have a very effective union that bargains for them and gains increasingly better conditions. At the time of your employment, you should make your own inquiry as to salary, hours, and other conditions as they apply to you. Job descriptions and requirements are less subject to change. In the next few pages we quote job descriptions as provided by the government.

Occupations in the Postal Service

The U.S. Postal Service handles billions of pieces of mail a year, including letters, magazines, and parcels. Close to a million workers are required to process and deliver this mail. The vast majority of Postal Service jobs are open to workers with 4 years of high school or less. The work is steady. Some of the jobs, such as mail carrier, offer a good deal of personal freedom. Other jobs, however, are more closely supervised and more routine.

NATURE AND LOCATION OF THE INDUSTRY

Most people are familiar with the duties of the mail carrier and the post office window clerk. Yet few are aware of the many different tasks required in processing mail and of the variety of occupations in the Postal Service.

At all hours of the day and night, a steady stream of letters, packages, magazines, and papers moves through the typical large post office. Mail carriers have collected some of this mail from neighborhood mailboxes; some has been trucked in from surrounding towns or from the airport. When a truck arrives at the post office, mail handlers unload the mail. Postal clerks then sort it according to destination. After being sorted, outgoing mail is loaded into trucks for delivery to the airport or nearby towns. Local mail is left for carriers to deliver the next morning.

To keep buildings and equipment clean and in good working order, the Postal Service employs a variety of service and maintenance workers, including janitors, laborers, truck mechanics, electricians, carpenters, and painters. Some workers specialize in repairing machines that process mail.

Postal inspectors audit the operations of post offices to see that they are run efficiently, that funds are spent properly, and that postal laws and regulations are observed. They also prevent and detect crimes such as theft, forgery, and fraud involving use of the mail.

Postmasters and supervisors are responsible for the day-to-day operation of the post office, for hiring and promoting employees, and for setting up work schedules.

The Postal Service also contracts with private businesses to transport mail. There are more than 12,500 of these "Star" route contracts. Most "Star" route carriers use trucks to haul mail, but in some remote areas horses or boats are used instead.

Almost 85 percent of all postal workers are in jobs directly related to processing and delivering mail. This group includes postal clerks, mail carriers, mail handlers, and truck drivers. Postmasters and supervisors make up nearly 10 percent of total employment, and maintenance workers about 4 percent. The remainder includes such workers as postal inspectors, guards, personnel workers, and secretaries.

The Postal Service operates more than 41,000 installations. Most are post offices, but some serve special purposes such as handling payroll records or supplying equipment.

Although every community receives mail service, employment is concentrated in large metropolitan areas. Post offices in cities such as New York, Chicago, and Los Angeles employ a great number of workers because they not only process huge amounts of mail for their own pop-

ulations, but also serve as mail processing points for the smaller communities that surround them. These large city post offices have sophisticated machines for sorting the mail. In these post offices, distribution clerks who have qualified as machine operators quickly scan addresses and send letters on their way automatically by pushing the proper button. These clerks must be able to read addresses quickly and accurately, must be able to memorize codes and sorting schemes and must demonstrate machine aptitude by their performance on the Number Series part of the exam.

TRAINING, OTHER QUALIFICATIONS, AND ADVANCEMENT

An applicant for a Postal Service job must pass an examination and meet minimum age requirements. Generally, the minimum age is 18 years, but a high school graduate may begin work at 16 years if the job is not hazardous and does not require use of a motor vehicle. Many Postal Service jobs do not require formal education or special training. Applicants for these jobs are hired on the basis of their examination scores.

Applicants should apply at the post office where they wish to work and take the entrance examination for the job they want. Examinations for most jobs include a written test. A physical examination is required as well. Applicants for jobs that require strength and stamina are sometimes given a special test. The names of applicants who pass the examinations are placed on a list in the order of their scores. Separate eligibility lists are maintained for each post office.

Every applicant must pass the exam to find a place on the eligibility list. As compensation for their service, veterans enjoy certain extra consideration in their placement on the list. Five extra points are added to the passing score of an honorably discharged veteran and 10 extra points to the score of a veteran wounded in combat or disabled. Disabled veterans who have a compensable, service-connected disability of 10 percent or more are placed at the top of the eligibility list. When a job opens, the appointing officer chooses one of the top three applicants. Others are left on the list so that they can be considered for future openings.

New employees are trained either on the job by supervisors and other experienced employees or in local training centers. Training ranges from a few days to several months, depending on the job.

Advancement opportunities are available for most postal workers because there is a management commitment to provide career development. Also, employees can get preferred assignments, such as the day shift or a more desirable delivery route, as their seniority increases. When an opening occurs, employees may submit written requests, called "bids," for assignment to the vacancy. The bidder who meets the qualifications and has the most seniority gets the job.

In addition, postal workers can advance to better paying positions by learning new skills. Training programs are available for low-skilled workers who wish to become technicians or mechanics.

Applicants for supervisory jobs must pass an examination. Additional requirements for promotion may include training or education, a satisfactory work record, and appropriate personal characteristics such as leadership ability. If the leading candidates are equally qualified, length of service also is considered.

Although opportunities for promotion to supervisory positions in smaller post offices are limited, workers may apply for vacancies in a larger post office and thus increase their chances.

EMPLOYMENT OUTLOOK

Employment of postal clerks is expected to grow slowly through the 1990s. Most openings will result from the need to replace clerks who retire, die, or transfer to other occupations.

Although the amount of mail post offices handle is expected to grow as both population and the number of businesses grow, modernization of post offices and installation of new equipment will increase the amount of mail each clerk can handle. For example, machines which semiautomatically mark destination codes on envelopes are now being tested. These codes can be read by computer-controlled letter-sorting machines which automatically drop each letter into the proper slot for its destination. With this system, clerks read addresses only once, at the time they are coded, instead of several times, as they now do. Eventually this equipment will be installed in all large post offices. Thus, while the total number of postal clerks may not increase, there will be greater need for distribution clerks who operate sorting machines, and job opportunities will open up in more and more cities.

Examination Announcement
Post Office Clerk-Carrier

The Post Office Clerk-Carrier Exam is not a regularly scheduled exam given on the same date all over the country. Rather, the Clerk-Carrier Exam is separately scheduled in each postal geographic area. An area may comprise a number of states or, in densely populated regions, may consist of only a portion of one county. The frequency of administration also varies, though generally the exam is offered every two or three years.

When an exam is about to open in a postal area, the postal examiner for the area sends notices to all the post offices serviced by that area. The examiner also places ads in local newspapers and commercials over local radio stations. State employment offices receive and post copies of the announcement, and Civil Service newspapers carry the information as well.

QUALIFICATION REQUIREMENTS

No experience is required. All applicants will be required to take a written examination designed to test aptitude for learning and performing the duties of the position. The test will consist of 2 parts: (1) Address Checking, (2)

Memory for Addresses. The test and completion of the forms will require approximately 1½ hours.

DUTIES

Clerks work indoors. Clerks have to handle sacks of mail weighing as much as 70 pounds. They sort mail and distribute it by using a complicated scheme which must be memorized. Some clerks work at a public counter or window doing such jobs as selling stamps and weighing parcels and are personally responsible for all money and stamps. Clerks may be on their feet all day. They also have to stretch, reach, and throw mail. Assignments to preferred positions, such as window clerks, typist and stenographic positions, etc., are filled by open bid and reassignment of the senior qualified clerk.

Carriers have to collect and deliver mail. Some carriers walk, other carriers drive. Carriers must be out in all kinds of weather. Almost all carriers have to carry mail bags on their shoulders; loads weigh as much as 35 pounds. Carriers sometimes have to load and unload sacks of mail weighing as much as 70 pounds.

The duties of newly appointed clerks and carriers are at times interchangeable. As representatives of the Postal Service, they must maintain pleasant and effective public relations with patrons and others, requiring a general familiarity with postal laws, regulations, and procedures commonly used.

Employees may be assigned to work in places exposed to public view. Their appearance influences the general public's confidence and attitude toward the entire Postal Service.

Employees appointed under this standard are, therefore, expected to maintain neat and proper personal attire and grooming appropriate to conducting public business, including the wearing of a uniform when required.

CARRIER POSITIONS REQUIRING DRIVING

Before eligibles may be appointed to carrier positions which require driving, they must demonstrate a Safe Driving record and must pass the Road Test to show they can safely drive a vehicle of the type used on the job.

Eligibles who fail to qualify in the Road Test will not be given the test again in the same group of hires. Those who fail the test a second time will not again be considered as a result of the same examination for appointment to a position that requires driving.

A valid driver's license from the state in which this post office is located must be presented at the time of appointment. Persons who do not have the license will not be appointed but their names will be restored to the register. They may not again be considered for carrier positions until they have obtained the required driver's license. After hire, individuals must also be able to obtain the required type of Government operator's permit.

SPECIAL PHYSICAL REQUIREMENTS

The distant vision for clerk and carrier positions not involving driving duties must test at least 20/30 (Snellen) in one eye, glasses permitted, and applicants generally must be able to hear ordinary conversation with or without a hearing aid, but some clerk positions may be filled by the deaf.

For carrier positions which require driving, applicants must have at least 20/30 (Snellen) in one eye and 20/50 (Snellen) in the other with or without a corrective device for unlimited operation of motor vehicles. Hearing must be at least 15/20 with or without a hearing aid.

A physical examination will be required before appointment.

Examination Announcement
Mail Handler

QUALIFICATION REQUIREMENTS

No experience is required. All applicants will be required to take a written examination designed to test (1) Address Checking, (2) Following Oral Directions, and (3) Understanding of Meaning of Words. The test and completion of the forms will require approximately 2 hours. Competitors will be rated on a scale of 100. They must score at least 70 on the examination as a whole.

DUTIES

Loads, unloads, and moves bulk mail, and performs duties incidental to the movement and processing of mail. Duties may include separation of mail sacks, facing letter mail, canceling stamps on parcel post; operating canceling machines, addressograph, mimeograph; operating fork-lift truck; rewrapping parcels, etc.

SPECIAL PHYSICAL REQUIREMENTS

Persons with amputation of arm, leg or foot should not apply. A physical examination will be required before appointment.

STRENGTH AND STAMINA TEST

When eligibles are within reach for appointment they will be required to pass a test of strength and stamina. In this test they will be required to lift, shoulder, and carry two 70-pound sacks—one at a time—15 feet and load them on a hand truck. They will be required to push that truck to where there are some 40-, 50-, and 60-pound sacks. They will be required to load those sacks onto the truck. They will then have to unload the truck and return the truck to its original location. Eligibles will be notified when and where to report for the test of strength and stamina.

Persons with certain physical conditions will not be permitted to take the test of strength and stamina without prior approval of a physician. These physical conditions are (a) hernia or rupture, (b) back trouble, (c) heart trouble, (d) pregnancy, (e) or any other condition which makes it dangerous to the eligible to lift and carry 70-pound weights. Persons with these physical conditions will be given special instructions at the time they are notified to report for the strength and stamina test.

An eligible being considered for an appointment who fails to qualify on the test will not be tested again in the same group of hires. If he fails the test a second time, his eligibility for the position of mail handler will be cancelled.

Mark-Up Clerk, Automated

DUTIES OF THE JOB

The mark-up clerk, automated, operates an electro-mechanical machine to process mail that is classified as "undeliverable as addressed." In doing this, the mark-up clerk operates the keyboard of a computer terminal to enter and extract data to several databases including change of address, mailer's database, and address-correction file. The mark-up clerk must select the correct program and operating mode for each application, must affix labels to mail either manually or with mechanical devices, and must prepare forms for address-correction services. Other duties may include distribution of processed markups to appropriate separations for further handling, operation of a photocopy machine, and other job-related tasks in support of primary duties.

QUALIFICATION REQUIREMENTS

An applicant for a mark-up clerk position must have had either six months of clerical or office-machine-operating experience or have completed high school or have had a full academic year (36 weeks) of business school. A mark-up clerk must also demonstrate the ability to type 40 wpm for five minutes with no more than 2 errors. The record of experience and training must show ability to use reference materials and manuals; ability to perform effectively under pressure; ability to operate any office equipment appropriate to the position; ability to work with others; and ability to read, understand, and apply certain regulations and procedures commonly used in processing mail undeliverable as addressed.

For appointment, a mark-up clerk must be eighteen years old, or sixteen years old if a high school graduate. An applicant who will reach his or her eighteenth birthday within two years from the date of the exam may participate. A mark-up clerk must be able to read, without strain, printed material the size of typewritten characters and must have 20/40 (Snellen) vision in one eye. Glasses are permitted. In addition, the applicant must pass an examination consisting of a clerical and verbal-abilities test and a computer administered alpha-numeric typing test.

Garageman-Driver, Tractor/Trailer Operator, Motor Vehicle Operator

DUTIES OF THE JOB

What all the above job titles have in common is driving various Postal Service vehicles on the highway and within the lots and properties of the Postal Service.

Garagemen are responsible for seeing that each vehicle is in the proper place at the proper time and that each vehicle is roadworthy before it is released. Garagemen must keep accurate records of all activity as it affects each vehicle and must follow through on what movement or maintenance is required.

Tractor/trailer operators drive the huge mail rigs from city to city along the super highways, delivering large quantities of mail as quickly as possible within the bounds of safety. The work of a Postal Service tractor/trailer operator is really no different from the work of a tractor/trailer operator for private industry.

Motor vehicle operators drive the various other Postal Service vehicles as needed, both within and between towns and cities.

QUALIFICATION REQUIREMENTS

The exam for all of these positions is designed to test powers of observation, ability to express oneself, accuracy in record keeping, familiarity with road signs, and ability to follow instructions. The exam is in two parts of 40 questions each. You will have sixty minutes to answer each part. The test requires concentration and careful attention to details. The sample questions that the Postal Service sends to applicants provide a good idea of what to expect from the exam itself.

Since all these positions require driving, applicants must be licensed drivers over the age of eighteen. In addition, applicants must have good eyesight and hearing and be in excellent health and physical condition. A physical exam and strength and stamina tests are part of the hiring process. Candidates must also take training and qualify for licensing on the vehicle they are required to drive.

Rural Carrier

DUTIES OF THE JOB

The work of the rural carrier combines the work of the window clerk and the letter carrier but also has special characteristics of its own. The rural carrier's day begins with sorting and loading the mail for delivery on his or her own route. Then comes a day's drive, which may be over unpaved roads and rough terrain. The rural carrier does most deliveries and pickups of outgoing mail from the car. Occasionally, however, bulky packages must be delivered directly to the homeowner's door. Since rural postal patrons may be far from the nearest post office, the rural carrier sells stamps, weighs and charges for packages to be mailed, and performs most other services performed by window clerks in post offices. At the end of the day, the rural carrier returns to the post office with outgoing mail and money collected in various transactions. The rural carrier must be able to account for the stamps, postcards, and other supplies with which he or she left in the morning and must "balance the books" each day.

A rural carrier enjoys a great deal of independence. No supervisor looks over his or her shoulder. On the other hand, there is no supervisor to turn to for advice on how to handle a new situation that may come up. Since the rural carrier is responsible for interpreting regulations and for handling money, the exam that applicants for this position must take is quite different from that taken by clerk-carrier applicants. The exam is designed to test for ability to handle the varied responsibilities of the job.

QUALIFICATION REQUIREMENTS

The qualifying exam for rural carrier is a three-part exam that takes nearly four hours to administer. The exam includes 35 Vocabulary questions, 25 Reading Comprehension questions, and 40 Mathematics Application questions. The Postal Service sends each applicant a set of sample questions along with the admission card for the exam and the detailed application form. At the test site, the applicant has a chance to try some sample questions before beginning the exam itself.

Since the rural carrier's job requires driving, the minimum age for a rural carrier is eighteen. The rural carrier must have a valid driver's license, good eyesight, and the ability to hear ordinary conversation (glasses and hearing aid are permitted). In addition, the rural carrier must demonstrate physical stamina and ability to withstand the rigors of the job.

Postal Police Officer

DUTIES OF THE JOB

A postal police officer is essentially a security guard at post offices and at other postal installations and facilities. The postal police officer may work inside postal buildings or out of doors at loading docks and in parking lots. A postal police officer may be armed.

QUALIFICATION REQUIREMENTS

An applicant for the position of postal police officer must be at least twenty years of age, and, unless a veteran, cannot be appointed until reaching the age of twenty-one years. The postal police officer must be physically able to perform the duties of the job, must have weight in proportion to height, must have good color vision and good distant vision (no weaker than 20/40 in one eye and 20/50 in the other eye correctable to 20/20), and must have keen hearing. Emotional and mental stability are essential for the armed officer, and a psychological interview is part of the qualification process. The candidate must demonstrate the ability to deal with the public in a courteous and tactful manner; to work in stress situations; to collect, assemble, and act on pertinent facts; to prepare clear and accurate records; to deal effectively with individuals and groups; and to express him or herself in both oral and written communications. A background investigation will be made on all otherwise qualified candidates. In order to be considered, each applicant must pass a written qualifying exam with a score of 70 or better out of a possible 100. The examination tests observation and memory, word knowledge, and the ability to arrange sentences in logical order.

THE ACWA GROUPS

ACWA stands for Administrative Careers With America. The ACWA exams were introduced into civil service testing in June of 1990. They are still undergoing development and refinement, job titles are being added to the group and others are being exempted. Basically, however, the ACWA groups consist of a great number of job titles at the GS-5 and GS-7 level.

The Federal Government needs persons with potential for advancement into responsible professional and administrative jobs. If you have a college degree or equivalent experience, this examination offers you the opportunity to compete for various positions with Federal agencies across the country. Many positions are filled at grade GS-5 and do not require specialized education or experience.

BASIC REQUIREMENTS

1. Grade GS-5 Positions:
   Four years of education leading to a bachelor's degree, 3 years of responsible experience, or an equivalent combination of education and experience.
2. Grade GS-7 Positions:
   a. A bachelor's degree and one of the following Superior Academic Achievement provisions:
      —A grade average of "B" (a GPA of 3.0 or higher) for all completed undergraduate courses, or those completed in the last 2 years of undergraduate study.
      —A grade average of "B+" (a GPA of 3.5 or higher) for all courses in your major field of study, or those courses in your major completed in the last 2 years of undergraduate study.
      —Rank in the upper one-third of your class in the college, university, or major subdivision.
      —Membership in a national honorary scholastic society (other than freshman honor societies) recognized by the Association of College Honor Societies; or
   b. One full year of graduate education, law school, or a graduate degree; or
   c. One year of work experience in a field related to the position. The experience must be equivalent to the GS-5 level or higher in the Federal service; or
   d. An equivalent combination of education and experience.

In addition to meeting the basic requirements, most applicants for ACWA positions must pass the competitive ACWA exam. Actually, there are six exams, slightly different from one another in content but very similar in style, format and difficulty. Preparation for any one ACWA exam is preparation for all ACWA exams. The only deviation from this rule is the exam for Writing and Public Information Occupations. This exam does not include any mathematics.

The following is a comprehensive listing of the jobs filled through each of the six examinations. Those positions followed by an asterisk are positions with specific coursework or experience requirements beyond the basic. If you are interested in a position with an asterisk, check with an OPM office or call the College Hotline at 900-990-9200 to learn about the specific qualification requirements.

BUSINESS, FINANCE AND MANAGEMENT OCCUPATIONS

Agricultural Programs*; *Includes*
  Agricultural Marketing
  Agricultural Program Specialist
Business: *Includes*
  Appraising and Assessing
  Bond Sales Promotion
  Budget Analysis
  Building Management
  Financial Administration and Programs
  Food Assistance Program Specialist
  General Business and Industry
  Housing Management
  Public Utilities Specialist
  Realty
  Wage and Hour Law Administration
Communication Specialist*
Contract Specialist*
Financial Institution Examining*
Finance*: *Includes*
  Financial Analysis
  Insurance Examining
  Loan Specialist
Industrial Programs*: *Includes*
  Industrial Property Management
  Industrial Specialist
  Quality Assurance Specialist

Supply: *Includes*
  Distribution Facilities and Storage
    Management
  General Supply
  Inventory Management
  Logistics Management
  Packaging
  Property Disposal
  Supply Cataloging
  Supply Program Management
Trade Specialist*
Transportation*: *Includes*
  Highway Safety Management
  Traffic Management
  Transportation Industry Analysis
  Transportation Operations
  Transportation Specialist
Unemployment Insurance*
An asterisk (*) denotes positions with specific qualification requirements.
Best Opportunities—The options offering the best opportunities for employment are: Business, Contract Specialist, Industrial Programs, and Supply.

BENEFITS REVIEW, TAX AND LEGAL OCCUPATIONS

Claims Examining: *Includes*
  Civil Service Retirement Claims Examining
  Contact Representative
  General Claims Examining
  Passport and Visa Examining
  Unemployment Compensation Claims
    Examining
  Veterans Claims Examining
  Workers' Compensation Claims Examining

Land Law Examining*
Paralegal Specialist
Social Insurance Administration
    (Representative)* and Social
    Insurance Claims Examining
Social Services
Tax Law Specialist*
Tax Technician*

PERSONNEL ADMINISTRATION AND COMPUTER OCCUPATIONS

Computer Specialists Trainee
Personnel: *Includes*

Contractor Industrial Relations
Employee Development

Employee Relations
Labor-Management Relations Examining
Labor Relations
Manpower Development
Military Personnel Management
Occupational Analysis
Personnel Management
Personnel Staffing
Position Classification

Salary and Wage Administration
Administration: *Includes*
 Administrative Officer
 Miscellaneous Administration and Programs
Program Analysis: *Includes*
 Management Analysis
 Program Analysis
Vocational Rehabilitation*

HEALTH, SAFETY, AND ENVIRONMENTAL OCCUPATIONS

Environmental Protection Specialist
Hospital Housekeeping Management*
Outdoor Recreation Planning*

Public Health Program Specialist
Safety and Occupational Health Management*

LAW ENFORCEMENT AND INVESTIGATION OCCUPATIONS

Alcohol, Tobacco, and Firearms Inspection
Civil Aviation Security Specialists
Criminal Investigator
Customs Inspector
Game Law Enforcement
General Investigator
Immigration Inspector
Internal Revenue Officer

Import Specialist and Security: *Includes*
 Import Specialist
 Intelligence
 Security Administration
Park Ranger*
Public Health Quarantine Inspection*
Securities Compliance Examining*
Wage and Hour Compliance

WRITING AND PUBLIC INFORMATION OCCUPATIONS

Agricultural Market Reporting*
Archives Specialist
General Arts and Information (excluding
 Fine and Applied Arts)

Public Affairs
Technical Information Services*
Technical Writing and Editing*
Writing and Editing

PART THREE

Useful Information About Civil Service Tests

TEST-TAKING TECHNIQUES

1. Give yourself enough time to prepare for the exam. Start studying weeks ahead of time; study every day; don't cram in the last twenty-four hours.
2. Arrive for your exam rested and relaxed. Get a good night's sleep before the exam. Leave home early enough so that you are not flustered by traffic or transit delays.
3. Arrive a bit early so that if you are not assigned a seat you can choose one away from drafts or a flickering light.
4. Wear a watch. Bring identification and admission ticket if one was issued to you.
5. Listen to instructions before the exam begins. Ask questions if there is anything that you do not fully understand.
6. Read directions carefully. Directions which state "Mark (D) if all three names being compared are alike" are very different from directions which state "Mark (D) if none of the three names being compared are alike." Misreading these directions will ruin your score.
7. Read every word of every question. Little words like "not," "most," "all," "every," and "except" can make a big difference.
8. Read all the answer choices before you mark your answer. Don't just choose the first answer that seems correct, read them all to find out which answer is best.
9. Mark your answers by completely blackening the space of your choice. Every answer must be recorded in a space on the answer sheet.
10. Mark only one answer for each question.
11. If you change your mind, erase completely and cleanly. Never cross out an answer.
12. Answer the questions in order. If you are not sure of an answer, eliminate those answers which are obviously wrong and guess from those remaining. Mark the question booklet so that you can return and rethink the guesses if you have time.
13. Check often to be certain that you are marking each question in the right space and that you have not skipped a space by mistake. The answer sheet is scored by a machine. Question 8 must be answered in space 8; question 52 in space 52.
14. Stay awake. Stay alert. Work steadily and carefully using all the time allowed to earn your best possible score.

SAMPLE TEST QUESTIONS FOR FEDERAL EXAMINATIONS

TESTS AND TESTING METHODS

The following section contains many of the types of questions which appear on federal examinations. The Office of Personnel Management utilizes aptitude testing to a large degree. This type of examination measures a candidate's ability to be trained to perform a specific job rather than evaluating a candidate's ability to perform from day one on the job as achievement tests are designed to accomplish. Many test factors like reasoning, non-verbal reasoning, and mechanical abilities can be, and are, used on a wide variety of aptitude tests for various positions. Other test factors are more specific and therefore are used for positions like Clerk, Stenographer, Typist, Postal Service positions, and professional and semi-professional positions. This type of testing includes questions specific to the duties of the position for which the examination is being held.

It is advocated however, that candidates for positions which call for specific testing should also review those test factors which are general in nature. This endeavor should serve to accomplish getting the candidate into shape for his or her examination through "mental gymnastics." A candidate is likely to profit by reviewing the entire section, ignoring only those sections which require technical knowledge that the candidate may not have.

Tests of Verbal Abilities

Answer Sheet

1 Ⓐ Ⓑ Ⓒ Ⓓ Ⓔ   3 Ⓐ Ⓑ Ⓒ Ⓓ Ⓔ   5 Ⓐ Ⓑ Ⓒ Ⓓ Ⓔ   7 Ⓐ Ⓑ Ⓒ Ⓓ Ⓔ

2 Ⓐ Ⓑ Ⓒ Ⓓ Ⓔ   4 Ⓐ Ⓑ Ⓒ Ⓓ Ⓔ   6 Ⓐ Ⓑ Ⓒ Ⓓ Ⓔ   8 Ⓐ Ⓑ Ⓒ Ⓓ Ⓔ

Tests of verbal abilities (often referred to in Civil Service usage as "general tests") are designed to test a wide range of abilities, including the ability to understand words, interpret the meaning of sentences and paragraphs, and recognize and apply the rules of grammar and spelling. There are many kinds of questions which could be used for this purpose; the ones most commonly used are shown on this page and the next few.

Vocabulary

These words are not limited only to words actually used on the job. Vocabulary questions are a good measure of a competitor's general ability, as well as his aptitude for work requiring skill with words.

There is no printed list of all words whose meanings are tested in civil service examinations. No study of a selected list of words is likely to help in preparing for an examination. The general improvement of your vocabulary will help, however, and you will find that this improvement will make other kinds of questions more understandable also.

Directions: In each of the following questions you are to find which one of five words or phrases offered as choices has most nearly the same meaning as the word or phrase in CAPITAL LETTERS or *italics*. On the answer sheet mark the letter of the suggested answer which you think is the best.

1. If a report is VERIFIED it is
   A) changed   D) discarded
   B) confirmed   E) corrected
   C) replaced

Since "confirmed," lettered B, means most nearly the same as "verified," the space under B is marked on the answer sheet for question 1.

2. A clerk who shows FORBEARANCE TOWARD THE OPINION OF OTHERS shows
   A) severity   D) quietness
   B) hypercriticism   E) thankfulness
   C) tolerance

3. *A controversy* between two persons is
   A) an agreement
   B) a dispute
   C) a partnership
   D) a plot
   E) an understanding

4. To say that a condition is *generally or extensively existing* means that it is
   A) artificial   D) timely
   B) prevalent   E) transient
   C) recurrent

5. *Authentic* means most nearly
   A) detailed   D) technical
   B) reliable   E) practical
   C) valuable

6. *The two farms lie close to each other, but are not in actual contact*. This sentence means most nearly that the two farms are
   A) adjoining   D) adjacent
   B) abutting   E) united
   C) touching

The space under D is marked for this question because "adjacent" best describes the meaning of the sentence in italics. The other choices all indicate that the farms are in contact in some degree or are touching each other.

Word Relations

In each of the following questions the first two words in capital letters go together in some way. Find how they are related. Then select from the last five words the one that goes with the third word in capital letters in the same way that the second word in capital letters goes with the first.

7. FOOD is to HUNGER as SLEEP is to
   A) night   D) health
   B) dream   E) rest
   C) weariness

Food relieves hunger and sleep relieves weariness. Therefore, C, the letter before "weariness," is marked on the answer sheet for this question.

8. SPEEDOMETER is related to POINTER as WATCH is related to
   A) case   D) spring
   B) hands   E) numerals
   C) dial

Answer Key

1. B	3. B	5. B	7. C
2. C	4. B	6. D	8. B

Interpretation of Paragraphs

Answer Sheet

1 Ⓐ Ⓑ Ⓒ Ⓓ Ⓔ   2 Ⓐ Ⓑ Ⓒ Ⓓ Ⓔ   3 Ⓐ Ⓑ Ⓒ Ⓓ Ⓔ   4 Ⓐ Ⓑ Ⓒ Ⓓ Ⓔ

Each question consists of a quotation followed by a series of five statements. Among the five statements there is only one that *must* be true if the quotation is true. Other statements among the five may or may not be true, but they are not necessary conclusions from the quotation. You are to select the *one* statement which is *best supported* by the quotation.

1. (*Reading*) "The application of the steam engine to the sawmill changed the whole lumber industry. Formerly the mills remained near the streams; now they follow the timber. Formerly the logs were floated downstream to their destination; now they are carried by the railroads."

What besides the method of transportation does the quotation indicate has changed in the lumber industry?
A) speed of cutting timber
B) location of market
C) type of timber sold
D) route of railroads
E) source of power

The quotation says nothing about the speed of steam-powered sawmills, location of the market for lumber, the type of timber sold, or the route of railroads. It does, however, mention "the application of the steam engine to the sawmill"—which gave a new source of power for sawmill operations. E is therefore the answer, and the space under E is blackened for question 1.

2. (*Reading*) "More patents have been issued for inventions relating to transportation than for those in any other line of human activity. These inventions have resulted in a great financial saving to the people and have made possible a civilization that could not have existed without them."

Select the alternative that is best supported by the quotation. Transportation
A) would be impossible without inventions
B) is an important factor in our civilization
C) is still to be much improved
D) is more important than any other activity
E) is carried on through the Patent Office

The space on the Answer Sheet under B is marked for question 2 because the statement lettered B is implied in the quotation. A is not strictly true, since manpower without inventions could supply transportation of a sort; C is probably true but is not in the quotation; D is exaggerated; E is not implied in the information given.

3. (*Reading*) "There exists a false but popular idea that a clue is some mysterious fact which most people overlook, but which some very keen investigator easily discovers and recognizes as having, in itself, a remarkable meaning. The clue is most often an ordinary fact which an observant person picks up—something which gains its significance when, after a long series of careful investigations, it is connected with a network of other clues."

According to the quotation, to be of value, clues must be
A) discovered by skilled investigators
B) found under mysterious circumstances
C) discovered soon after the crime

D) observed many times

E) connected with other facts

The quotation does not say that the clue must be (A) discovered by an investigator in order to make it of value; it does not mention (B) the circumstances under which a clue must be found; nothing in the paragraph implies that the value of a clue depends upon the (C) time of its discovery, nor upon the (D) number of times it is observed. E is the answer, because the quotation does say that a clue gains its significance, or value, when *connected with other clues or facts.*

4. (*Reading*) "Just as the procedure of a col-

lection department must be clear-cut and definite, the steps being taken with the sureness of a skilled chess player, so the various paragraphs of a collection letter must show clear organization, giving evidence of a mind that, from the beginning, has had a specific end in view."

The quotation best supports the statement that a collection letter should always

A) show a spirit of sportsmanship

B) be divided into several paragraphs

C) express confidence in the debtor

D) be brief, but courteous

E) be carefully planned

Answer Key

1. E   2. B   3. E   4. E

Proverbs

Answer Sheet

1 Ⓐ Ⓑ Ⓒ Ⓓ Ⓔ   3 Ⓐ Ⓑ Ⓒ Ⓓ Ⓔ   5 Ⓐ Ⓑ Ⓒ Ⓓ Ⓔ

2 Ⓐ Ⓑ Ⓒ Ⓓ Ⓔ   4 Ⓐ Ⓑ Ⓒ Ⓓ Ⓔ   6 Ⓐ Ⓑ Ⓒ Ⓓ Ⓔ

These questions test ability to understand meanings and apply generalizations. The answer is the sentence which means the same thing as the saying quoted.

1. The saying "Many hands make light work" means most nearly

   A) Most people prefer easy jobs.

   B) When several work together, each finds his task easy.

   C) Much light work can be done by hand.

   D) There are often too many to help.

   E) One does his best work when working alone.

The statement lettered B means most nearly the same as "Many hands make light work." Therefore this answer should be selected.

2. The saying "To know the road, ask of those who have traveled it" means most nearly

   A) Know your destination before you start.

   B) Seek counsel of experienced persons.

   C) When in doubt, stop.

   D) The traveled road is the easiest route.

   E) If you would advance profit by your past.

Judgment

These questions are based on a variety of facts, sometimes on facts with which the candidate would be expected to be familiar, sometimes on facts explained in the question itself. The questions are of various degrees of difficulty. In some cases judgment items may pertain to a particular field of subject matter, knowledge of which is necessary for the job.

3. Hospital beds are usually higher than beds in private homes. Which of the following is the BEST reason for this fact?
   A) Hospital beds are in use all day, instead of at night only.
   B) Many hospital patients are children.
   C) Private homes seldom have space enough for high beds.
   D) The care of patients is less difficult when the beds are high.
   E) The danger of falling out of bed is greater where there are no nurses.

The suggestion lettered D is the answer and is marked on the answer sheet. Of all the suggestions given as possible reasons why hospital beds are higher than other kinds, the one lettered D is clearly the most reasonable and best.

4. Objects are visible because
   A) they are opaque
   B) they are partially in shadow
   C) they absorb light from the sun
   D) light falls on them and is reflected to the eye
   E) light rays penetrate their surfaces

5. In starting a load, a horse has to pull harder than he does to keep it moving, because
   A) the load weighs less when it is moving
   B) there is no friction after the load is moving
   C) the horse has to overcome the tendency of the wagon to remain at rest
   D) the wheels stick to the axles
   E) the horse becomes accustomed to pulling the load

6. Which of the following would be the *surest* indication that a druggist may have violated the legal requirement that narcotic drugs be dispensed only on a physician's prescription?
   A) A number of people known to have purchased other drugs from him are believed to possess narcotics, but no prescriptions issued to these persons are in the druggist's file.
   B) He is himself an addict.
   C) His wholesaler refuses to sell him narcotics.
   D) The total of his present narcotics stock and the amount legally accounted for is much less than his purchases.
   E) The supply of narcotics in stock is less than the amount which he recently reported.

The facts related in A do not indicate that these customers have secured their narcotics from this druggist—the narcotics may have been obtained from some other druggist on a proper prescription; B is no indication that prescriptions did not cover all the narcotics he has dispensed, either for his own use or for other people; C might be true for many reasons—for example, his credit may be bad; and E could be explained by legal sales made since his last report. The answer is D, because violation of the requirement mentioned is a likely explanation of the large difference; therefore D should be selected.

Answer Key

1. B	3. D	5. C
2. B	4. D	6. D

Grammar and English Usage

In each of questions 1 and 2, select the sentence that is preferable with respect to grammar and good usage in a formal letter or report.

1. A) They do not ordinarily present these kind of reports in detail like this.
   B) Reports like this is not generally given in such great detail.
   C) A report of this kind is not hardly ever given in such detail as this one.
   D) This report is more detailed than what such reports ordinarily are.
   E) A report of this kind is not ordinarily presented in such detail as this one.

2. A) Although that statement is true, I did not leave it influence my decision.
   B) My decision is not effected by that statement, even though it is true.
   C) Although true, I have not let that statement influence my decision
   D) That statement is true, but it does not affect my decision.
   E) Because that statement is true does not have any effect on my decision.

In questions 3 and 4, four words or phrases have been underlined and lettered A, B, C, and D. If there is an error in usage in one of the underlined words or phrases, mark on the answer sheet the letter of the one in which the error occurs. If there is no error, mark the E space.

3. The gasoline tank <u>bust</u> and <u>escaping</u> gaso-
               A   B

   line <u>became</u> ignited in an unknown <u>manner</u>.
       C   D

4. The truck <u>was</u> in good <u>mechanical</u> condition
               A   B

   <u>when examined</u> ten hours <u>before</u> the acci-
        C   D

   dent occurred.

Spelling

5. Select the one misspelled word.
   A) reliable   D) accurrate
   B) detailed   E) sanctioned
   C) different

In questions like the following, find the correct spelling of the word and blacken the proper space on your answer sheet. If none of the suggested spellings is correct, choice D should be selected.

6. A) occassion   C) ocassion
   B) occasion   D) none of these

The correct spelling of the word is *occasion*. Since the B spelling is correct, it should be selected as your answer.

Look at each word in the following list and decide whether the spelling is *all right* or *bad*. On the answer sheet blacken space
   A if the spelling is ALL RIGHT
   B if the spelling is BAD

7. running

8. indien

9. skool

In questions like 10, a sentence is given in which one word, which is underlined, is spelled as it is pronounced. Write the correct spelling of the word in the blank. Then decide which one of the suggested answers, A, B, C, or D, is the correct answer to the question. (Sometimes the question will refer to one letter in the word, sometimes to a combination of letters.)

10. The new treasurer uses the same system that his <u>pred-eh-sess'-urr</u> did. In the correct spelling, —————————————, what is the tenth letter?

A) s

B) e

C) o

D) none of these

The correct spelling of the underlined word is *predecessor*. Since the tenth letter is "o," which is given as answer C, this should be your answer.

Answer Key

1. E	3. A	5. D	7. A	9. B
2. D	4. E	6. B	8. B	10. C

Tests of Reasoning

Answer Sheet

1 Ⓐ Ⓑ Ⓒ Ⓓ Ⓔ   3 Ⓐ Ⓑ Ⓒ Ⓓ Ⓔ   5 Ⓐ Ⓑ Ⓒ Ⓓ Ⓔ   7 Ⓐ Ⓑ Ⓒ Ⓓ Ⓔ

2 Ⓐ Ⓑ Ⓒ Ⓓ Ⓔ   4 Ⓐ Ⓑ Ⓒ Ⓓ Ⓔ   6 Ⓐ Ⓑ Ⓒ Ⓓ Ⓔ

In some jobs, it is necessary to understand, interpret, and apply rules and principles. In others, it is necessary also to discover principles from available data or information. These types of reasoning ability can be tested by different kinds of tests—for example, questions on the relationship of words, understanding of paragraphs, or solving of numerical problems.

Other types of questions that have been found useful in testing reasoning abilities are illustrated on these two pages. Here the competitor is asked to find relationships between elements (numbers, letters, or patterns), to find the rule by which they are bound together in groups or arranged in a certain order, and to select or arrange other elements according to that rule.

Number Series

Each of these three questions gives a series of six numbers. Each series of numbers is made up according to a certain rule or order. You are to find what the next number in the series should be; then blacken the space on the answer sheet that is lettered the same as the correct suggested answer.

1. 2 4 6 8 10 12
   A) 14
   B) 16
   C) 18
   D) 20
   E) none of these

In question 1, the rule is to add 2 to each number (2 + 2 = 4; 4 + 2 = 6; etc.). The next number in the series is 14 (12 + 2 = 14). Since *14* is lettered A among the suggested answers, the space lettered A is blackened on the answer sheet for question 1.

2. 7 8 6 7 5 6
   A) 2
   B) 3
   C) 4
   D) 5
   E) none of these

In question 2, the rule is to add 1 to the first number, subtract 2 from the next, add 1, subtract 2, and so on. The next number in the series is 4. On the answer sheet, the letter C should be blackened for question 2.

3. 3 6 9 12 15 18
   A) 39
   B) 40
   C) 45
   D) 59
   E) none of these

In question 3, the rule is to add 3, making 21 the next number in the series. The correct answer to question 3 is *none of these*, since 39, 40, 45, and 59 are all incorrect answers; therefore E is marked on the answer sheet.

The next two questions are more difficult. In these, the arrangement is more complicated, and the answer is chosen from groups of two numbers, of which one group gives the next two numbers in the series.

4. 1 1 2 1 3 1 4 1
   A) 1 5   D) 5 5
   B) 4 1   E) 6 1
   C) 5 1

The series consists of 1's alternating with numbers in ascending numerical order. The next two numbers would be 5 and 1; therefore C is the correct answer.

5. 2 8 3 7 5 6 8 5
   A) 10 6   D) 12 4
   B) 11 3   E) 12 6
   C) 11 4

This series consists of a subseries for which the rule is to add 1, add 2, add 3, add 4, alternating with another subseries in descending numerical order. The next number in the first subseries would be 8 + 4, or 12; and the next number in the descending series would be 4. Therefore D is the correct choice.

Letter Series

In each of these questions there is a series of letters which follow some definite order, and at the right there are five sets of two letters each. Look at the letters in the series and determine what the order is; then from the suggested answers at the right, select the set that gives the next two letters in the series in their correct order. Mark the space that has the same letter as the set you have chosen.

6. X C X D X E X   A) F X   B) F G   C) X F   D) E F   E) X G

The series consists of X's alternating with letters in alphabetical order. The next two letters would be F and X; therefore, A is the correct answer.

7. A B D C E F H A) **G H** B) **I G** C) **G I** D) **K L** E) **I H**

If you compare this series with the alphabet, you will find that it goes along in pairs, the first pair in their usual order and the next pair in reverse order. The last letter given in the series is the second letter of the pair G—H, which is in reverse order. The first missing letter must, therefore, be G. The next pair of letters would be I—J, in that order; the second of the missing letters is I. The alternative you look for, then, is G I, which is lettered c.

Answer Key

1. A	3. E	5. D	7. C
2. C	4. C	6. A	

Symbol Series

> ### Answer Sheet
>
> 1 Ⓐ Ⓑ Ⓒ Ⓓ Ⓔ   2 Ⓐ Ⓑ Ⓒ Ⓓ Ⓔ

Questions 1 and 2 consist of a series of five symbols at the left and five other symbols labeled A, B, C, D, and E at the right.

In each question, first study the series of symbols at the left; then from the symbols at the right, labeled A, B, C, D, and E, select the one which continues the series most completely. Next to the question number on the answer sheet blacken the space lettered the same as the symbol which you have chosen.

1.

Each symbol in the series at the left has two coils. The symbols differ from one another in the number of loops that each coil has. In the first symbol, each coil has five loops; in the second, the left-hand one has four and the right-hand one has five; in the third, each coil has four. In this series, first the left-hand coil loses a loop and then the right-hand coil loses one.

Since the fifth symbol has three loops in each coil, the next symbol in this series must have two loops in the left-hand coil and three in the right-hand coil. Since symbol A is the only one which has two loops in the left-hand coil and three in the right-hand coil, A is the answer, and you should blacken space A for question 1 on the answer sheet.

2.

Question 2 is harder. The first five symbols show an alternation from small to large to small; and a quarter-turn in a counterclockwise direction each time. The answer should be a large circle, therefore (which eliminates B from the alternatives), with the larger rectangle at the bottom of the circle (which eliminates D and E). A second look at A shows that the rectangles within it are larger than any of the rectangles in the other circles; this change has no basis in the series. Thus C is left as the correct answer.

Answer Key

1. **A**   2. **C**

Clerical Tests

Clerk

Answer Sheet

1 Ⓐ Ⓑ Ⓒ Ⓓ Ⓔ   3 Ⓐ Ⓑ Ⓒ Ⓓ Ⓔ   5 Ⓐ Ⓑ Ⓒ Ⓓ Ⓔ

2 Ⓐ Ⓑ Ⓒ Ⓓ Ⓔ   4 Ⓐ Ⓑ Ⓒ Ⓓ Ⓔ   6 Ⓐ Ⓑ Ⓒ Ⓓ Ⓔ

ALPHABETIZING: In each of the following questions there is a name enclosed in a box, followed by a series of four names in proper alphabetic order. The spaces between the names are lettered A, B, C, D, and E. Decide in which space the boxed name belongs in that series; then blacken the proper space on the answer sheet.

1. | Kessler, Neilson |

   A) →
      Kessel, Oscar
   B) →
      Kessinger, D. J.
   C) →
      Kessler, Karl
   D) →
      Kessner, Lewis
   E) →

2. | Olsen, C. C. |

   A) →
      Olsen, C. A.
   B) →
      Olsen, C. D.
   C) →
      Olsen, Charles
   D) →
      Olsen, Christopher
   E) →

3. | Robeson, Carl |

   A) →
      Robey, Clarke
   B) →
      Robinette, Claude
   C) →
      Robinson, Claude
   D) →
      Robinton, Charles
   E) →

COMPUTATIONS: Work each problem and compare your answer with suggested answers A, B, C, and D. On the Sample Answer Sheet, blacken the proper space. If your answer does not agree with any of the first four suggested answers, blacken space E on the answer sheet.

4. Add:
   9 6 3
   2 5 7
   4 1 6
   ———

Answers
A) 1,516
B) 1,526
C) 1,636
D) 1,726
E) none of these

5. Divide:
$$2\,7\,\overline{)\,4\,3\,7\,9\,.\,4}$$

A) 160.2
B) 160.22
C) 1,620.2
D) 1,622
E) none of these

6. From a shipment of supplies, an inspector accepts 32 boxes and rejects 8 boxes. What percentage of the boxes of supplies is accepted?

A) 20   D) 80
B) 25   E) none of these
C) 75

Answer Key

1. D   4. C
2. B   5. E
3. A   6. C

Accounting Clerk

Answer Sheet

1 Ⓐ Ⓑ Ⓒ Ⓓ Ⓔ   3 Ⓐ Ⓑ Ⓒ Ⓓ Ⓔ   5 Ⓐ Ⓑ Ⓒ Ⓓ Ⓔ   7 Ⓐ Ⓑ Ⓒ Ⓓ Ⓔ

2 Ⓐ Ⓑ Ⓒ Ⓓ Ⓔ   4 Ⓐ Ⓑ Ⓒ Ⓓ Ⓔ   6 Ⓐ Ⓑ Ⓒ Ⓓ Ⓔ   8 Ⓐ Ⓑ Ⓒ Ⓓ Ⓔ

The following sample questions show the types of questions that will be used in the written tests. They show also how the questions in the tests are to be answered. Read the directions below; then answer the sample questions.

Each sample question has a number of suggested answers lettered A, B, C, D, and E. Decide which one is the best answer to the question. Then, on the Sample Answer Sheet, find the answer space numbered to correspond with the number of the question and blacken the space lettered the same as the best suggested answer.

For each question like 1 and 2, choose the one of the five suggested answers that means most nearly the same as the word or group of words in *italics*.

1. A small crane was used to *raise* the heavy parts. *Raise* means most nearly
   A) drag
   B) unload
   C) deliver
   D) lift
   E) guide

2. The reports were *consolidated* by the secretary. *Consolidated* means most nearly
   A) combined
   B) concluded
   C) distributed
   D) protected
   E) weighed

3. (*Reading*) "What constitutes skill in any line of work is not always easy to determine; economy of time must be carefully distinguished from economy of energy, as the quickest method may require the greatest expenditure of muscular effort, and may not be essential or at all desirable."

The quotation best supports the statement that
   A) energy and time cannot both be conserved in the performing of a single task
   B) the most efficiently executed task is not always the one done in the shortest time
   C) if a task requires muscular energy, it is not being performed economically
   D) skill in performing a task should not be acquired at the expense of time
   E) a task is well done when it is performed in the shortest time

Regulation (on which Questions 4 and 5 are based):
Full-time employees shall earn and be credited with sick leave at the rate of 1¼ days per calendar month.

Directions (for Questions 4 and 5):
The following table gives the sick-leave records of two full-time employees for the calendar year 1980. For each of these employees, the workweek consisted of five 8-hour days. For each question, determine the balance of accumulated sick leave to the credit of the employee at the end of December 1980. At the right side of the table are four suggested answers, designated by A, B, C, and D at the top of the columns. If one of these suggested answers is correct, blacken the proper space on the Answer Sheet. If the correct answer is not given under A, B, C, or D, blacken the space indicating E on the Answer Sheet.

Questions:

Employee	Accumulated Sick Leave 12/31/79	Sick Leave Used in 1980	Balance of Accumulated Leave 12/31/80				
			A	B	C	D	E
	Days — Hours	Days — Hours	Days — Hours	Days — Hours	Days — Hours	Days — Hours	
4. No. 4	8 – 4	2 – 1	6 – 3	7 – 5	17 – 5	21 – 3	None of these
5. No. 5	60 – 0	8 – 7	51 – 1	51 – 7	60 – 0	66 – 3	

6. A voucher contained the following items:

6 desks	@ $89.20	$525.20
8 chairs	@ $32.50	260.00
	Total	$885.20

The terms were given on the voucher as 3%, 10 days; net, 30 days. Verify the computations, which may be incorrect, and calculate the correct amount to be paid. If payment is made within the discount period, the amount to be paid is

A) $761.64

B) $771.34

C) $795.20

D) $858.64

E) none of these

Questions 7 and 8 are based on the following portion of a withholding tax table:

If the payroll period with respect to an employee is WEEKLY

And wages are—		And number of withholding exemptions claimed is—				
At least	But less than	0	1	2	3	4
		The amount of income tax to be withheld shall be				
$172	$176	$31.30	$21.30	$11.30	$1.30	0
176	180	32.00	22.00	12.00	2.00	0
180	184	32.80	22.80	12.80	2.80	0

7. K received a monthly wage of $176.40 the first 3 weeks of the year and $182.50 the next 9 weeks. He claimed 3 exemptions for the first 4 weeks and 4 for the next 8 weeks. What was the total income tax withheld during the 12 week period?

A) $0.00

B) $6.00

C) $8.80

D) $11.20

E) none of these

8. L, who has 2 exemptions receives a weekly wage of $175.50. If no amounts other than income tax were withheld, his weekly take-home pay would be

A) $154.20

B) $164.20

C) $174.20

D) $175.50

E) none of these

Answer Key

| 1. D | 3. B | 5. E | 7. C |
| 2. A | 4. D | 6. B | 8. B |

Storekeeping Clerk

Answer Sheet

1 Ⓐ Ⓑ Ⓒ Ⓓ Ⓔ   3 Ⓐ Ⓑ Ⓒ Ⓓ Ⓔ   5 Ⓐ Ⓑ Ⓒ Ⓓ Ⓔ   7 Ⓐ Ⓑ Ⓒ Ⓓ Ⓔ

2 Ⓐ Ⓑ Ⓒ Ⓓ Ⓔ   4 Ⓐ Ⓑ Ⓒ Ⓓ Ⓔ   6 Ⓐ Ⓑ Ⓒ Ⓓ Ⓔ

Answer questions like 11 through 17 in the following way.

Assume that a stockroom floor is divided into three sections—West, Central, and East. There are a number of bins in each of these sections. Each bin is numbered and holds one particular type of stock item which has the same number as the bin in which it is kept. For example, bin number 3 holds a supply of stock item number 3. The bins and stock items are located in the three sections as follows:

LOCATION PLAN

Section	Bin and Item Numbers
West	1—10
Central	11—20
East	21—30

Each question contains several numbers, which are the stock numbers of the items to be taken from the bins to fill an order. To answer each question, decide which section or sections contain the bins from which the items are to be taken. Select

A if the order is filled from only ONE section
B if the order is filled from the WEST and CENTRAL sections only
C if the order is filled from the WEST and EAST sections only
D if the order is filled from the CENTRAL and EAST sections only
E if the order is filled from ALL THREE sections

Now do the following sample questions and mark your answers on the Answer Sheet.

1. 26, 28, 29
   The answer to question 11 is A, because all three items in this order are found in only ONE section.

2. 2, 12, 25, 29
   The answer here is E, because items must be taken from ALL THREE sections to fill this order.

3. 12, 15, 27
   Here D is the answer, because items must be taken from the CENTRAL and EAST sections.

4. 2, 8, 21, 25

5. 19, 20, 21

From time to time bins, with the items they hold, will be moved from one section to another. Also, items may become unavailable and other items will have to be substituted for them. Write the Location Plan on scratch paper, and make a record of all changes in the Plan.

Change I. The following shifts are made in the stock:

Bins and items 11 and 12 are moved from the Central section to the West section.

Bin and item 21 are moved from the East section to the Central section.

The following substitutions are to be made:

Discontinued	Replaced by
Item 15	Item 25
Item 27	Item 3

Your changed Location Plan should read:

Section	Bin and Item Numbers		
West	~~1—10~~	1—12	For 15 use 25
Central	~~11—20~~	13—21	For 27 use 3
East	~~21—30~~	22—30	

After you have made these changes, answer questions 16 and 17 on the basis of the changed Location Plan.

16. 2, 11, 22, 23

17. 15, 24, 29

The answer to question 16 is c, because, in accordance with the above changes, the order will be filled from the WEST and EAST sections.

The answer to question 17 is a, because Item 25 will be used for Item 15 and the order will, therefore, be filled from only ONE section.

Now compare your answers with the Answer Key.

Answer Key

1.	A	5.	D
2.	E	6.	C
3.	D	7.	A
4.	C		

Office Machine Operator

The following sample questions show the types and approximate difficulty of the questions that will be used. They also show how the questions are to be answered by those who take the tests.

Read the directions; then look over the sample questions and try to answer them. (For the actual examination, you will be given separate answer sheets on which your answers can be scored by an electric machine.) Each number on the answer sheet stands for the question with the same number. For each question, make a solid black mark in the appropriate space which corresponds to the number of the question. Compare your answers with those given in the Answer Key.

In the test that has questions like 1 through 10 below, each question is a line of three names or three numbers that are much alike. Compare the three names or numbers and decide which ones are exactly alike. On the Answer Sheet, blacken the space lettered

    A if ALL THREE names or numbers are exactly ALIKE
    B if only the FIRST and SECOND names or numbers are exactly ALIKE
    C if only the FIRST and THIRD names or numbers are exactly ALIKE
    D if only the SECOND and THIRD names or numbers are exactly ALIKE
    E if ALL THREE names or numbers are DIFFERENT

1.	Davis M. Hazen	David M. Hozen	David M. Hazen
2.	Lois Berger Appel	Lois Berger Appel	Lois Berger Apfel
3.	June McPherson Allan	Jane McPherson Allan	Jane McPherson Allan
4.	Annabel K. Dove	Annabel H. Dove	Annabel K. Dove
5.	J. Menninger Baxter	J. Menninger Baxter	J. Menninger Baxter
6.	3449212	3449212	3449112
7.	2153107	2153017	2153117
8.	1023576	1023576	1023576
9.	32614513	32164513	32614513
10.	412893778	412893378	412893378

Answer Key

1. E	3. D	5. A	7. E	9. C
2. B	4. C	6. B	8. A	10. D

Typing Test

In the typing test you are to show how well you know the alphabetic keyboard.

Set your *marginal stop* for a left-hand margin of about 2½ inches. You will type only *one column, down the center* of your page.

Set your machine to *double space* between lines. Allow one space between words; use the space bar for this purpose.

If you notice that you have made an error, double space and begin the same line again. *Do not make any erasures* or other corrections.

As soon as you have typed a line correctly, double space and begin the next line. When taking the examination, if you finish all the lines before time is called, begin copying the list a second time.

Since the machines that some appointees will operate do not make any difference between capital letters and small letters, it makes *no difference whether you use capitals* in this test. You may type a line all in capitals or all in small letters, or in any combination. Similarly, although there is no punctuation in the list, you will not be charged with an error if you happen to type a comma or a period.

If you were copying from a list like the Practice List at the bottom of this page and you abandoned incorrect lines, you would be credited for having the first three lines of the list correctly typed if your paper looked like this—

```
Nesbit ED ELECTRICIAN Transit Belmont

Foley Jno survv

Foley John

foley jno surveyor bayside co. norfolk

Lewis Don lineman HydroPower B

LEWIS DON LINEMAN HYDRO POWER BEDFORD
```

PRACTICE LIST

```
Nesbit Ed electrician Transit Belmont     Proctor S drycleaning service manager

Foley Jno surveyor Bayside Co Norfolk     Adam Fred assembler and bench grinder

Lewis Don lineman Hydro Power Bedford     Brown Cal automobile mechanic skilled

Burkert T miner Penn Colliery Glencoe     Wetmore S demonstrator office devices

Nesbitt F welder United Steel Phoenix     Loman Leo calculating machine repairs
```

In the examination, you will be given these directions and time to copy the Practice List in order to exercise your fingers and to see that your machine is working properly. For the actual test, you will be given a longer list and be allowed 10 minutes for making correct copies of as many lines as you can.

Supervision

Answer Sheet

1 Ⓐ Ⓑ Ⓒ Ⓓ Ⓔ   2 Ⓐ Ⓑ Ⓒ Ⓓ Ⓔ

Each question has five suggested answers, lettered A, B, C, D, and E. For each question, decide which one of the suggested answers is the best answer to the question.

1. A supervisor is planning a discussion with his workers as part of a training course. To which one of the following factors should he give most attention?
   A) preparing in advance questions that will promote the discussion of important matters
   B) getting as many workers as possible to attend the meeting
   C) inviting only those workers who do not hesitate to speak in a group
   D) making certain that the meeting will not drag out too long
   E) selecting about six workers to make speeches which they will prepare in advance

2. A group of employees has recently been hired to perform simple, routine tasks. The use of which one of the following statements in the training of the group would be most likely, in general, to create interest in this work?
   A) emphasis upon the pleasant working conditions and special services which the company offers its employees
   B) explanation of the inspection system by which all work is reviewed in order to make certain that it conforms with requirements
   C) demonstration that the work is extremely simple and therefore there can be no excuse for failure to perform it properly
   D) a frank statement that the work is monotonous but must be done even if it is not interesting
   E) explanation of the relationship and the importance of the work to the total work of the organization

Answer Key

1. A   2. E

Electronic Computer Operator

Answer Sheet

1 Ⓐ Ⓑ Ⓒ Ⓓ Ⓔ   2 Ⓐ Ⓑ Ⓒ Ⓓ Ⓔ   3 Ⓐ Ⓑ Ⓒ Ⓓ Ⓔ

Each of the next three questions has two boxes at the left. The symbols in the first box are like each other in some way, and the symbols in the second box are like each other in some way. But whatever it is that makes the symbols alike in one box makes them different from those in the other box. There is a question mark in the second box to indicate that a symbol is missing. You are to choose from the lettered symbols in the third box the one which best fits into the second box.

Look at question 1. In this question, all the symbols in the first box are curved lines; in the second box they are straight lines. Of the answer choices, only B is straight, so B should be marked on the Answer Sheet. (Note that some of the lines are "dotted"; but this is not the *difference* between the two boxes, for if it were it would also be the *likeness* between the symbols in the second box—they would both be dotted lines.) Now do questions 2 and 3.

NOTE: There is not supposed to be a *series* or progression in these symbol questions. If you look for a progression in the first box and try to find the missing figure to fill out a similar progression in the second box, you will be wasting time. For example, look at question 1. A competitor who saw that both boxes had a horizontal figure followed by an oblique one might try to find a vertical figure to match the last one in the first box. If he chose D he would be missing the real point of the question. Remember, look for a *likeness* within each box and a *difference* between the two boxes.

Answer Key

1. **B**   3. **B**
2. **D**

STENOGRAPHY *(Only Stenographers take this):*

A practice dictation and a test exercise will be dictated at the rate of 80 words a minute.

The sample printed below shows the length and the difficulty of material to be used by the examiner in giving the dictation. If each pair of lines is dictated in exactly 10 seconds, the dictation will be at the rate of 80 words a minute. Have someone dictate the exercise to you at the rate shown, so that you may have some idea as to how well prepared you are to take the examination. The periods should be dictated; the commas should not be dictated, but the passage should be read with the expression that the commas indicate.

Sample Dictation:

In recent years there has been a great increase in the need for capable stenographers,	10 sec.
not only in business offices but also in public service agencies, both	20 sec.
governmental and private. (Period) The high schools and business schools in many parts of	30 sec.
the country have tried to meet this need by offering complete commercial courses. (Period)	40 sec.
The increase in the number of persons who are enrolled in these courses shows that	50 sec.
students have become aware of the great demand for stenographers. (Period) A person	1 min.
who wishes to secure employment in this field must be able to take dictation	10 sec.
and to transcribe the notes with both speed and accuracy. (Period) The rate of	20 sec.
speed at which dictation is given in most offices is somewhat less than that of	30 sec.
ordinary speech. (Period) Thus, one who has had a thorough training in shorthand	40 sec.
should have little trouble in taking complete notes. (Period) Skill in taking dictation	50 sec.
at a rapid rate is of slight value if the stenographer cannot also type her notes	2 min.
in proper form. (Period) A businessman sometimes dictates a rough draft of the ideas	10 sec.
he wishes to have included in a letter, and leaves to the stenographer the task	20 sec.
of putting them in good form. (Period) For this reason, knowledge of the essentials	30 sec.
of grammar and of composition is as important as the ability to take	40 sec.
dictation. (Period) In addition, a stenographer should be familiar with the sources of	50 sec.
general information that are most likely to be used in office work. (Period)	3 min.

Shown below, the TRANSCRIPT and WORD LIST for part of the preceding dictation are similar to those each competitor will receive for the dictation exercise. Many words have been left out of the TRANSCRIPT. Compare your notes with it and, when you come to a blank space in the TRANSCRIPT, decide what word (or words) belongs in the space. For example, you will find that the word "there" belongs in blank No. 1.

Look at the WORD LIST to see whether you can find the missing word. Notice what letter (A, B, C, or D) is printed beside it, and write that letter in the blank. For example, the word "there" is listed, followed by the letter C. We have already written C in blank No. 1 to show you how you are to record your choice. Now decide what belongs in each of the other blanks. You are to write E if the exact answer is NOT listed. You may also write the word (or words), or the shorthand for it, if you wish. The same choice may belong in more than one blank.

ALPHABETIC WORD LIST

Write E if the answer is NOT listed.

advertising—A	many—D
agencies—D	marked—A
almost—C	met—A
also—C	most—C
and—D	need—D
business—B	offering—D
but—A	only—B
claimed—B	opening—A
colleges—C	parts—A
complete—B	private—C
country—A	schools—D
demand—B	sections—B
especially—D	the need—A
even—B	their—D
government—B	there—C
great—C	to complete—C
has been—D	to meet—C
high schools—A	to offer—B
in—C	trained—C
in government—A	tried—A

TRANSCRIPT

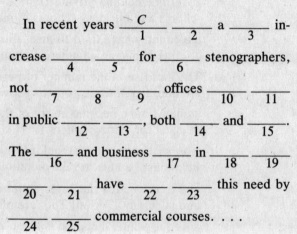

In recent years ___C___ _____ a _____ increase _____ _____ for _____ stenographers,
not _____ _____ _____ offices _____ _____
in public _____ _____, both _____ and _____.
The _____ and business _____ in _____ _____
_____ _____ have _____ _____ this need by
_____ _____ commercial courses. . . .

(For the next sentences there would be another word list, if the entire sample dictation were transcribed.)

You will be given a special answer sheet like the sample on page 155, on which your answers can be scored by an electric machine. Each number on the answer sheet stands for the blank with the same number in the transcript. Blacken the space with the letter that is the same as the letter you wrote in the transcript. If you have not finished writing letters in the blanks in the transcript, or if you wish to make sure that you have lettered them correctly, *you may continue to use your notes after you begin marking the answer sheet.*

Answer Sheet for Sample Transcript

1 Ⓐ Ⓑ Ⓒ Ⓓ Ⓔ	14 Ⓐ Ⓑ Ⓒ Ⓓ Ⓔ
2 Ⓐ Ⓑ Ⓒ Ⓓ Ⓔ	15 Ⓐ Ⓑ Ⓒ Ⓓ Ⓔ
3 Ⓐ Ⓑ Ⓒ Ⓓ Ⓔ	16 Ⓐ Ⓑ Ⓒ Ⓓ Ⓔ
4 Ⓐ Ⓑ Ⓒ Ⓓ Ⓔ	17 Ⓐ Ⓑ Ⓒ Ⓓ Ⓔ
5 Ⓐ Ⓑ Ⓒ Ⓓ Ⓔ	18 Ⓐ Ⓑ Ⓒ Ⓓ Ⓔ
6 Ⓐ Ⓑ Ⓒ Ⓓ Ⓔ	19 Ⓐ Ⓑ Ⓒ Ⓓ Ⓔ
7 Ⓐ Ⓑ Ⓒ Ⓓ Ⓔ	20 Ⓐ Ⓑ Ⓒ Ⓓ Ⓔ
8 Ⓐ Ⓑ Ⓒ Ⓓ Ⓔ	21 Ⓐ Ⓑ Ⓒ Ⓓ Ⓔ
9 Ⓐ Ⓑ Ⓒ Ⓓ Ⓔ	22 Ⓐ Ⓑ Ⓒ Ⓓ Ⓔ
10 Ⓐ Ⓑ Ⓒ Ⓓ Ⓔ	23 Ⓐ Ⓑ Ⓒ Ⓓ Ⓔ
11 Ⓐ Ⓑ Ⓒ Ⓓ Ⓔ	24 Ⓐ Ⓑ Ⓒ Ⓓ Ⓔ
12 Ⓐ Ⓑ Ⓒ Ⓓ Ⓔ	25 Ⓐ Ⓑ Ⓒ Ⓓ Ⓔ
13 Ⓐ Ⓑ Ⓒ Ⓓ Ⓔ	

Correct Answers for Sample Transcript

1 Ⓐ Ⓑ ● Ⓓ Ⓔ	14 Ⓐ Ⓑ Ⓒ Ⓓ ●
2 Ⓐ Ⓑ Ⓒ ● Ⓔ	15 Ⓐ Ⓑ ● Ⓓ Ⓔ
3 Ⓐ Ⓑ ● Ⓓ Ⓔ	16 ● Ⓑ Ⓒ Ⓓ Ⓔ
4 Ⓐ Ⓑ ● Ⓓ Ⓔ	17 Ⓐ Ⓑ Ⓒ ● Ⓔ
5 ● Ⓑ Ⓒ Ⓓ Ⓔ	18 Ⓐ Ⓑ Ⓒ ● Ⓔ
6 Ⓐ Ⓑ Ⓒ Ⓓ ●	19 ● Ⓑ Ⓒ Ⓓ Ⓔ
7 Ⓐ ● Ⓒ Ⓓ Ⓔ	20 Ⓐ Ⓑ Ⓒ Ⓓ ●
8 Ⓐ Ⓑ ● Ⓓ Ⓔ	21 ● Ⓑ Ⓒ Ⓓ Ⓔ
9 Ⓐ ● Ⓒ Ⓓ Ⓔ	22 ● Ⓑ Ⓒ Ⓓ Ⓔ
10 ● Ⓑ Ⓒ Ⓓ Ⓔ	23 Ⓐ Ⓑ ● Ⓓ Ⓔ
11 Ⓐ Ⓑ ● Ⓓ Ⓔ	24 Ⓐ Ⓑ Ⓒ ● Ⓔ
12 Ⓐ Ⓑ Ⓒ Ⓓ ●	25 Ⓐ ● Ⓒ Ⓓ Ⓔ
13 Ⓐ Ⓑ Ⓒ ● Ⓔ	

COPYING FROM PLAIN COPY *(Both Typists and Stenographers take this):*

The sample given on page 156 shows the kind of material that competitors must copy. See whether you can copy it twice in 10 minutes and how many errors your copies contain. Competitors will be required to meet a certain minimum in accuracy as well as in speed. Above the minimum speed and accuracy requirements, accuracy counts twice as much as speed in determining whether the competitor is eligible on Copying from Plain Copy.

Space, paragraph, spell, punctuate, capitalize, and begin and end each line precisely as shown in the exercise.

In the examination you will have 10 minutes in which to make copies of the test exercise, keeping in mind that your eligibility will depend upon accuracy as well as speed. Each time you complete the exercise, simply double space once and begin again. Use both sides of the paper.

Your typing must go a little over halfway through a second copy of the exercise to make you eligible in speed. With that minimum speed, your paper must not have more than 9 errors. The number of errors permitted increases with the amount typed.

This practice exercise is similar in length and difficulty to the one that you will be required to typewrite for the Plain Copy test. You are to space, capitalize, punctuate, spell, and begin and end each line precisely as in the copy. Directions regarding erasures will be given when you take the Plain Copy Test. Follow carefully all directions given at the time of the examination. Practice typewriting this material on scratch paper until the examiner tells you to stop, remembering that for this examination it is more important to typewrite accurately than to typewrite rapidly.

There are several ways in which a typist can prepare herself to be an efficient worker in a business office. First of all, she should know her typewriter thoroughly, the location of all the keys, even those used infrequently, and the use of the marginal stops and extra devices furnished on modern typewriters. In addition to being completely familiar with the typewriter, she should be equipped with knowledge of the correct spellings and correct use of a large number of words. Although a letter has been typewritten neatly, without omissions or insertions, it will still be considered unsatisfactory if it contains any misspellings whatsoever.

Engineering and Other Physical Sciences

Engineers and scientists hired by the Government at the lower professional grades are sometimes given a written test covering their branch of science, as well as the aptitude tests appropriate for the type of work. The written test nearly always requires a knowledge of whatever branch of mathematics is involved in the scientific field.

1. A plane figure consists of a square 10 inches on a side and an isosceles triangle whose base is the left edge of the square and whose altitude dropped from the vertex opposite the 10-inch base of the triangle common to the square is 6 inches. Approximately how far in inches from the left side of the square is the center of gravity of the whole figure located?
   A) 2.92   D) 3.75
   B) 3.15   E) 4.28
   C) 3.38

2. The stiffness of a rectangular beam varies
   A) as the depth
   B) inversely as the depth
   C) as the square of the depth
   D) as the cube of the depth
   E) inversely as the cube of the depth

3. At atmospheric pressure, steam at 100° C. is passed into 400 grams of water at 10° C. until the temperature of the water rises to 40° C. It is then found that the weight of the water has increased to 420 grams due to the condensing steam. The heat of vaporization of steam in calories per gram at 100° C. is
   A) 60   D) 600
   B) 300   E) none of these
   C) 540

4. The addition of HCl to a solution of sodium acetate causes
   A) the precipitation of sodium chloride
   B) a decrease in the concentration of acetate ion
   C) an increase in the concentration of sodium ion
   D) an increase in the concentration of hydroxide ion
   E) no change in the concentration of hydroxide ion

Psychology

5. In experiments on the localization of sound in space, the sounds which can be most accurately located by the hearer are those sounds originating at points

   A) in the plane equidistant from the two ears of the hearer
   B) in front of the hearer
   C) above and below the hearer
   D) to the left and to the right of the hearer
   E) behind the hearer

6. In the field of measurement of interests, the Preference Record is associated with the name of
   A) Remmers   D) Viteles
   B) Kuder   E) Bell
   C) Bingham

Statistics

7. If 4 is added to every observation in a sample, the mean is
   A) increased by 4
   B) increased by 4 times the number of observations
   C) increased by 4 divided by the number of observations
   D) decreased by 4
   E) not affected

8. A distribution for which one of the following variables would constitute a discrete series?
   A) weight of eighth-grade pupils
   B) width of the visual field
   C) "items right" score on a history test
   D) auditory reaction time
   E) age at marriage of 850 charwomen

9. Of the following measures, which one is the most stable under conditions of random sampling?
   A) mode   D) harmonic mean
   B) median   E) geometric mean
   C) arithmetic mean

10. The standard deviation is a measure of which one of the following characteristics of a population
    A) skewness   D) randomness
    B) symmetry   E) variability
    C) normality

Answer Key

1. C	3. C	5. D	7. A	9. C
2. D	4. B	6. B	8. C	10. E

Accounting

Answer Sheet

1 (A) (B) (C) (D) (E)　　　3 (A) (B) (C) (D) (E)　　　5 (A) (B) (C) (D) (E)　　　7 (A) (B) (C) (D) (E)

2 (A) (B) (C) (D) (E)　　　4 (A) (B) (C) (D) (E)　　　6 (A) (B) (C) (D) (E)

An accounting position in the Federal Government may involve one or more of the following activities, with varying degrees of responsibility: Cost accounting, tax accounting, auditing, bookkeeping, analysis and interpretation of financial statements, constructive accounting, and fund or governmental accounting. Very few positions require a specialized knowledge of governmental accounting; most positions require experience or training in commercial accounting principles and practices.

Examinations may be announced for accountants or for accountants and auditors in general; the test in such cases will be based on principles generally applicable to all accounting activities. Occasionally, an examination for a specialized position will test the accounting principles more directly applicable to the duties of that position.

1. An operating mining company properly charged $1,200 to expense to reflect the wear and tear on its equipment. The corresponding credit should have been made to
   A) reserve for contingent liability
   B) reserve for depletion
   C) reserve for depreciation
   D) surplus reserve
   E) earned surplus

2. The Jones Company had a merchandise inventory of $24,625 on January 1, 1950. During the year the company purchased $60,000 worth of goods, sales were $85,065, and the cost of goods sold was $28,060. The inventory on December 31, 1950, was
   A) $28,065.00　　　D) $57,005.00
   B) $28,500.00　　　E) none of these
   C) $49,690.00

The answer to question 2 is $56,565, which is not given as A, B, C, or D. The answer sheet is marked under E, therefore.

Weather Forecasting

Weather forecasting is an increasingly important science, which uses many skilled workers, both professional and subprofessional. Ordinarily the persons selected for trainee jobs are given aptitude tests continuing mechanical and physical problems. A knowledge of algebra and physics is sometimes required. Professional tests contain questions in the science of weather, or meteorology.

3. Particles of dust, smoke, or microbes often cause the air to be
   A) hazy　　　D) dry
   B) clear　　　E) cold
   C) humid
   C) found in the atmosphere in very small quantities
   D) found in the Arctic region in largest proportion
   E) found only over the ocean

4. Helium, neon, krypton, and xenon are
   A) never found in the atmosphere
   B) found in place of hydrogen in the upper atmosphere

5. The air is warmed to the greatest extent by
   A) the sun's rays directly
   B) only conduction from the earth

c) hot vapors
d) dust particles

e) both convection and conduction from the earth

Safety

Examinations for the position of safety inspector or foreman in dangerous occupations, such as mining, stress knowledge of safety devices, rules, and precautions.

6. An electrical detonator is
   A) an instrument used to measure electrical energy
   B) a part of an electrical signaling apparatus
   C) a device used for detecting sound
   D) a device used to fire explosives
   E) a part of an electric-light bulb

7. Most authorities in the field of safety planning agree that the ultimate success of any safety program depends on the
   A) individual worker
   B) foreman
   C) management
   D) state government
   E) safety instructor

Answer Key

1. C   3. A   5. E   7. A
2. E   4. C   6. D

Mathematics

Answer Sheet

1 Ⓐ Ⓑ Ⓒ Ⓓ Ⓔ   2 Ⓐ Ⓑ Ⓒ Ⓓ Ⓔ   3 Ⓐ Ⓑ Ⓒ Ⓓ Ⓔ

In some positions, even at the trainee level, a working knowledge of algebra or geometry is needed to perform the duties of the job or to complete the training course. Mathematicians are given more difficult material, including trigonometry, differential equations, and other branches.

1. The product of $(3m - n)$ and $3m$ is
   A) $9m^2 - 3mn$
   B) $9m^2 - mn$
   C) $9m - 3n$
   D) $9m^2 - n^2$
   E) $3m^2 - 3mn$

2. Find the total differential of $(x^2 + y^2)^{\frac{1}{2}}$.
   A) $x(x^2 + y^2) - \frac{1}{2}$
   B) $y(x^2 + y^2) - \frac{1}{2}$
   C) $xdx + ydy$

   D) $\dfrac{xdx}{\sqrt{x^2 + y^2}} + \dfrac{ydy}{\sqrt{x^2 + y^2}}$
   E) $xdx - ydy$

3. The length l of a spiral spring supporting a pan is increased c centimeters for x grams of weight placed on the pan. What is the length of the spring if w grams are placed on the pan?
   A) $lc + \dfrac{x}{w}$
   B) $l + \dfrac{w}{cx}$
   C) $l + \dfrac{cw}{x}$
   D) $\dfrac{l + cw}{x}$
   E) $\dfrac{l + cx}{w}$

Sometimes the use of a slide rule is permitted in examinations which contain problems that could be worked with its aid. If there is a statement in the announcement of examination, or in the card of admission to the examination room, that the use of a slide rule, protractor, scale, or any other device is permitted, the applicant must furnish the instrument himself if he wishes to use it. If any instrument or device is *required* to be furnished by the applicant, the announcement or admission card will say so. If it is not required but simply permitted, it is up to the applicant to decide whether he will use it or not.

Answer Key

1. A   2. D   3. C

Mechanical and Nonverbal Tests

Answer Sheet

1 Ⓐ Ⓑ Ⓒ Ⓓ Ⓔ   3 Ⓐ Ⓑ Ⓒ Ⓓ Ⓔ   5 Ⓐ Ⓑ Ⓒ Ⓓ Ⓔ   7 Ⓐ Ⓑ Ⓒ Ⓓ Ⓔ   9 Ⓐ Ⓑ Ⓒ Ⓓ Ⓔ

2 Ⓐ Ⓑ Ⓒ Ⓓ Ⓔ   4 Ⓐ Ⓑ Ⓒ Ⓓ Ⓔ   6 Ⓐ Ⓑ Ⓒ Ⓓ Ⓔ   8 Ⓐ Ⓑ Ⓒ Ⓓ Ⓔ   10 Ⓐ Ⓑ Ⓒ Ⓓ Ⓔ

"Nonverbal" describes tests that do not depend on knowledge of language or understanding of words, so much as on the ability to work with numbers, diagrams, and other symbols.

Shop Arithmetic

In each of the following machine-scored problems, five different answers are suggested. Sometimes the last one is "none of these." In question 9, none of the figures given is the correct answer; hence the proper letter to choose is E, which is the letter preceding the answer "none of these."

1. When 100, 125, 75, and 20 are added the answer is

   A) 220   D) 320
   B) 270   E) 420
   C) 325

The sum of these numbers is 320. Look at the choices given and you will find the number 320 after the letter (D). Therefore, to answer question 1, the space of the letter D on the answer sheet should be blackened.

2.

X is what part of the whole sheet?

   A) ⅙   D) ⅕
   B) ⅓   E) none of these
   C) ¼

3.

The area of the triangle in question 3 in square inches is

   A) 56   D) 22
   B) 112   E) 448
   C) 122

4.

What is the greatest number of pieces 9″ × 2″ that could be cut from the given sheet of metal?

   A) 18   D) 80
   B) 21   E) 28
   C) 26

5.

The volume of the rectangular solid in cubic inches is

   A) 224   D) 56
   B) 28   E) 32
   C) 896

6. ½ of ¼ is
   A) ¹/₁₂   D) ¼
   B) ⅛   E) 8
   C) ½

7. A circular saw cuts 8 boards per minute. If there are 1,440 boards to be cut, the number of *hours* required to cut these boards is
   A) 2⅓   D) 3⅔
   B) 2⅔   E) 3
   C) 4

8. A drawing of a certain building is 10 inches by 15 inches. On this drawing 1 inch represents 5 feet. If the same drawing had been made 20 inches by 30 inches, 1 inch on the drawing would represent
   A) 7½ feet   D) 3⅓ feet
   B) 5 feet   E) 2½ feet
   C) 10 feet

9. During his first 8-hour day, an apprentice earned 40 percent as much as a master mechanic. If the master mechanic earned $112.00, what was the apprentice's average *hourly* earning?
   A) $6.40   D) $4.48
   B) $9.60   E) none of these
   C) $6.72

10. An opening 6 yards long and 3 feet wide is to be covered by sheathing. Enough lumber is available to cover two-thirds of the area of the opening. How many square feet will remain uncovered?
    A) 2   D) 12
    B) 4   E) none of these
    C) 6

Answer Key

1. D	3. A	5. A	7. E	9. E
2. C	4. E	6. B	8. E	10. E

Mechanical and Nonverbal Tests

Messenger and Guard

Answer Sheet

1 Ⓐ Ⓑ Ⓒ Ⓓ Ⓔ		3 Ⓐ Ⓑ Ⓒ Ⓓ Ⓔ		5 Ⓐ Ⓑ Ⓒ Ⓓ Ⓔ		7 Ⓐ Ⓑ Ⓒ Ⓓ Ⓔ	
2 Ⓐ Ⓑ Ⓒ Ⓓ Ⓔ		4 Ⓐ Ⓑ Ⓒ Ⓓ Ⓔ		6 Ⓐ Ⓑ Ⓒ Ⓓ Ⓔ		8 Ⓐ Ⓑ Ⓒ Ⓓ Ⓔ	

For some positions in the lower pay grades of messenger and guard, no experience is necessary; but for the higher pay grades, experience either in one of the armed services or in a position whose duties were similar to those which a messenger or guard must fulfill is required.

A test of word meaning is given in addition to the test described below.

Each box below contains several names. You will be given a few minutes to memorize the arrangement, and then you will be given a list of names. For each name, you will mark on the answer sheet the letter of the box in which the name appears. For example, question 1 is Gaynor. Gaynor is in box c, so the answer sheet is marked to show that c is the answer to question 1.

A	B	C	D	E
Reed	Bliss	Ryder	Mead	Stroud
Molton	Case	Gaynor	Hook	Barry
Robbins	Osmer	Richmond	Blum	Cole
Sheldon	Harris	Bruce	Hortmer	Rakow

1. Gaynor	3. Sheldon
2. Stroud	4. Bruce

5. Molton	7. Mead
6. Case	8. Osmer

Sometimes questions testing knowledge of mechanical facts are included in tests for mechanical positions. Often, however, such positions, particularly those at the apprentice level, require aptitude rather than knowledge. Many types of questions, some measuring aptitude, others measuring knowledge and ability, are likely to be found in mechanical tests.

Tools and Mechanical Principles and Information and Judgment

Answer Sheet

1 Ⓐ Ⓑ Ⓒ Ⓓ Ⓔ   3 Ⓐ Ⓑ Ⓒ Ⓓ Ⓔ   5 Ⓐ Ⓑ Ⓒ Ⓓ Ⓔ   7 Ⓐ Ⓑ Ⓒ Ⓓ Ⓔ

2 Ⓐ Ⓑ Ⓒ Ⓓ Ⓔ   4 Ⓐ Ⓑ Ⓒ Ⓓ Ⓔ   6 Ⓐ Ⓑ Ⓒ Ⓓ Ⓔ   8 Ⓐ Ⓑ Ⓒ Ⓓ Ⓔ

Tools and Mechanical Principles

1. In which, if either, of the figures shown above can the man lift more weight?
   A) A
   B) B
   C) The men in figures A and B can lift equal weights.
   D) The man who can lift more weight cannot be determined.

The position of the fulcrum gives the man in figure A a greater mechanical advantage so answer A is correct.

2. In the gears shown above, as gear X turns in a counterclockwise direction, gear Y turns
   A) clockwise at the same speed
   B) clockwise at a faster speed
   C) counterclockwise at a slower speed
   D) counterclockwise at the same speed

3. In order to smooth and standardize a straight or tapered hole, the best of the following tools to use is a
   A) reamer
   B) drill
   C) tap
   D) cold chisel
   E) compass saw

4. The tool illustrated above is a
   A) counterbore
   B) tap
   C) center punch
   D) rose countersink
   E) pin punch

5. Which one of the following frequencies is most commonly used in the United States in alternating-current lighting circuits?
   A) 10 cycles   D) 60 cycles
   B) 25 cycles   E) 110 cycles
   C) 40 cycles

6. The device used to mix the air and the fuel in a gasoline engine is called the
   A) carburetor
   B) cylinder
   C) distributor
   D) manifold
   E) valve

7. Which one of the following would cause excessive backlash in the rear axle assembly?
   A) bent rear axle shaft
   B) chipped differential gears
   C) improper lubrication

D) worn differential gears and thrust washers
E) ring gear adjusted too close to pinion

8. As a driver brought his truck into a long curve to the left at 40 miles per hour, he made a moderate application of his air brakes, and at that point he felt a pull to the right on the steering wheel. Which one of the following could *not* have caused that pull?
   A) sudden loss of air from right front tire
   B) lack of superelevation on curve
   C) lack of adequate tread on front tires
   D) unbalanced adjustment of brakes

Answer Key

1. A	3. A	5. D	7. D
2. B	4. C	6. A	8. C

Identical Forms

In each question there are five drawings lettered A, B, C, D, and E. Four of the drawings are alike in every way. Find the one that differs from the rest and select it as your answer.

1.

In question 1 the object in drawing E has a wall across the back of the shelf-like space. All the other objects are open at the back. The answer E for question 1 is correct.

2.

3.

Touching Cubes

Questions 4 and 5 are based on one group of touching cubes, and questions 6 and 7 on another group. All the cubes are exactly the same size, and there are only enough hidden cubes to support the ones you can see. The question number is on a cube in the group. You are to find how many cubes in that group touch the numbered cube.

A cube is considered to touch the numbered cube if any part, even an edge or a corner, touches. Then select the answer that shows how many cubes touch the numbered cube by selecting

A if the answer is 1 or 6 or 11 cubes
B if the answer is 2 or 7 or 12 cubes
C if the answer is 3 or 8 or 13 cubes
D if the answer is 4 or 9 or 14 cubes
E if the answer is 5 or 10 or 15 cubes

In question 4, there are three cubes that touch the cube marked 4—the one right behind it which you cannot see, the one on top of that, and the one marked 5. Because the answer is three cubes, the space marked c should be blackened.

Answer Key

1. E	3. C	5. A	7. E
2. B	4. C	6. B	

Graph and Meter Reading

Many jobs require ability to read graphs and charts, or to make graphs and charts from collected information so that others can find the information there.

The following questions can be answered by reading the bar graph at the right.

OUTPUT OF RADIO SETS AND TELEVISION SETS BY FACTORY "K"
1977–1981

1. In the year in which the total output of the factory was the least, the percentage of that output which consisted of television sets was approximately
   A) 10%
   B) 20%
   C) 25%
   D) 30%
   E) 40%

2. In which year did the production of television sets total approximately 20,000?
   A) 1977
   B) 1978
   C) 1979
   D) 1980
   E) 1981

Meter Reading

3. The position of the pointer on the meter scale is nearest to
   A) 2.6
   B) 3.1
   C) 3.2
   D) 3.3

An examination of the meter scale shows, first, that only the even numbers are given on the dial. Between each pair of numbers are 10 small subdivisions. The position of the odd numbers is indicated by the slightly longer subdivision mark. Since there are five subdivisions between the positions of two successive whole numbers, each subdivision indicates ⅕ or .2.

The pointer in the example is closest to one subdivision beyond 3; the correct reading of the meter would be 3 + ⅕, or 3.2.

For a reading of 3.1, the pointer would be midway between the mark corresponding to 3 and the mark corresponding to 3.2.

Answer Key

1. A   2. D   3. C

Matching Parts and Figures

Answer Sheet

1 Ⓐ Ⓑ Ⓒ Ⓓ Ⓔ   2 Ⓐ Ⓑ Ⓒ Ⓓ Ⓔ   3 Ⓐ Ⓑ Ⓒ Ⓓ Ⓔ   4 Ⓐ Ⓑ Ⓒ Ⓓ Ⓔ

These questions test understanding of spatial relations. They also present problems found in making templates and patterns. The first two questions show, at the left side, two or more flat pieces. In each question select the arrangement lettered A, B, C, or D that shows how these pieces can be fitted together without gaps or overlapping. The pieces may be *turned around* or *turned over* in any way to make them fit together. Select as your answer that letter which you decide is correct.

From these pieces   *which one of these arrangements can you make?*

1.

                             A   B   C   D

In sample question 1, for instance, only the arrangement lettered D could be formed by fitting together the pieces on the left. Note that the pieces are turned around to make D. None of the other arrangements shows pieces of the given size and shape.

From these pieces   *which one of these arrangements can you make?*

2.

                             A   B   C   D

The next questions are based on the four solid patterns shown on page 171.

Each of the questions shows *one* of these four patterns cut up into pieces. For each question, decide which one of the four patterns could be made by fitting *all of the pieces* together without having any edges overlap and without leaving any space between pieces. Some of the pieces may need to be *turned around* or *turned over* to make them fit. The pattern must be made in its exact size and shape.

Look at sample question 3. If the two pieces were fitted together they would make pattern D. The piece on the left fits at the bottom of pattern D, and the piece at the right is turned around and over to make the top of the pattern.

Answer Key

1. D   2. B   3. D   4. B

Perception of Form

Look at the rows of drawings below. In each row, the design at the left is contained in *one or more* of the more complex drawings. A drawing is to be marked as an answer if it contains the exact design in the same position. The designs in the drawings need not be alined with the original design, but they are not to be *turned*. The designs and drawings are two-dimensional. In some rows more than one drawing contains the exact design in the correct position.

Look at question 1. The design at the left is contained in the more complex drawings B and C, so these are marked as answers for question 1. The design is also in drawing D, but not in the correct position, so this is not an answer.

Matching Solid Figures and Parts

In each question the object pictured at the left is a combination of two pieces. One *set* of the five sets of pieces at the right can be combined to make the object at the left. Watch both the sizes and shapes of the pieces.

4.

OBJECT   A   B   C   D   E

5.

OBJECT   A   B   C   D   E

Answer Key

1. B–C   2. B   3. A–C   4. A   5. E

Cube Turning

The drawing at the left in each of the two following sample questions represents a cube. There is a different design on each of the six faces of the cube. Four other drawings of cubes are lettered A, B, C, and D.

You are asked to show, by marking the correct space on your Answer Sheet, which *one* of the four could possibly be the cube on the left turned to a different position. (The cube at the left may have been turned *over*, it may have been turned *around*, or it may have been turned *both* over and around, and faces not seen in the drawing on the left may become visible.)

1.

                                 A   B   C   D

In sample question 1 you will notice that only B could be the same cube as that shown on the left. Study the sample carefully and be sure you understand why B is the cube on the left turned to a different position. Also, be sure you understand why A, C, and D could *not* be the same cube. For instance, A is wrong because when the block is turned with the square on the right and the cross in front, the triangle would be on top, but it would point toward the cross instead of away from it.

If the cube were turned upside down, the cross and triangle would appear as they do in C, but the square would be on the bottom and would not show; the former bottom, now the top, would have a different design, since no two faces are alike. Or if the original cube were given a quarter-turn clockwise, the square would still be on top and the cross would be in front as in C—but again a new face would show, which could not be a triangle. D is not the answer either, since the triangle ought to point toward the cross, and in D it points toward a circle.

2.

                                 A   B   C   D

Pattern Folding

In questions like No. 3, you are to select the *one* object, A, B, C, or D, that could be made from the flat piece shown at the left, if this flat piece were folded on the dotted lines shown in the drawing, or rolled so that the edges meet.

3.

Answer Key

1. B   2. A   3. A

Elevations and Perspective

An elevation is a drawing of one side of an object. Think of an object inside a glass box. The tracing of the object's shape on the top of the box would be a "top elevation" or "top view." Tracings can be made from any side. In mechanical drawing, usually three views are given.

Directions: In the following questions you are given a top view, a front view, and a view of the right side of a solid object. The problem is to find the *one* of the four objects lettered A, B, C, and D that would look like these views.

1.

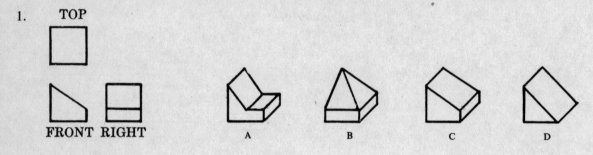

In question 1, both A and C have the correct right view; both C and D have the top view shown; but only C looks like the view marked "FRONT." C is therefore the answer to the question.

2.

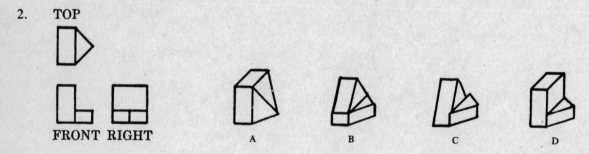

When you work these problems, you may check any one of the views first; one or more of the objects may show up as being clearly different from this view. Then compare the other views with the remaining objects. You will find that only one object finally remains which looks like all three of the given views.

In question 2, for example, beginning with the front view: A is ruled out at first glance, B has one line in the wrong place, but C and D are left. Now a check of the top view shows that C should have a line which is not in the given top view, and a final check of the right side view against D shows that D is the answer.

If you had started with the top view in question 2, you would have had A and D remaining as possibilities. Then a check of either the front or right view would have eliminated A, and D would be the correct letter to mark on the answer sheet. If you had started with the right view, you could have found the answer on the first try. There is no way to tell which order will prove to be the quickest for any given question—as you see in question 1, the front view would have given the answer at once. It is best, if you have the time, to check all views of each object so that you are sure you have found the *one* answer.

3.

TOP

FRONT RIGHT   A   B   C   D

Question 3 is harder. A, C, and D all look alike from both top and front. B is evidently incorrect, since it does not check with any of the views shown. To find the correct answer among A, C, and D, however, it is necessary to check all views, and it can then be seen that only C has the correct side view.

Answer Key

1. C   2. D   3. C

Inspection Tests

CODE FOR
INSPECTION TEST

Bin A – All Right

Bin B – Bashed In

Bin C – Combination
of Same

Bin D – Different
Numbers

Bin E – Empty

The ability to inspect, sort, and examine objects of many kinds can be tested by some pencil and paper tests. Two of these are described here.

The diagram at the left shows five bins into which pairs of parts are to be sorted. In each pair of parts, one part should be round and the other square; both should have the same number.

Bin A is for pairs that are ALL RIGHT.

Bin B is for pairs that have a part which is BASHED IN.

Bin C is for a COMBINATION of two round or two square parts.

Bin D is for pairs in which the parts have DIFFERENT numbers.

Bin E is for pairs in which the number spaces are EMPTY.

Look at each pair of parts below, and decide which bin they go into. The letter of that bin should be recorded on the answer sheet. (To save space, the answer sheet is not reproduced here, but the correct answers are indicated.)

Answer Sheet

1 Ⓐ Ⓑ Ⓒ Ⓓ Ⓔ   2 Ⓐ Ⓑ Ⓒ Ⓓ Ⓔ   3 Ⓐ Ⓑ Ⓒ Ⓓ Ⓔ   4 Ⓐ Ⓑ Ⓒ Ⓓ Ⓔ   5 Ⓐ Ⓑ Ⓒ Ⓓ Ⓔ   6 Ⓐ Ⓑ Ⓒ Ⓓ Ⓔ

For another type of inspection test the competitor counts small objects. Each question asks for the number of x's or o's, or both, in a certain area of the diagram shown. Count the objects as directed. If an x or o falls across a line dividing one area from another, count it as being in the area in which most of it falls. Look for the answer sheet accordingly. If your answer is not listed, mark E.

1. How many x's are there in Row 1, Col. 2?   A) 12 B) 13 C) 14 D) 15 E) none of these
2. How many o's in Row 1, Columns 1 and 2?   A) 13 B) 14 C) 15 D) 17 E) none of these
3. How many x's in Row 2, Col. 1?   A) 11 B) 13 C) 14 D) 16 E) none of these
4. How many o's in Row 3, Col. 3?   A) 11 B) 13 C) 15 D) 16 E) none of these
5. How many x's and o's in Row 3, Col. 2?   A) 22 B) 23 C) 24 D) 25 E) none of these
6. How many o's in Row 2, Col. 3?   A) 9 B) 10 C) 11 D) 12 E) none of these

Answer Key

1. B   2. D   3. C   4. E   5. A   6. B

Observation and Memory

This kind of test is used in examinations for various kinds of investigators, for example, Treasury Enforcement Agent. Read the directions under the picture.

Study the picture for 5 minutes. Observe all the details of the scene—what the people are wearing, what kinds of furniture and equipment are in the room, and where each object is. Do not make any written notes.

After 5 minutes, turn the page and see if you can answer the questions at the top of the next page without looking back at the picture.

Observation and Memory—Continued

Do not read these questions until you have studied the picture on the other side of this sheet. After you have studied the picture for 5 minutes, you must not look back at it for the answers to the questions. *After* you have answered the questions, check them with the answer key.

1. Which one of these things can be seen in the picture?
   A) a telephone
   B) an initialed belt buckle
   C) a list of names on the blackboard
   D) a brief case
   E) a calendar with one date circled

2. The man on the left is
   A) holding a pencil in his left hand
   B) smoking a pipe
   C) holding a slide rule in his right hand
   D) pointing to the blackboard
   E) opening a loose-leaf notebook

3. The woman in this picture
   A) wears no jewelry
   B) has a light-colored dress
   C) is writing in a loose-leaf binder
   D) wears a short-sleeved dress
   E) is looking at the blackboard

4. The man who is smoking a pipe is also
   A) pointing to a statistical chart
   B) leaning on the table
   C) wearing a bow tie
   D) writing on the map
   E) wearing rimless glasses

Answer Key

1. E   2. C   3. D   4. B

Knowledge Tests for Professional and Semiprofessional Positions

Supervision

Answer Sheet

1 Ⓐ Ⓑ Ⓒ Ⓓ Ⓔ   3 Ⓐ Ⓑ Ⓒ Ⓓ Ⓔ   5 Ⓐ Ⓑ Ⓒ Ⓓ Ⓔ

2 Ⓐ Ⓑ Ⓒ Ⓓ Ⓔ   4 Ⓐ Ⓑ Ⓒ Ⓓ Ⓔ   6 Ⓐ Ⓑ Ⓒ Ⓓ Ⓔ

1. In general, the most important advantage of good employee morale is that it results in
   A) high production
   B) decreased work for the supervisor
   C) increased ease in rating workers' efficiency
   D) high standing for the supervisor with management
   E) less desire for wage increases among employees

2. Which one of the following types of information would be most useful to a supervisor in determining which employee should lose his job in case lay-offs are necessary?
   A) length of service with the supervisor
   B) marital status
   C) education
   D) age
   E) job performance rating

Administration

3. A number of national organizations require the approval of the headquarters office on all actions originating in the field offices, instead of following the alternate procedure of delegating authority for such actions. This requirement of headquarters' review and approval is frequently unsatisfactory to the headquarters office itself. In general, the most frequent reason for the *dissatisfaction* in the headquarters office is that
   A) headquarters may lack the information necessary for approving these cases
   B) field offices resent the review
   C) the review causes delay
   D) it is felt that authority should be commensurate with responsibility
   E) clearance through a large number of divisions is required in most headquarters offices

Occupational Analysis

4. In the machine shop of a manufacturing firm, a job with the title of Foreman has the following duties:

"Installs cutting tools in various types of semiautomatic machinery. Adjusts the guides, stops, working tables of machines, and other controls to handle the size of stock to be machined. Operates and adjusts machine until accurate production (based on blueprint specifications, patterns, or templates) has been achieved. Checks production with precision gages, often to tolerances of 0.0005 inch. Turns machine over to regular operator when it is producing satisfactorily."

Which of the following would be the most descriptive title for this job?
A) cutting-machine mechanic
B) dimensional checker
C) job setter
D) machinist
E) tool and die maker

Public Affairs

5. The most important way in which geographic factors influence rural community structure is by
   A) influencing the size of the farms and thus the density of the population
   B) influencing the birth rate
   C) dictating the habits of the people
   D) influencing the temperament of the people in such a way as to make them cooperative or non-cooperative
   E) being the most important determinants of community boundaries

6. The following table indicates the distribution, by type of economic activity, of those employed in a country. Which of the following five countries most probably has the occupational distribution indicated in this table?

Employment by Activity

Agriculture and Fishing	655,190
Mining	51,449
Manufacturing	926,997
Construction	257,466
Transport and Communications	296,737
Commerce, Banking, Insurance	447,242
Domestic Service	243,555
Total Employment	3,185,816

A) Bulgaria   D) Portugal
B) Hungary   E) Turkey
C) Netherlands

Answer Key

1. A	3. A	5. A
2. E	4. C	6. C

SAMPLE ANSWER SHEET
GROSS DEXTERITY TEST AND
FOLLOWING ORAL INSTRUCTIONS

1 Ⓐ Ⓑ Ⓒ Ⓓ Ⓔ	26 Ⓐ Ⓑ Ⓒ Ⓓ Ⓔ	51 Ⓐ Ⓑ Ⓒ Ⓓ Ⓔ	76 Ⓐ Ⓑ Ⓒ Ⓓ Ⓔ	101 Ⓐ Ⓑ Ⓒ Ⓓ Ⓔ
2 Ⓐ Ⓑ Ⓒ Ⓓ Ⓔ	27 Ⓐ Ⓑ Ⓒ Ⓓ Ⓔ	52 Ⓐ Ⓑ Ⓒ Ⓓ Ⓔ	77 Ⓐ Ⓑ Ⓒ Ⓓ Ⓔ	102 Ⓐ Ⓑ Ⓒ Ⓓ Ⓔ
3 Ⓐ Ⓑ Ⓒ Ⓓ Ⓔ	28 Ⓐ Ⓑ Ⓒ Ⓓ Ⓔ	53 Ⓐ Ⓑ Ⓒ Ⓓ Ⓔ	78 Ⓐ Ⓑ Ⓒ Ⓓ Ⓔ	103 Ⓐ Ⓑ Ⓒ Ⓓ Ⓔ
4 Ⓐ Ⓑ Ⓒ Ⓓ Ⓔ	29 Ⓐ Ⓑ Ⓒ Ⓓ Ⓔ	54 Ⓐ Ⓑ Ⓒ Ⓓ Ⓔ	79 Ⓐ Ⓑ Ⓒ Ⓓ Ⓔ	104 Ⓐ Ⓑ Ⓒ Ⓓ Ⓔ
5 Ⓐ Ⓑ Ⓒ Ⓓ Ⓔ	30 Ⓐ Ⓑ Ⓒ Ⓓ Ⓔ	55 Ⓐ Ⓑ Ⓒ Ⓓ Ⓔ	80 Ⓐ Ⓑ Ⓒ Ⓓ Ⓔ	105 Ⓐ Ⓑ Ⓒ Ⓓ Ⓔ
6 Ⓐ Ⓑ Ⓒ Ⓓ Ⓔ	31 Ⓐ Ⓑ Ⓒ Ⓓ Ⓔ	56 Ⓐ Ⓑ Ⓒ Ⓓ Ⓔ	81 Ⓐ Ⓑ Ⓒ Ⓓ Ⓔ	106 Ⓐ Ⓑ Ⓒ Ⓓ Ⓔ
7 Ⓐ Ⓑ Ⓒ Ⓓ Ⓔ	32 Ⓐ Ⓑ Ⓒ Ⓓ Ⓔ	57 Ⓐ Ⓑ Ⓒ Ⓓ Ⓔ	82 Ⓐ Ⓑ Ⓒ Ⓓ Ⓔ	107 Ⓐ Ⓑ Ⓒ Ⓓ Ⓔ
8 Ⓐ Ⓑ Ⓒ Ⓓ Ⓔ	33 Ⓐ Ⓑ Ⓒ Ⓓ Ⓔ	58 Ⓐ Ⓑ Ⓒ Ⓓ Ⓔ	83 Ⓐ Ⓑ Ⓒ Ⓓ Ⓔ	108 Ⓐ Ⓑ Ⓒ Ⓓ Ⓔ
9 Ⓐ Ⓑ Ⓒ Ⓓ Ⓔ	34 Ⓐ Ⓑ Ⓒ Ⓓ Ⓔ	59 Ⓐ Ⓑ Ⓒ Ⓓ Ⓔ	84 Ⓐ Ⓑ Ⓒ Ⓓ Ⓔ	109 Ⓐ Ⓑ Ⓒ Ⓓ Ⓔ
10 Ⓐ Ⓑ Ⓒ Ⓓ Ⓔ	35 Ⓐ Ⓑ Ⓒ Ⓓ Ⓔ	60 Ⓐ Ⓑ Ⓒ Ⓓ Ⓔ	85 Ⓐ Ⓑ Ⓒ Ⓓ Ⓔ	110 Ⓐ Ⓑ Ⓒ Ⓓ Ⓔ
11 Ⓐ Ⓑ Ⓒ Ⓓ Ⓔ	36 Ⓐ Ⓑ Ⓒ Ⓓ Ⓔ	61 Ⓐ Ⓑ Ⓒ Ⓓ Ⓔ	86 Ⓐ Ⓑ Ⓒ Ⓓ Ⓔ	111 Ⓐ Ⓑ Ⓒ Ⓓ Ⓔ
12 Ⓐ Ⓑ Ⓒ Ⓓ Ⓔ	37 Ⓐ Ⓑ Ⓒ Ⓓ Ⓔ	62 Ⓐ Ⓑ Ⓒ Ⓓ Ⓔ	87 Ⓐ Ⓑ Ⓒ Ⓓ Ⓔ	112 Ⓐ Ⓑ Ⓒ Ⓓ Ⓔ
13 Ⓐ Ⓑ Ⓒ Ⓓ Ⓔ	38 Ⓐ Ⓑ Ⓒ Ⓓ Ⓔ	63 Ⓐ Ⓑ Ⓒ Ⓓ Ⓔ	88 Ⓐ Ⓑ Ⓒ Ⓓ Ⓔ	113 Ⓐ Ⓑ Ⓒ Ⓓ Ⓔ
14 Ⓐ Ⓑ Ⓒ Ⓓ Ⓔ	39 Ⓐ Ⓑ Ⓒ Ⓓ Ⓔ	64 Ⓐ Ⓑ Ⓒ Ⓓ Ⓔ	89 Ⓐ Ⓑ Ⓒ Ⓓ Ⓔ	114 Ⓐ Ⓑ Ⓒ Ⓓ Ⓔ
15 Ⓐ Ⓑ Ⓒ Ⓓ Ⓔ	40 Ⓐ Ⓑ Ⓒ Ⓓ Ⓔ	65 Ⓐ Ⓑ Ⓒ Ⓓ Ⓔ	90 Ⓐ Ⓑ Ⓒ Ⓓ Ⓔ	115 Ⓐ Ⓑ Ⓒ Ⓓ Ⓔ
16 Ⓐ Ⓑ Ⓒ Ⓓ Ⓔ	41 Ⓐ Ⓑ Ⓒ Ⓓ Ⓔ	66 Ⓐ Ⓑ Ⓒ Ⓓ Ⓔ	91 Ⓐ Ⓑ Ⓒ Ⓓ Ⓔ	116 Ⓐ Ⓑ Ⓒ Ⓓ Ⓔ
17 Ⓐ Ⓑ Ⓒ Ⓓ Ⓔ	42 Ⓐ Ⓑ Ⓒ Ⓓ Ⓔ	67 Ⓐ Ⓑ Ⓒ Ⓓ Ⓔ	92 Ⓐ Ⓑ Ⓒ Ⓓ Ⓔ	117 Ⓐ Ⓑ Ⓒ Ⓓ Ⓔ
18 Ⓐ Ⓑ Ⓒ Ⓓ Ⓔ	43 Ⓐ Ⓑ Ⓒ Ⓓ Ⓔ	68 Ⓐ Ⓑ Ⓒ Ⓓ Ⓔ	93 Ⓐ Ⓑ Ⓒ Ⓓ Ⓔ	118 Ⓐ Ⓑ Ⓒ Ⓓ Ⓔ
19 Ⓐ Ⓑ Ⓒ Ⓓ Ⓔ	44 Ⓐ Ⓑ Ⓒ Ⓓ Ⓔ	69 Ⓐ Ⓑ Ⓒ Ⓓ Ⓔ	94 Ⓐ Ⓑ Ⓒ Ⓓ Ⓔ	119 Ⓐ Ⓑ Ⓒ Ⓓ Ⓔ
20 Ⓐ Ⓑ Ⓒ Ⓓ Ⓔ	45 Ⓐ Ⓑ Ⓒ Ⓓ Ⓔ	70 Ⓐ Ⓑ Ⓒ Ⓓ Ⓔ	95 Ⓐ Ⓑ Ⓒ Ⓓ Ⓔ	120 Ⓐ Ⓑ Ⓒ Ⓓ Ⓔ
21 Ⓐ Ⓑ Ⓒ Ⓓ Ⓔ	46 Ⓐ Ⓑ Ⓒ Ⓓ Ⓔ	71 Ⓐ Ⓑ Ⓒ Ⓓ Ⓔ	96 Ⓐ Ⓑ Ⓒ Ⓓ Ⓔ	121 Ⓐ Ⓑ Ⓒ Ⓓ Ⓔ
22 Ⓐ Ⓑ Ⓒ Ⓓ Ⓔ	47 Ⓐ Ⓑ Ⓒ Ⓓ Ⓔ	72 Ⓐ Ⓑ Ⓒ Ⓓ Ⓔ	97 Ⓐ Ⓑ Ⓒ Ⓓ Ⓔ	122 Ⓐ Ⓑ Ⓒ Ⓓ Ⓔ
23 Ⓐ Ⓑ Ⓒ Ⓓ Ⓔ	48 Ⓐ Ⓑ Ⓒ Ⓓ Ⓔ	73 Ⓐ Ⓑ Ⓒ Ⓓ Ⓔ	98 Ⓐ Ⓑ Ⓒ Ⓓ Ⓔ	123 Ⓐ Ⓑ Ⓒ Ⓓ Ⓔ
24 Ⓐ Ⓑ Ⓒ Ⓓ Ⓔ	49 Ⓐ Ⓑ Ⓒ Ⓓ Ⓔ	74 Ⓐ Ⓑ Ⓒ Ⓓ Ⓔ	99 Ⓐ Ⓑ Ⓒ Ⓓ Ⓔ	124 Ⓐ Ⓑ Ⓒ Ⓓ Ⓔ
25 Ⓐ Ⓑ Ⓒ Ⓓ Ⓔ	50 Ⓐ Ⓑ Ⓒ Ⓓ Ⓔ	75 Ⓐ Ⓑ Ⓒ Ⓓ Ⓔ	100 Ⓐ Ⓑ Ⓒ Ⓓ Ⓔ	125 Ⓐ Ⓑ Ⓒ Ⓓ Ⓔ

ANSWER KEY
GROSS DEXTERITY TEST AND
FOLLOWING ORAL INSTRUCTIONS

1 Ⓐ Ⓑ Ⓒ Ⓓ Ⓔ	26 Ⓐ ● Ⓒ ● Ⓔ	51 Ⓐ Ⓑ Ⓒ Ⓓ ●	76 Ⓐ Ⓑ Ⓒ ● Ⓔ	101 Ⓐ Ⓑ Ⓒ Ⓓ Ⓔ
2 Ⓐ Ⓑ Ⓒ Ⓓ Ⓔ	27 Ⓐ Ⓑ ● ● Ⓔ	52 Ⓐ Ⓑ Ⓒ Ⓓ ●	77 Ⓐ Ⓑ Ⓒ Ⓓ ●	102 ● Ⓑ Ⓒ Ⓓ Ⓔ
3 Ⓐ Ⓑ Ⓒ Ⓓ ●	28 Ⓐ Ⓑ ● Ⓓ ●	53 Ⓐ ● Ⓒ Ⓓ Ⓔ	78 ● Ⓑ ● Ⓓ Ⓔ	103 Ⓐ Ⓑ Ⓒ Ⓓ Ⓔ
4 Ⓐ ● Ⓒ Ⓓ Ⓔ	29 ● Ⓑ Ⓒ ● ●	54 Ⓐ Ⓑ Ⓒ Ⓓ Ⓔ	79 Ⓐ ● ● Ⓓ ●	104 Ⓐ Ⓑ Ⓒ ● Ⓔ
5 Ⓐ Ⓑ Ⓒ Ⓓ Ⓔ	30 Ⓐ Ⓑ Ⓒ Ⓓ Ⓔ	55 Ⓐ ● Ⓒ Ⓓ Ⓔ	80 Ⓐ ● ● Ⓓ ●	105 ● Ⓑ Ⓒ Ⓓ Ⓔ
6 Ⓐ Ⓑ ● Ⓓ Ⓔ	31 Ⓐ Ⓑ Ⓒ ● Ⓔ	56 Ⓐ ● Ⓒ Ⓓ ●	81 ● Ⓑ Ⓒ Ⓓ Ⓔ	106 ● Ⓑ ● Ⓓ Ⓔ
7 Ⓐ Ⓑ Ⓒ ● ●	32 Ⓐ Ⓑ ● Ⓓ Ⓔ	57 Ⓐ Ⓑ ● Ⓓ Ⓔ	82 Ⓐ Ⓑ Ⓒ Ⓓ Ⓔ	107 Ⓐ Ⓑ Ⓒ Ⓓ ●
8 Ⓐ ● Ⓒ Ⓓ ●	33 ● Ⓑ Ⓒ Ⓓ ●	58 ● Ⓑ Ⓒ Ⓓ ●	83 Ⓐ Ⓑ Ⓒ Ⓓ ●	108 Ⓐ Ⓑ Ⓒ Ⓓ ●
9 Ⓐ Ⓑ Ⓒ Ⓓ ●	34 Ⓐ Ⓑ Ⓒ ● ●	59 Ⓐ Ⓑ Ⓒ Ⓓ Ⓔ	84 Ⓐ ● Ⓒ Ⓓ ●	109 Ⓐ Ⓑ Ⓒ Ⓓ Ⓔ
10 Ⓐ Ⓑ Ⓒ ● ●	35 ● Ⓑ ● ● Ⓔ	60 Ⓐ Ⓑ Ⓒ ● Ⓔ	85 Ⓐ Ⓑ Ⓒ Ⓓ Ⓔ	110 Ⓐ Ⓑ Ⓒ ● Ⓔ

Gross Dexterity Test

This is a timed test that shows how quickly and accurately you can work by finding and filling in the spaces on the answer sheet. Look at the sample answer sheet on page 183 and notice that the answer sheet has an upper and a lower section. Since there are 25 numbers in each column, the upper section has the first 10 of each group of 25—that is, numbers 1 to 10, 26 to 35, 51 to 60, 76 to 85, and 101 to 110. All the questions given here are to be marked only in the upper section. In a real examination the questions would be scattered all over the page.

26. B	77. E	8. B	7. D	60. D	55. B
57. C	81. A	104. D	106. A	4. B	107. E
31. D	105. A	6. C	108. E	83. E	79. B
9. E	53. B	80. C	51. E	102. A	35. A
110. D	106. C	34. E	78. A	29. D	27. D

Following Oral Directions

This is another test which uses only the answer sheet. In this test the examiner reads directions aloud, and the competitors mark their answer sheets as directed. You can use this material for practice by reading each sentence aloud and covering the directions while you follow them, or by copying the directions and having someone else read them to you. Try to work quickly. In the examination room the reading of each paragraph is timed carefully so that all competitors have the same time to work. (Note: If you have worked the Gross Dexterity Test above on the sample answer sheet, you do not have to erase your answers—the samples for Following Oral Directions will not interfere with them.)

"Mark E for 7, 8, 10, (slight pause) 3, and 52. (Pause.)
"Mark C for 32, 35, and 78. (Pause.)
"Mark D as in dog for 26, 35, (slight pause) 76, and 10. (Pause.)
"For the next set of questions, mark space E and also mark the letter I call, unless E is already marked. If E is already marked for that number, do not make any mark for that number.
"Mark B as in boy for 56, 3, (slight pause) 80, and 84. (Pause.)
"Mark A for 33, 29, (slight pause) 8, and 58. (Pause.)
"Mark C for 79, 52, (slight pause) and 28."
The same answer paper is to be used for both the Gross Dexterity Test and Following Oral Instructions.

POSTAL EXAMS

Official Sample Questions for the
Postal Clerk-Carrier Exam

Applicants for the positions of postal clerk and mail carrier take the same exam, the clerk-carrier exam. The following sample questions are official sample questions sent to applicants by the Postal Service along with the admission card for the exam.

ADDRESS CHECKING TEST

In this test you will have to decide whether two addresses are alike or different. If the two addresses are exactly *alike* in every way, darken space (A) for the question. If the two addresses are *different* in any way, darken space (D) for the question.

Mark your answers to these sample questions on the sample answer sheet below.

1. 2134 S 20th St   2134 S 20th St

Since the two addresses are exactly alike, mark (A) for question 1 on the sample answer sheet.

2. 4608 N Warnock St   4806 N Warnock St
3. 1202 W Girard Dr   1202 W Girard Rd
4. Chappaqua NY 10514   Chappaqua NY 10514
5. 2207 Markland Ave   2207 Markham Ave

Sample Answer Sheet

1. Ⓐ Ⓓ	**4.** Ⓐ Ⓓ
2. Ⓐ Ⓓ	**5.** Ⓐ Ⓓ
3. Ⓐ Ⓓ	

The correct answers for questions 2 to 5 are:

2. **D**	4. **A**
3. **D**	5. **D**

MEMORY FOR ADDRESSES TEST

In this test you will have to memorize the locations (A, B, C, D, or E) of twenty-five addresses shown in five boxes, such as those below. For example, "Sardis" is in Box C, "5200-5799 West" is in Box B, etc. (The addresses in the actual test are, of course, different.)

| A | B | C | D | E |

A	B	C	D	E
4700-5599 Table Lismore 4800-5199 West Hesper 5500-6399 Blake	6800-6999 Table Kelford 5200-5799 West Musella 4800-5499 Blake	5600-6499 Table Joel 3200-3499 West Sardis 6400-7299 Blake	6500-6799 Table Tatum 3500-4299 West Porter 4300-4799 Blake	4400-4699 Table Ruskin 4300-4799 West Somers 7300-7499 Blake

Study the locations of the addresses for five minutes. As you study, sound them to your-self. Then cover the boxes and try to answer the questions below. Mark your answers for each question by darkening the space as was done for questions 1 and 2.

1. Musella
2. 4300-4799 Blake
3. 4700-5599 Table
4. Tatum

5. 5500-6399 Blake
6. Hesper
7. Kelford
8. Somers

9. 6400-7299 Blake
10. Joel
11. 5500-6399 Blake
12. 5200-5799 West

13. Porter
14. 7300-7499 Blake

Sample Answer Sheet

1 Ⓐ ● Ⓒ Ⓓ Ⓔ	6 Ⓐ Ⓑ Ⓒ Ⓓ Ⓔ	11 Ⓐ Ⓑ Ⓒ Ⓓ Ⓔ
2 Ⓐ Ⓑ Ⓒ ● Ⓔ	7 Ⓐ Ⓑ Ⓒ Ⓓ Ⓔ	12 Ⓐ Ⓑ Ⓒ Ⓓ Ⓔ
3 Ⓐ Ⓑ Ⓒ Ⓓ Ⓔ	8 Ⓐ Ⓑ Ⓒ Ⓓ Ⓔ	13 Ⓐ Ⓑ Ⓒ Ⓓ Ⓔ
4 Ⓐ Ⓑ Ⓒ Ⓓ Ⓔ	9 Ⓐ Ⓑ Ⓒ Ⓓ Ⓔ	14 Ⓐ Ⓑ Ⓒ Ⓓ Ⓔ
5 Ⓐ Ⓑ Ⓒ Ⓓ Ⓔ	10 Ⓐ Ⓑ Ⓒ Ⓓ Ⓔ	

The correct answers for questions 3 to 14 are:

| 3. A | 5. A | 7. B | 9. C | 11. A | 13. D |
| 4. D | 6. A | 8. E | 10. C | 12. B | 14. E |

Official Sample Questions for the
Postal Distribution Clerk Exam

The following sample questions show the types of questions that will be used on the test. They show also how the questions in the test are to be answered.

NUMBER SERIES TEST

DIRECTIONS: For each Number Series question, there is a series of numbers that follow some definite order and below this, five sets of two numbers each. You are to look at the numbers in the series and find out what order they follow. Then decide what the next two num-bers in that series would be if the same order were continued. Mark your answers on the sample answer sheet provided.

1. 1 2 3 4 5 6 7 ...

(A) 1 2   (B) 5 6   (C) 8 9   (D) 4 5   (E) 7 8

The numbers in this series are increasing by 1. If the series were continued for two more numbers, it would read: 1 2 3 4 5 6 7 [8 9]. Therefore, the correct answer is 8 and 9, and you should have darkened (C) for question 1.

2. 15 14 13 12 11 10 9 ...

(A) 2 1   (B) 17 16   (C) 8 9   (D) 8 7   (E) 9 8

The numbers in this series are decreasing by 1. If the series were continued for two more numbers, it would read: 15 14 13 12 11 10 9 [8 7]. Therefore, the correct answer is 8 and 7, and you should have darkened (D) for question 2.

3. 20 20 21 21 22 22 23 ...

(A) 23 23   (B) 23 24   (C) 19 19   (D) 22 23   (E) 21 22

Each number in this series is repeated and then increased by 1. If the series were continued for two more numbers, it would read: 20 20 21 21 22 22 23 [23 24]. Therefore, the correct answer is 23 and 24, and you should have darkened (B) for question 3.

4. 17 3 17 4 17 5 17 ...

(A) 6 17   (B) 6 7   (C) 17 6   (D) 5 6   (E) 17 7

This series is the number 17 separated by numbers increasing by 1, beginning with the number 3. If the series were continued for two more numbers, it would read: 17 3 17 4 17 5 17 [6 17]. Therefore, the correct answer is 6 and 17, and you should have darkened (A) for question 4.

5. 1 2 4 5 7 8 10 ...

(A) 11 12   (B) 12 14   (C) 10 13   (D) 12 13   (E) 11 13

The numbers in this series are increasing first by 1 (plus 1) and then by 2 (plus 2). If the series were continued for two more numbers, it would read: 1 2 4 5 7 8 10 [(plus 1) 11 (plus 2) 13]. Therefore, the correct answer is 11 and 13, and you should have darkened (E) for question 5.

Now read and work sample questions 6 through 10.

6. 21 21 20 20 19 19 18 ...

(A) 18 18   (B) 18 17   (C) 17 18   (D) 17 17   (E) 18 19

7. 1 22 1 23 1 24 1 ...

(A) 26 1   (B) 25 26   (C) 25 1   (D) 1 26   (E) 1 25

8. 1 20 3 19 5 18 7 ...

    (A) 8 9   (B) 8 17   (C) 17 10   (D) 17 9   (E) 9 18

9. 4 7 10 13 16 19 22 ...

    (A) 23 26   (B) 25 27   (C) 25 26   (D) 25 28   (E) 24 27

10. 30 2 28 4 26 6 24 ...

    (A) 23 9   (B) 26 8   (C) 8 9   (D) 26 22   (E) 8 22

Sample Answer Sheet

1 Ⓐ Ⓑ Ⓒ Ⓓ Ⓔ	6 Ⓐ Ⓑ Ⓒ Ⓓ Ⓔ
2 Ⓐ Ⓑ Ⓒ Ⓓ Ⓔ	7 Ⓐ Ⓑ Ⓒ Ⓓ Ⓔ
3 Ⓐ Ⓑ Ⓒ Ⓓ Ⓔ	8 Ⓐ Ⓑ Ⓒ Ⓓ Ⓔ
4 Ⓐ Ⓑ Ⓒ Ⓓ Ⓔ	9 Ⓐ Ⓑ Ⓒ Ⓓ Ⓔ
5 Ⓐ Ⓑ Ⓒ Ⓓ Ⓔ	10 Ⓐ Ⓑ Ⓒ Ⓓ Ⓔ

The correct answers for questions 6 through 10 are:

6. **B**   8. **D**   10. **E**
7. **C**   9. **D**

The remaining questions on the Distribution Clerk Exam are similar to the questions on the Clerk-Carrier Exam.

Official Sample Questions for the Mail Handler Exam

The following samples show the types of questions you will see on the written tests. Read the directions, answer the sample questions, and mark your answers on the sample answer sheet. Then compare your answers with those given in the correct answers section.

ADDRESS CHECKING TEST

DIRECTIONS: In the Address Checking test, you will have to decide whether two addresses are alike or different. If the two addresses are exactly *alike* in every way, darken choice (A) on the answer sheet for the question. If the two addresses are *different* in any way, darken choice (D) on the answer sheet. Questions 1 to 5 are samples of this test. Use the sample answer sheet below to mark your answers.

1. Acme La   Acme La

Since the two addresses are exactly alike, mark (A) for question 1 on the sample answer sheet.

2. Orleans Mass	Orleans Mich
3. Saxe Va	Saxis Va
4. Chappaqua NY 10514	Chappaqua NY 10514
5. Los Angeles Calif 90013	Los Angeles Calif 90018

MEANING OF WORDS TEST

DIRECTIONS: The Meaning of Words test asks you what a word or phrase means. In each question, a word or phrase is in italics. Five other words or phrases—lettered A, B, C, D, and E—are given as possible meanings. Only one is *right*. You are to pick out the one that is right. Then, on the answer sheet, find the answer space numbered the same as the question and darken the space with the letter of the right answer. Questions 6 and 7 are samples of this test. Mark your answers to questions 6 and 7 on the sample sheet below.

6. The letter was *short*. *Short* means most nearly

(A) tall   (B) wide   (C) brief   (D) heavy   (E) dark

For this question, you should darken space choice (C) because *brief* is the suggested answer that means most nearly the same as *short*, the word in italics.

7. A small crane was used to *raise* the heavy part. *Raise* means most nearly

(A) lift   (B) drag   (C) drop   (D) deliver   (E) guide

Sample Answer Sheet	
1. Ⓐ ●	5. Ⓐ Ⓓ
2. Ⓐ Ⓓ	6. Ⓐ Ⓑ Ⓒ Ⓓ Ⓔ
3. Ⓐ Ⓓ	7. Ⓐ Ⓑ Ⓒ Ⓓ Ⓔ
4. Ⓐ Ⓓ	

The correct answers for questions 2 to 7 are:

2. **D**	4. **A**	6. **C**
3. **D**	5. **D**	7. **A**

FOLLOWING ORAL DIRECTIONS TEST

DIRECTIONS: In the test of Following Oral Directions, you will be told to follow directions by writing in a test booklet and then on an answer sheet. The test booklet will have lines of material like the following samples. To practice this test, tear off this page. Then have somebody read the instructions on page 19 to you. Follow the instructions. When you are told to darken the spaces on the sample answer sheet, use the one below.

SAMPLE 8.   5 _____

SAMPLE 9.   1   6   4   3   7

SAMPLE 10.   D   B   A   E   C

SAMPLE 11.   (8__)   (5__)   (2__)   (9__)   (10__)

SAMPLE 12.   (7__)   [6__]   (1__)   [12__]

Sample Answer Sheet

1	Ⓐ Ⓑ Ⓒ Ⓓ Ⓔ	7	Ⓐ Ⓑ Ⓒ Ⓓ Ⓔ
2	Ⓐ Ⓑ Ⓒ Ⓓ Ⓔ	8	Ⓐ Ⓑ Ⓒ Ⓓ Ⓔ
3	Ⓐ Ⓑ Ⓒ Ⓓ Ⓔ	9	Ⓐ Ⓑ Ⓒ Ⓓ Ⓔ
4	Ⓐ Ⓑ Ⓒ Ⓓ Ⓔ	10	Ⓐ Ⓑ Ⓒ Ⓓ Ⓔ
5	Ⓐ Ⓑ Ⓒ Ⓓ Ⓔ	11	Ⓐ Ⓑ Ⓒ Ⓓ Ⓔ
6	Ⓐ Ⓑ Ⓒ Ⓓ Ⓔ	12	Ⓐ Ⓑ Ⓒ Ⓓ Ⓔ

These instructions are to be read aloud by someone else. (The words in parentheses should NOT be read aloud.) The person taking the test must NOT read these instructions.

You are to follow the instructions that I shall read to you. I cannot repeat them.

Look at the samples. Sample 8 has a number and a line beside it. On the line write an A. (Pause 2 seconds.) Now on the sample answer sheet, find number 5 (pause 2 seconds) and darken the space for the letter you just wrote on the line. (Pause 2 seconds.)

Look at Sample 9. (Pause slightly.) Draw a line under the third number. (Pause 2 seconds.) Now look on the sample answer sheet, find the number under which you just drew a line, and darken space B as in baker for that number. (Pause 5 seconds.)

Look at the letters in Sample 10. (Pause slightly.) Draw a line under the third letter in the line. (Pause 2 seconds.) Now on your answer sheet, find number 9 (pause 2 seconds) and darken the space for the letter under which you drew a line. (Pause 5 seconds.)

Look at the five circles in sample 11. (Pause slightly.) Each circle has a number and a line in it. Write D as in dog on the blank in the last circle. (Pause 2 seconds.) Now on the sample answer sheet, darken the space for the number-letter combination that is in the circle in which you just wrote. (Pause 5 seconds.)

Look at Sample 12. (Pause slightly.) There are two circles and two boxes of different sizes with numbers in them. (Pause slightly.) If 4 is more than 2 and if 5 is less than 3, write A in the smaller circle. (Pause slightly.) Otherwise write C in the larger box. (Pause 2 seconds.) Now on the sample answer sheet, darken the space for the number-letter combination in the box or circle in which you just wrote. (Pause 5 seconds.)

Now look at the sample answer sheet. (Pause slightly.) You should have darkened spaces 4B, 5A, 9A, 10D, and 12C on the sample answer sheet. (If the person preparing to take the examination made any mistakes, try to help the candidate see why he or she made wrong marks.)

Official Sample Questions for the Rural Carrier Exam

In order to provide equal opportunity to all competitors, this test is more general in nature than a test based only on postal work, but it requires the same abilities as that work. A rural carrier must be able to understand written instructions and to make and check computations. The written examination tests those abilities; it does not require postal experience.

WRITTEN TEST

DIRECTIONS: The following sample questions are like those that will be used in the written test. Each question has four suggested answers lettered A, B, C, and D. Decide which one is the best answer to the question. Then, on the sample answer sheet below, blacken the lettered space that corresponds with your answer for the question. After you have answered all the questions, compare your answers with the correct answers given. The questions test word knowledge and ability to understand written material.

1. The office work in most commercial firms is concerned primarily with making and using records of the business, and in preserving the records for future reference. The records are the history of transactions of the business and include accounts, correspondence, contracts, and orders, as well as inventories and plans.

The quotation best supports the statement that the records of most commercial firms

(A) are made and kept for possible later use
(B) can be maintained only by constantly reusing past records
(C) are of most value when they are relatively new
(D) usually give a correct history of the various transactions of a business

Explanation: (B) is not the answer because the paragraph does not indicate that constant reuse is necessary to maintain the records; (C) is not the answer because there is nothing in the quotation to show when the records are of most value; (D) is not the answer because the paragraph does not indicate how often one can expect the records to be correct; (A) is the correct answer because the quotation shows that making and preserving records for future reference is a part of the office work of most commercial firms. Therefore, you should blacken (A) for question 1.

2. To say that parcels and other bulky mail must be *consolidated* means most nearly that they must be

(A) weighed
(B) dispatched
(C) protected
(D) combined

Explanation: Since "combined," answer choice (D), best shows what is meant by *consolidated* as it is used, blacken (D) on the sample answer sheet for question 2.

Sample Answer Sheet

1 Ⓐ Ⓑ Ⓒ Ⓓ Ⓔ   2 Ⓐ Ⓑ Ⓒ Ⓓ Ⓔ

The correct answers for questions 1 and 2 are:

1. **A**   2. **D**

COMPUTATIONS TEST

DIRECTIONS: In many ways a postal worker and an employee of a mailing and shipping department of an industrial concern have similar duties and need similar abilities. Both have to compute, using tables and price lists. The following sample questions test ability to make and check computations. Base all answers wholly on the information contained in the questions, the table of Postage Rates for Mailing Packages, and the Price List. Use the sample answer sheet that follows the test.

Use the table below to find the cost of mailing a package of the weight shown in the first column at the left to the different areas shown at the tops of the columns.

POSTAGE RATES FOR MAILING PACKAGES

Weight, 1 pound and not exceeding	Local Area	Areas 1 & 2	Area 3	Area 4	Area 5	Area 6
2 pounds	$0.28	$0.41	$0.32	$0.30	$0.34	$0.29
3 pounds	.30	.54	.40	.37	.43	.34
4 pounds	.33	.67	.48	.45	.52	.39
5 pounds	.36	.80	.57	.52	.61	.45
6 pounds	.39	.94	.68	.60	.72	.51

Note: The postal rates given on this table are deliberately inaccurate so that persons who have worked in shipping and mailing departments and who may have memorized rates have no advantage over other competitors.

Postage and packing charges are not added to bills sent to customers unless specified. Do not assume that a bill is sent unless specifically instructed. Bills are based on this price list:

PRICE LIST
Group A

Article No.	Price
1 or 2	$1.20 an ounce
3	1.15 an ounce
4	0.87 each

Group B

All articles cost $0.13 for the first 2 ounces or less, and 5¢ for each additional ounce or fraction of an ounce.

Box Packing Charges
(To be added to bill in addition to price when specifically required):

Size 1 or 2 box	$0.05
Size 3, 4, or 5 box	.10
Size 6 or over box	.15

1. What is the cost of thirty 4-cent stamps and seven 8-cent stamps?

   (A) $0.76
   (B) $1.75
   (C) $6.80
   (D) none of these

Explanation: The cost of thirty 4-cent stamps is $1.20, and the cost of seven 8-cent stamps is 56 cents. The sum of $1.20 and 56 cents is $1.76. Since none of the answers given in (A) through (C) is correct; (D), none of these, is the correct answer. The sample answer sheet has been properly marked to show that (D) is the answer to question 1.

2. What is the total postage on four 6-pound packages to area 3, and six 3-pound packages to area 2? Use the table of Postage Rates for mailing packages to calculate your answers.

(A) $1.22
(B) $3.26
(C) $5.96
(D) none of these

Explanation: The Table of Postage Rates for Mailing Packages shows that postage on one 6-pound package to area 3 is 68 cents. The postage for 4 packages would be 4 times 68 cents, or $2.72. The postage on one 3-pound package to area 2 is 54 cents. The postage for 6 packages would be 6 times 54 cents, or $3.24. The sum of $2.72 and $3.24 is $5.96. The correct answer choice is (C).

3. What is the amount of the bill for three Group A, No. 2 articles each weighing 4 ounces and each packed in a size-5 box? Use the Price List for Group A articles and the list of Box Packing Charges to calculate your answer.

(A) $14.40
(B) $14.70
(C) $14.80
(D) none of these

Explanation: No. 2 articles in Group A cost $1.20 an ounce. One 4-ounce article would cost 4 times $1.20, or $4.80. Three such articles would cost 3 times $4.80, or $14.40. Packing in a size-5 box would add 10 cents for each article, or 30 cents for 3 articles. The sum of $14.40 and $0.30 is $14.70. The correct answer choice is (B).

Sample Answer Sheet

1. Ⓐ Ⓑ Ⓒ ●   3. Ⓐ Ⓑ Ⓒ Ⓓ
2. Ⓐ Ⓑ Ⓒ Ⓓ

The correct answers for questions 1 through 3 are:

1. **D**   2. **C**   3. **B**

Official Sample Questions for the Mark-up Clerk, Clerk-Typist, and Clerk-Stenographer Exam

Applicants for all three positions—mark-up clerk, automated; clerk-typist; and clerk-stenographer take the same written examination. The first part of this exam tests verbal abilities; the second part tests clerical abilities. Applicants for positions as clerk-typists and clerk-stenographers take the plain-copy typing test, for which the official sample is included. Mark-up clerk candidates do not take the plain-copy typing test; their typing test is administered by computer. The Postal Service does not distribute sample questions for the computer-administered typing test. Mark-up clerk applicants receive the same sample typing test as all other registrants for this exam. The stenography test is given only to applicants for clerk-stenographer positions. Only clerk-stenographer applicants receive the sample questions for the stenography test.

The following sample questions show the types of questions that will be used in the written test. They show also how the questions in the test are to be answered. Read the directions below; then answer the sample questions. Record your answers on the sample answer sheet.

> *DIRECTIONS:* Each question has several answers lettered A, B, C, D, E. Decide which one is the best answer to the question. On the sample answer sheet, find the answer space numbered the same as the question and darken the space lettered the same as the best suggested answer. Then compare your answers with the correct answers given below.

Sample Questions 1 to 5—Verbal Abilities

1. BARREN means most nearly

   (A) nobleman   (C) bauble
   (B) productive   (D) empty

2. *(Reading)* "The secretarial profession is a very old one and has increased in importance with the passage of time. In modern times, the vast expansion of business and industry has greatly increased the need and opportunities for secretaries, and for the first time in history their number has become large."

   The quotation best supports the statement that the secretarial position

   (A) is older than business and industry
   (C) did not exist in ancient times
   (B) demands higher training than it did formerly
   (D) has greatly increased in size

In the following question, the first two words in capital letters go together in some way. The third word in capital letters is related in the same way to one of the words lettered A, B, C, or D.

3. ACTOR is to THEATER as MINISTER is to

   (A) children   (C) church
   (B) people   (D) aisle

Find the correct spelling of the word and darken the proper answer space. If no suggested spelling is correct, darken the space (D).

4. (A) careacteristic   (C) cheracteristic
   (B) characteristic   (D) none of these

Decide which sentence is preferable with respect to grammar and usage for a formal letter or report.

5. (A) This booklet is designed to inform teachers about training requirements.
   (B) According to the announcement, the new director's interest were many and varied.
   (C) He arrived at about noon.
   (D) I expect the report is true.

Sample Questions 6 to 8—Arithmetic

Work each problem and compare your answers with suggested answers A, B, C, D. If your answer does not agree with any of these suggested answers, darken space E.

6. Multiply: 26
        × 6

(A) 120
(B) 136
(C) 146
(D) 156
(E) none of these

7. Add: 24
        + 35

(A) 48
(B) 49
(C) 58
(D) 59
(E) none of these

8. Subtract: 27
        − 6

(A) 20
(B) 21
(C) 33
(D) 35
(E) none of these

Sample Answer Sheet

1 Ⓐ Ⓑ Ⓒ Ⓓ Ⓔ   5 Ⓐ Ⓑ Ⓒ Ⓓ Ⓔ
2 Ⓐ Ⓑ Ⓒ Ⓓ Ⓔ   6 Ⓐ Ⓑ Ⓒ Ⓓ Ⓔ
3 Ⓐ Ⓑ Ⓒ Ⓓ Ⓔ   7 Ⓐ Ⓑ Ⓒ Ⓓ Ⓔ
4 Ⓐ Ⓑ Ⓒ Ⓓ Ⓔ   8 Ⓐ Ⓑ Ⓒ Ⓓ Ⓔ

The correct answers for questions 1 to 8 are:

1. **D**   3. **C**   5. **A**   7. **D**
2. **D**   4. **B**   6. **D**   8. **B**

Sample Questions 9 to 30—Clerical Aptitude

Sample questions 9 to 13 require name and number comparisons. In each line across the page there are three names or numbers that are much alike. Compare the three names or numbers and decide which ones are exactly alike. On the sample answer sheet at the right, mark the answer:

A if ALL THREE names or numbers are exactly ALIKE
B if only the FIRST and SECOND names or numbers are exactly ALIKE
C if only the FIRST and THIRD names or numbers are exactly ALIKE
D if only the SECOND and THIRD names or numbers are exactly ALIKE
E if ALL THREE names or numbers are DIFFERENT

9. Maria Ferster	Maria Fester	Marie Ferster
10. Beth Spring	Beth Spring	Beth Springs
11. Jan Foot	Jan Foote	Jan Foote
12. 21346	21346	21346
13. 54836	54386	54836

In the next group of sample questions, there is a name in a box at the left, and four other names in alphabetical order at the right. Find the correct space for the boxed name so that it will be in alphabetical order with the others, and mark the letter of that space as your answer.

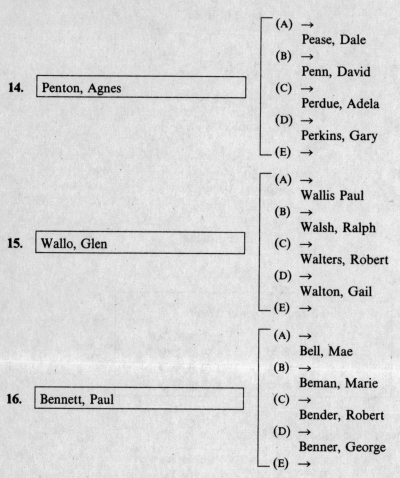

14. | Penton, Agnes |

(A) →
   Pease, Dale
(B) →
   Penn, David
(C) →
   Perdue, Adela
(D) →
   Perkins, Gary
(E) →

15. | Wallo, Glen |

(A) →
   Wallis Paul
(B) →
   Walsh, Ralph
(C) →
   Walters, Robert
(D) →
   Walton, Gail
(E) →

16. | Bennett, Paul |

(A) →
   Bell, Mae
(B) →
   Beman, Marie
(C) →
   Bender, Robert
(D) →
   Benner, George
(E) →

Sample Answer Sheet

9 Ⓐ Ⓑ Ⓒ Ⓓ Ⓔ	**13** Ⓐ Ⓑ Ⓒ Ⓓ Ⓔ
10 Ⓐ Ⓑ Ⓒ Ⓓ Ⓔ	**14** Ⓐ Ⓑ Ⓒ Ⓓ Ⓔ
11 Ⓐ Ⓑ Ⓒ Ⓓ Ⓔ	**15** Ⓐ Ⓑ Ⓒ Ⓓ Ⓔ
12 Ⓐ Ⓑ Ⓒ Ⓓ Ⓔ	**16** Ⓐ Ⓑ Ⓒ Ⓓ Ⓔ

The correct answers for questions 9 to 16 are:

9. **E**   11. **D**   13. **C**   15. **B**
10. **B**   12. **A**   14. **C**   16. **E**

In the following questions, do whatever the question says, and find your answer among the list of suggested answers for that question. Mark the sample answer sheet A, B, C, or D, for the answer you obtained; or if your answer is not among these, mark E for that question.

17. Add: 23
               + 34

    (A) 46
    (B) 47
    (C) 56
    (D) 57
    (E) none of these

18. Subtract: 26
               − 5

    (A) 20
    (B) 21
    (C) 31
    (D) 33
    (E) none of these

19. Multiply: 26
               × 7

    (A) 120
    (B) 146
    (C) 176
    (D) 182
    (E) none of these

20. Divide: $8\overline{)168}$

    (A) 20
    (B) 22
    (C) 24
    (D) 26
    (E) none of these

There is a set of five suggested answers for each group of sample questions that appears below. Do not try to memorize these answers, because there will be a different set on each page in the test.

To find the answer to each question, find which one of the suggested answers contains numbers and letters all of which appear in that question. These numbers and letters may be in any order in the question, but all four must appear. If no suggested answer fits, mark E for that question.

21.	O	Q	M	1	I	V	6	8	
22.	V	I	9	B	8	N	5	M	
23.	B	9	I	M	5	1	0	Q	
24.	5	M	1	6	8	I	B	N	
25.	B	Q	9	5	O	M	V	1	

Suggested Answers
{
A = 9, 1, I, M
B = 0, 1, V, B
C = 8, 9, M, B
D = 8, 0, I, V
E = none of these
}

26.	1	R	N	2	A	W	7	9	
27.	W	2	0	C	9	P	6	N	
28.	C	0	J	N	6	2	1	R	
29.	6	N	2	7	9	J	C	P	
30.	C	R	0	6	1	N	W	B	

Suggested Answers
{
A = 0, 2, J, N
B = 1, 2, W, C
C = 9, 0, N, C
D = 9, 1, J, W
E = none of these
}

Sample Answer Sheet

17 Ⓐ Ⓑ Ⓒ Ⓓ Ⓔ		24 Ⓐ Ⓑ Ⓒ Ⓓ Ⓔ
18 Ⓐ Ⓑ Ⓒ Ⓓ Ⓔ		25 Ⓐ Ⓑ Ⓒ Ⓓ Ⓔ
19 Ⓐ Ⓑ Ⓒ Ⓓ Ⓔ		26 Ⓐ Ⓑ Ⓒ Ⓓ Ⓔ
20 Ⓐ Ⓑ Ⓒ Ⓓ Ⓔ		27 Ⓐ Ⓑ Ⓒ Ⓓ Ⓔ
21 Ⓐ Ⓑ Ⓒ Ⓓ Ⓔ		28 Ⓐ Ⓑ Ⓒ Ⓓ Ⓔ
22 Ⓐ Ⓑ Ⓒ Ⓓ Ⓔ		29 Ⓐ Ⓑ Ⓒ Ⓓ Ⓔ
23 Ⓐ Ⓑ Ⓒ Ⓓ Ⓔ		30 Ⓐ Ⓑ Ⓒ Ⓓ Ⓔ

The correct answers for questions 17 to 30 are:

17. **D**	19. **D**	21. **D**	23. **A**	25. **B**	27. **C**	29. **E**
18. **B**	20. **E**	22. **C**	24. **E**	26. **E**	28. **A**	30. **E**

Official Sample Questions for the Postal Police Officer Exam

OBSERVATION AND MEMORY TEST

DIRECTIONS: In this test you will be allowed three minutes to study a picture. At the end of that time you will not be allowed to look at the picture again, but will answer questions about it based on what you can remember. To practice, then, study the picture below for three minutes. When you are through, turn to the next page and answer questions 1 and 2 without looking back at the picture. Mark your answers to these, and the other sample questions in this section, on the sample answer sheet provided.

1. The words "2 BILLION PIECES OF MAIL" appear on the same panel as

   (A) stars
   (B) a triangle
   (C) a circle
   (D) squares

2. The top section of the panel is blank on the panel that reads

   (A) THE POSTAL SERVICE
   (B) 2 BILLION PIECES OF MAIL
   (C) STAMP SALES
   (D) AMERICA

Sample Answer Sheet

1 Ⓐ Ⓑ Ⓒ Ⓓ Ⓔ   4 Ⓐ Ⓑ Ⓒ Ⓓ Ⓔ
2 Ⓐ Ⓑ Ⓒ Ⓓ Ⓔ   5 Ⓐ Ⓑ Ⓒ Ⓓ Ⓔ
3 Ⓐ Ⓑ Ⓒ Ⓓ Ⓔ   6 Ⓐ Ⓑ Ⓒ Ⓓ Ⓔ

The correct answers for questions 1 and 2 are:

1. **B**   2. **D**

VOCABULARY TEST

3. The company *exhibited* its new products. *Exhibited* means most nearly

   (A) produced
   (B) manufactured
   (C) displayed
   (D) offered

4. He had no *authority* to speak for all of us. *Authority* means most nearly

   (A) right
   (B) reason
   (C) method
   (D) judgment

   The correct answers for questions 3 and 4 are:

   3. **C**   4. **A**

SCRAMBLED SENTENCES TEST

DIRECTIONS: For each question, four paragraphs are labeled A, B, C, and D. Select the paragraph in which the sentences appear in the most logical order to make the best sense. Then mark the sample answer sheet by darkening the space with the same letter as the best paragraph. Mark only one choice for each set of four paragraphs.

5. (A) Security police officers are now checking packages being carried by employees into the facility. This checking resulted in discovery and confiscation of a revolver on December 18. The suspect stated that he carried it to keep it away from his children. The weapon was turned over to postal inspectors for further investigation.

   (B) The weapon was turned over to postal inspectors for further investigation. The suspect stated that he carried it to keep it away from his children. This checking resulted in discovery and confiscation of a revolver on December 18. Security police officers are now checking packages being carried by employees into the facility.

   (C) This checking resulted in discovery and confiscation of a revolver on December 18. Security police officers are now checking packages being carried by employees into the facility. The suspect stated that he carried it to keep it away from his children. The weapon was turned over to postal inspectors for further investigation.

   (D) Security police officers are now checking packages being carried by employees into the facility. The suspect stated that he carried it to keep it away from his children. This checking resulted in discovery and confiscation of a revolver on December 18. The weapon was turned over to postal inspectors for further investigation.

6. (A) They observed a vehicle accident with several injured persons lying on the freeway. The security patrol immediately requested that an ambulance be dispatched to the scene. Prompt action was taken to establish traffic control to protect the injured parties from further injury. Two security police on vehicle patrol were traveling on a local freeway.

   (B) Two security police on vehicle patrol were traveling on a local freeway. They observed a vehicle accident with several injured persons lying on the freeway. The security patrol immediately requested that an ambulance be dispatched to the scene. Prompt action was taken to establish traffic control to protect the injured parties from further injury.

   (C) Prompt action was taken to establish traffic control to protect the injured parties from further injury. The security patrol immediately requested that an ambulance be dispatched to the scene. They observed a vehicle accident with several injured persons lying on the freeway. Two security police on vehicle patrol were traveling on a local freeway.

   (D) Two security police on vehicle patrol were traveling on a local freeway. The security patrol immediately requested that an ambulance be dispatched to the scene. They observed a vehicle accident with several injured persons lying on the freeway. Prompt action was taken to establish traffic control to protect the injured parties from further injury.

   The correct answers for questions 5 and 6 are:

   5. **A**   6. **B**

OFFICIAL SAMPLE QUESTIONS FOR AN OPM EXAM

The following sample questions are typical of the questions on such exams as those for Border Patrol Agents, Customs Aids, and Federal Protective Officers—all administered by the Office of Personnel Management.

DIRECTIONS: Each question has five suggested answers, lettered A, B, C, D, and E. Decide which one is the best answer to the question. Then darken completely the space corresponding to the letter that is the same as the letter of your answer. Keep your mark within the space. If you have to erase a mark, be sure to erase it completely. Mark only one answer for each question.

Sample Answer Sheet

1 Ⓐ Ⓑ Ⓒ Ⓓ Ⓔ	4 Ⓐ Ⓑ Ⓒ Ⓓ Ⓔ	7 Ⓐ Ⓑ Ⓒ Ⓓ Ⓔ	10 Ⓐ Ⓑ Ⓒ Ⓓ Ⓔ	13 Ⓐ Ⓑ Ⓒ Ⓓ Ⓔ
2 Ⓐ Ⓑ Ⓒ Ⓓ Ⓔ	5 Ⓐ Ⓑ Ⓒ Ⓓ Ⓔ	8 Ⓐ Ⓑ Ⓒ Ⓓ Ⓔ	11 Ⓐ Ⓑ Ⓒ Ⓓ Ⓔ	14 Ⓐ Ⓑ Ⓒ Ⓓ Ⓔ
3 Ⓐ Ⓑ Ⓒ Ⓓ Ⓔ	6 Ⓐ Ⓑ Ⓒ Ⓓ Ⓔ	9 Ⓐ Ⓑ Ⓒ Ⓓ Ⓔ	12 Ⓐ Ⓑ Ⓒ Ⓓ Ⓔ	15 Ⓐ Ⓑ Ⓒ Ⓓ Ⓔ

Sample Questions 1 through 3. In each of the sample questions below, select the one of the five suggested answers that is closest in meaning to the word in *italics*. Then darken the proper space on the sample answer sheet.

1. The new training program is much better than any of the *previous* ones. *Previous* means most nearly

(A) abandoned
(B) former
(C) unused
(D) recent
(E) ineffective

2. The officer made several phone calls in an attempt to *verify* the report. To *verify* means most nearly to

(A) examine
(B) explain
(C) confirm
(D) believe
(E) improve

3. The driver's only *option* was to turn right at the intersection. *Option* means most nearly

- (A) use
- (B) direction
- (C) hope
- (D) choice
- (E) opportunity

Sample Questions 4 through 6. In each of the next three sample questions, select the one of the five suggested answers that is best supported by the paragraph. Then darken the proper space on the sample answer sheet.

4. Just as the procedure of a collection department must be clear cut and definite, the steps being taken with the sureness of a skilled chess player, so the various paragraphs of a collection letter must show clear organization, giving evidence of a mind that, from the beginning, has had a specific end in view.

The paragraph best supports the statement that a collection letter should always

- (A) show a spirit of sportsmanship
- (B) be divided into several paragraphs
- (C) be brief, but courteous
- (D) be carefully planned
- (E) be written by the head of the collection department

5. To prevent industrial accidents it is not only necessary that safety devices be used to guard exposed machinery, but also that mechanics be instructed in safety rules which they must follow for their own protection and that the lighting in the plant be adequate.

The paragraph best supports the statement that industrial accidents

- (A) may be due to ignorance
- (B) are always avoidable
- (C) usually result from unsafe machinery
- (D) cannot be entirely overcome
- (E) usually result from inadequate lighting

6. Through advertising, manufacturers exercise a high degree of control over consumers' desires. However, the manufacturer assumes enormous risks in attempting to predict what consumers will want and in producing goods in quantity and distributing them in advance of final selection by the consumers.

The paragraph best supports the statement that manufacturers

- (A) can eliminate the risk of overproduction by advertising
- (B) distribute goods directly to the consumers
- (C) must depend on the final consumers for the success of their undertakings
- (D) can predict with great accuracy the success of any product they put on the market
- (E) are more concerned with advertising than with the production of goods

Sample Questions 7 through 9. Each of the next three sample questions contains five sentences. Decide which one of the five sentences would be most suitable in a formal letter or report with respect to grammar and usage. Then darken the proper space on the sample answer sheet.

7. (A) The officer should of answered courteously the questions asked by the callers.
   (B) The officer must answer courteously the questions of all them callers.
   (C) The officer must answer courteously the questions what are asked by the callers.
   (D) There would have been no trouble if the officer had have always answered courteously.
   (E) The officer should answer courteously the questions of all callers.

8. (A) There are less mistakes in his work since he took the training course.
   (B) The training course being completed, he makes very few mistakes in his work.
   (C) Since he has completed the training course, he makes few mistakes in his work.
   (D) After taking the training course, his work was found to contain hardly any mistakes.
   (E) After he completed the training course, he seldom ever made any mistakes in his work.

9. (A) If properly addressed, the letter will reach my supervisor and I.
   (B) The letter had been addressed to myself and my supervisor.
   (C) I believe the letter was addressed to either my supervisor or I.
   (D) My supervisor's name, as well as mine, was on the letter.
   (E) My supervisor and me will receive the letter if it is probably addressed.

Samples Questions 10 through 12. In each of these sample questions, use your judgment and general knowledge to select the *best* or *most important* answer from the five suggested answers. Then darken the proper space on the sample answer sheet.

10. From the standpoint of the prisoners, the *chief* advantage to be derived from a properly administered parole system is the

    (A) freedom from fear of being returned to prison
    (B) opportunity to adjust themselves to release from imprisonment
    (C) removal of the temptation to commit crime
    (D) reduced cost of supervising prisoners
    (E) opportunity to save whatever they are able to earn

11. An officer of the law may arrest a person without a warrant upon reasonable suspicion that the person has committed a felony. The *chief* purpose of this rule is to

    (A) prevent the person's escape while his or her guilt is being investigated
    (B) prevent the person from committing more crimes immediately
    (C) give the person a chance to confess
    (D) permit observation of the person's behavior
    (E) increase the rate of arrest in proportion to the number of crimes committed

12. Acquaintance with all types of ammunition commonly in use is extremely valuable to the worker in crime detection *chiefly* because

- (A) all criminals possess this knowledge
- (B) a broad background is desirable for success in investigative work
- (C) the worker's safety is thus insured in time of danger
- (D) the worker can thus eventually become a specialist in this line
- (E) such knowledge often simplifies the problem of investigation

Sample Questions 13 through 15. Each of these sample questions consists of five related events followed by five suggested orders in which the events could have occurred. Each suggested order represents the sequence in which the five sentences should be read, i.e., 3–5–1–2–4 indicates that the third sentence should be read first, the fifth sentence second, the first sentence third, etc. Select the one of the five suggested orders, lettered A, B, C, D, and E, in which the events most probably happened. Then darken the proper space on the sample answer sheet.

13. 1. The maid discovered the body and called the police.
   2. The police found Mary at the home of her sister.
   3. A man was shot while swimming in his private pool.
   4. A gun was found in Mary's pocketbook and was identified as the murder weapon.
   5. The police questioned the maid and discovered that the victim had had a heated argument with his wife, Mary, the night before.

- (A) 1–3–5–4–2
- (B) 3–5–1–4–2
- (C) 3–1–5–2–4
- (D) 1–5–2–4–3
- (E) 3–1–2–4–5

14. 1. In addition to the paper, a printing press and a stack of freshly printed $10 bills were found in Mr. Hayes' basement.
   2. A detective saw Mr. Hayes leave a printing shop with a large package.
   3. Mr. Hayes was arrested for counterfeiting and taken to the station.
   4. The owner of the shop said Mr. Hayes had bought very high quality paper.
   5. Mr. Hayes was under surveillance as a suspect in a counterfeiting case.

- (A) 2–4–1–5–3
- (B) 5–2–4–1–3
- (C) 3–2–4–1–5
- (D) 2–5–1–4–3
- (E) 5–2–3–4–1

15. 1. The inspector realized that Ms. Smith was wearing a wig and had her searched.
2. The inspector decided to search Ms. Smith's luggage.
3. Although the inspector could not place the face, he knew that Ms. Smith looked familiar.
4. Narcotics were found sewn to the crown of Ms. Smith's wig.
5. The inspector found nothing in Ms. Smith's luggage, but her passport photograph revealed her identity as a suspected smuggler.

(A) 2–5–3–1–4
(B) 3–1–4–2–5
(C) 1–4–2–5–3
(D) 3–2–5–1–4
(E) 2–1–3–5–4

The correct answers are:

1. **B**	4. **D**	7. **E**	10. **B**	13. **C**
2. **C**	5. **A**	8. **C**	11. **A**	14. **B**
3. **D**	6. **C**	9. **D**	12. **E**	15. **D**

Explanations of Answers to OPM Exam

1. **(B)** *Previous* means coming or occurring before something else.

2. **(C)** To *verify* means to prove or to determine the truth or correctness of something.

3. **(D)** *Option* means something that may be or is chosen.

4. **(D)** The correct answer, D, is supported by the paragraph's statement that a collection letter should show clear organization and be written with a specific end in view. There is nothing in the paragraph to support alternatives A or E. Although the paragraph does imply that collection letters may contain several paragraphs (alternative B), it does not state that they should *always* be so divided. Also, the paragraph says nothing about the length or tone of a collection letter (alternative C), but only refers to the letter's clarity of thought and organization.

5. **(A)** The correct answer, A, is supported by the paragraph's statement that instructing mechanics in safety rules can help prevent industrial accidents, which implies that in some cases accidents may be due to ignorance of these rules. The paragraph does not support the statements that, in actual practice, industrial accidents are either *always* avoidable (alternative B) or that they cannot be entirely overcome (alternative D); it merely states the requirements of successful accident prevention. Although the paragraph does imply that industrial accidents can be caused by unsafe machinery (alternative C) and inadequate lighting (alternative E), it does not support the statements that such accidents *usually* result from these causes.

6. **(C)** The correct answer, C, is supported by the paragraph's statement that although advertising gives manufacturers considerable control over the consumers' demand for their products, there are still big risks involved in producing and distributing their goods in advance of the consumers' final selection, which implies that manufacturers' ultimate success depends on the consumers. The paragraph's statement that there are such risks, in spite of advertising, contradicts alternatives A and D; nor is there any support for the statements that manufacturers distribute goods *directly* to consumers (alternative B) or that they are more concerned with advertising than production (alternative E).

7. **(E)** Alternative A is incorrect because the word *have* should have been used instead of the word *of*. Alternative B is incorrect because the word *those* should have been used instead of the word *them*. Alternative C is incorrect because the word *that* should have been used instead of the word *what*. Alternative D is incorrect because the phrase *had have* is incorrect grammar; only the word *had* should have been used.

8. **(C)** Alternative A is incorrect because the word *fewer* should have been used instead of the word *less*. Alternative B is incorrect because poor word usage makes it seem as if *he* refers to the *training course*. Alternative D is incorrect because the word *few* should have been used instead of the phrase *hardly any*. Alternative E is incorrect because it is poor usage for the word *ever* to follow the word *seldom*.

9. **(D)** In alternative A, "my supervisor and me" is the object of the verb. In alternative C, "my supervisor and me" is the object of the preposition. In alternative B, the word *myself* should be replaced with the word *me*. In alternative E, "my supervisor and I" is the subject of the sentence.

10. **(B)** The *chief* advantage of a properly administered parole system from the prisoners' standpoint is the opportunity it provides them for information and assistance concerning their reentry into society. A parole system cannot guarantee that released prisoners will never return to prison in the future (alternative A), that they will not be tempted to commit crime (alternative C), or that they will have the opportunity to save whatever they earn (alternative E), since these possibilities are largely in the hands of the prisoners themselves. While alternative D may be a result of the parole system, it is not the chief advantage from the standpoint of the prisoners.

11. **(A)** The *chief* purpose of arresting a person suspected of committing a felony is to insure that the suspect does not escape while further investigation takes place. While there may be some truth in all of the other alternatives, none of them can be considered to be the primary reason for this rule.

12. **(E)** The *chief* advantage of familiarity with all types of ammunition for the worker in crime detection lies in the fact that such knowledge can be a valuable aid in discovering and following up clues during the process of investigation. Alternatives A and C are untrue, and while alternatives B and D may be true in some cases, neither one is the most important reason why acquaintance with ammunition is valuable to the worker in crime detection.

13. **(C)** The most logical order of the five events is that first the man was shot (3); second, his body was discovered by the maid and the police were called (1); third, the police questioned the maid and learned of the couple's argument of the previous night (5); fourth, the police found Mary at her sister's home (2); and fifth, a gun was found in Mary's pocketbook and identified as the murder weapon (4). The answer is not A because the maid could not have

discovered the body (1) before the man was shot (3). The answer is not B because the police could not have questioned the maid (5) before she called them (1). The answer is not D because the first four events could not have taken place before the man was shot (3). The answer is not E because the police could not have looked for Mary (2) before learning from the maid that she was the victim's wife (5).

14. **(B)** The most logical order of the five events is that first Mr. Hayes was under surveillance (5); second, a detective saw him leave a printing shop with a large package (2); third, the shop owner said he had bought high quality paper (4); fourth, a printing press and freshly printed bills were found in Mr. Hayes' basement along with the paper (1); and fifth, he was arrested for counterfeiting (3). The answer is not A or D because the detective would not have seen Mr. Hayes leave the printing shop (2) if he had not been under surveillance (5). The answer is not C or E because Mr. Hayes could not have been arrested for counterfeiting (3) before any evidence was discovered (1).

15. **(D)** The most logical order of the five events is that first the inspector saw that Ms. Smith looked familiar (3); second, he decided to search her luggage (2); third, he found nothing in her luggage but identified her from her passport photograph as a suspected smuggler (5); fourth, he realized that she was wearing a wig and had her searched (1); and fifth, narcotics were found in her wig (4). The answer is not A because the inspector would not have decided to search Ms. Smith's luggage (2) unless his suspicions were aroused by the fact that she looked familiar (3). The answer is not B, C, or E because the inspector would not have realized Ms. Smith was wearing a wig (1) before seeing her passport photograph (5).

ACWA SAMPLE QUESTIONS

The questions selected as sample questions for the written test are similar to the questions you will find in the actual test in terms of difficulty and form. In general, the test questions deal with topics related to Government business which you would be likely to encounter.

PART A: VOCABULARY AND READING

The total time alloted for Part A is 50 minutes. Part A will consist of fifteen vocabulary questions and twenty reading questions. It should take you about 5 minutes to answer the vocabulary questions, which would leave you 45 minutes for the reading questions. Do not spend much more than five minutes on the vocabulary questions, since this would cut into the time you have for answering the reading questions. However, if you finish Part A before the allotted time is over, you should review your answers in both the Vocabulary and the Reading sections, especially any answers about which you were uncertain.

VOCABULARY QUESTIONS

Federal jobs require you to communicate well both in written and spoken language. Consequently, a good vocabulary is important for successful job performance. The following questions present a key word and five suggested answers. Your task is to find the suggested answer that is closest in meaning to the key word. Wrong answers may have some connection with the word, but their meanings will be essentially different from that of the key word. Sample questions 1 and 2 are examples of the vocabulary questions in the test.

1. To *collaborate* means most nearly to work

(A) rapidly   (D) overtime
(B) together   (E) carefully
(C) independently

The word *collaborate* means to work with another, especially on a project of mutual interest. Therefore, response B, *together*, is the best answer. Responses A, D, and E are clearly unrelated to the meaning of *collaborate,* and response C, *independently*, is opposite in meaning.

2. *Altruistic* means most nearly

(A) unselfish   (D) organized
(B) extended   (E) appealing
(C) unimaginative

To be *altruistic* means to be concerned for or devoted to the welfare of others. Therefore, response A, *unselfish*, is an excellent synonym. Response B could be viewed as slightly related, since *altruistic* people often extend themselves to help others. However, the basic meaning of *extended*—stretched out—is completely different from the meaning of *altruistic*. Responses C and D are clearly unrelated to the meaning of *altruistic*. A vague connection exists between *altruistic* and response E, *appealing*. *Altruistic* people often make appeals on behalf of those less fortunate than themselves. Simultaneously, the generosity of *altruistic* people often makes them very *appealing* to other people. Although this vague connection exists between *altruistic* and *appealing*, they do not share a similar meaning.

READING QUESTIONS

In each of these questions you will be given a paragraph which contains all the information necessary to infer the correct answer. Use **only** the information provided in the paragraph. Do not speculate or make assumptions that go beyond this information. Also, assume that all information given in the paragraph is true, even if it conflicts with some fact known to you. Only one correct answer can be validly inferred from the information contained in the paragraph.

Pay special attention to negated verbs (for example, "are *not*") and negative prefixes (for example, "*in*complete" or "*dis*organized"). Also pay special attention to quantifiers, such as "all," "none," and "some." For example, from a paragraph in which it is stated that "it is not true that all contracts are legal" one can validly infer that "some contracts are not legal," or that "some contracts are illegal," or that "some illegal things are contracts," but one **cannot** validly infer that "no contracts are legal," or that "some contracts are legal." Similarly, from a paragraph that states "all contracts are legal" and "all contracts are two-sided agreements," one can infer that "some two-sided agreements are legal," but one **cannot** validly infer that "all two-sided agreements are legal."

Bear in mind that in some tests, universal quantifiers such as "all" and "none" often give away incorrect response choices. That is **not** the case in this test. Some correct answers will refer to "all" or "none" of the members of a group.

Be sure to distinguish between essential information and unessential, peripheral information. That is to say, in a real test question, the example above ("all contracts are legal" and "all contracts are two-sided agreements") would appear in a longer, full-fledged paragraph. It would be up to you to separate the essential information from its context, and then to realize that a response choice that states "some two-sided agreements are legal" represents a valid inference and hence the correct answer.

Sample questions 3 and 4 are examples of the reading questions in the text.

3. Personnel administration begins with the process of defining the quantities of people needed to do the job. Therefore, people must be recruited, selected, trained, directed, rewarded, transferred, promoted, and perhaps released or retired. However, it is not true that all organizations are structured so that workers can be dealt with as individuals. In some organizations, employees are represented by unions, and managers bargain directly only with these associations.

The paragraph best supports the statement that

(A) no organizations are structured so that workers cannot be dealt with as individuals
(B) some working environments other than organizations are structured so that workers can be dealt with as individuals
(C) all organizations are structured so that employees are represented by unions
(D) no organizations are structured so that managers bargain with unions
(E) some organizations are not structured so that workers can be dealt with as individuals

- The correct answer is response E. This conclusion can be derived from information contained in the third sentence of the paragraph, which states that *it is not true that all organizations are structured so that workers can be dealt with as individuals.* From this statement, it can be inferred that *some organizations are not structured so that workers can be dealt with as individuals.*

- Response A is incorrect because it contradicts the information in the third and fourth sentences of the paragraph. With its double negation, response A is in effect saying that all organizations are structured so that workers can be dealt with as individuals. This flatly contradicts the third sentence and also contradicts the fourth sentence, which says that *in some organizations, employees are represented by unions, and managers bargain with these associations.*

- Response B is not supported by the paragraph because the paragraph gives no information about working environments other than organizations.

- Response C is not supported by the paragraph because the paragraph says only that employees are represented by unions in *some* organizations. One cannot generalize from this to say that employees are represented by unions in *all* organizations.

- Response D is incorrect because it contradicts the fourth sentence, which says that managers bargain with unions in some organizations.

Note that in this question, the correct answer follows basically from one sentence in the paragraph—the third sentence. The rest of the paragraph presents additional information about personnel administration which is relevant to the discussion, but not necessary to make the inference. Part of your task in the Reading section is to *understand* what you read, and then to *discern* what conclusions follow logically from statements in the paragraph. Consequently, in this test, you will find some questions in which it is necessary to use all or most of the statements presented in the paragraph, while in others, such as this one, only one statement is needed to infer the correct answer.

4. Many kinds of computer programming languages have been developed over the years. Initially, programmers had to write instructions in machine language. If a computer programming language is a machine language, then it is a code which can be read directly by a computer. Most high-level computer programming languages, such as Fortran and Cobol, use strings of common English phrases which communicate with the computer only after being converted or translated into a machine code.

The paragraph best supports the statement that

(A) all high-level computer programming languages use strings of common English phrases which are converted to a machine code.

(B) if a computer programming language is a machine language, then it is not a code which can be read directly by a computer

(C) if a computer programming language is a code which can be read directly by a computer, then it is not a machine language

(D) if a computer programming language is not a code which can be read directly by a computer, then it is not a machine language

(E) if a computer programming language is not a machine language, then it is a code which can be read directly by a computer

- The correct answer is response D. The answer can be derived from the information presented in the third sentence. That sentence states that *if a computer programming language is a machine language, then it is a code which can be read directly by a computer.* From this statement it can be seen that all machine languages are codes which can be read directly by a computer, and that if a computer programming language is not such a code, then it is not a machine language.

- Response A goes beyond the information presented in the paragraph, which states only that *most* high level computer programming languages use strings of common English phrases.
- Response B represents a complete contradiction of the third sentence of the paragraph.
- Response C contradicts the paragraph. We know from the paragraph that at least some coded languages which can be read directly by a computer are machine languages.
- Response E is incorrect because the paragraph does not say whether or not computer languages that are *not* machine languages are codes which can be read directly by a computer.

PART B: TABULAR COMPLETION AND ARITHMETIC REASONING

The total time allotted to Part B is 50 minutes. Part B will consist of ten tabular completion questions and fifteen arithmetic reasoning questions. It should take you no more than 15 minutes to answer the tabular completion questions, which would leave you 35 minutes for the arithmetic reasoning questions. Some problems in Part B may be solved by more than one method. When this is the case, use whatever method is fastest and easiest for you. Keep in mind, however, that each question has only **one** correct answer. If you finish Part B before the allotted time is over, you should review your answers in both the Tabular Completion and Arithmetic Reasoning sections, especially any answers about which you were uncertain. *The use of calculators will NOT be permitted during the actual test; therefore, they should not be used to solve these sample questions.*

TABULAR COMPLETION QUESTIONS

These questions are based on information presented in tables. Only *two* sample questions of this type appear below, although, in the actual test, you will have to find *five* unknown values in each table. You must calculate these unknown values by using the known values given in the table. In some questions, the exact answer will not be given as one of the response choices. In such cases, you should select response E, "none of these." Sample questions 5 and 6, which are based on the accompanying table, are examples of the tabular completion questions in this test.

FEDERAL BUDGET RECEIPTS OUTLAYS, AND DEBT
FISCAL YEARS 1981-1985
(In millions of dollars)

ITEM	FISCAL YEAR				
	1981	1982	1983	1984	1985
Total Receipts	I	298,060	355,559	399,561	463,302
Federal funds..................	187,505	201,099	241,312	270,490	316,366
Trust funds.....................	116,683	131,750	150,560	165,569	186,988
Interfund transactions..........	−25,098	−34,789	−36,313	−36,498	−40,052
Total Outlays	324,244	364,473	400,507	448,368	490,997
Federal funds..................	240,080	269,921	295,757	331,991	362,396
Trust funds.....................	109,262	II	141,063	152,875	168,653
Interfund transactions..........	−25,098	−34,789	−36,313	−36,498	−40,052
Total Surplus or Deficit (−).......	−45,154	−66,413	−44,948	−48,807	V
Federal funds..................	−52,576	−68,822	−54,444	−61,501	−40,030
Trust funds.....................	7,422	2,409	9,496	12,694	12,336
Gross Federal Debt	544,131	631,866	III	780,425	833,751
Held by Government agencies ...	147,225	151,566	157,295	169,477	189,162
Held by the public..............	396,906	480,300	551,843	610,948	644,589
Federal Reserve System	84,993	94,714	105,004	IV	115,594
Other	311,913	385,586	446,839	495,468	528,995

Hypothetical data.

5. What is the value of I in millions of dollars?

  (A) 91,585
  (B) 162,407
  (C) 279,090
  (D) 304,188
  (E) none of these

    The correct answer is C. It can be calculated by adding the Receipt values for *Federal funds, Trust funds,* and *Interfund transactions.* Numerically, 187,505 + 116,683 + (−25,098) = 279,090.

6. What is the value of II in millions of dollars?

  (A)   329,684
  (B)   129,341
  (C)   94,552
  (D) −101,202
  (E) none of these

    The correct answer is B. It can be calculated by subtracting the Outlay values for *Federal funds* and *Interfund transactions* from the value for *Total Outlays.* Numerically, 364,473 − (269,921) − (−34,789) = 129,341.

ARITHMETIC REASONING QUESTIONS

In this part of the test you will have to solve problems formulated in both verbal and numeric form. You will have to analyze a paragraph in order to set up the problem, and then solve it. If the exact answer is not given as one of the response choices, you should select response E, "none of these." Sample questions 7 and 8 are examples of the arithmetic reasoning questions in this test.

7. An interagency task force has representatives from three different agencies. Half of the task force members represent Agency A, one-third represent Agency B, and three represent Agency C. How many people are on the task force?

   (A) 12
   (B) 15
   (C) 18
   (D) 24
   (E) none of these

The correct answer is response C. It can be obtained by computing the following:

$$1/2 \ X + 1/3 \ X + 3 = X$$

X is equal to the total number of task force members; 1/2 X represents the number from Agency A; 1/3 X represents the number from Agency B; and 3 is the number from Agency C. The first two terms on the left side of the equation can be combined by computing their lowest common denominator, which is 6. Therefore:

$$1/2 \ X = 3/6 \ X \text{ and } 1/3 \ X = 2/6 \ X$$

The sum of 3/6 X and 2/6 X is 5/6 X, which, when subtracted from X (or 6/6 X), yields the results:

$$1/6 \ X = 3 \text{ and } X = 18$$

Responses A, B, and D are the result of erroneous computations.

8. It has been established in recent productivity studies that, on the average, it takes a filing clerk 2 hours and 12 minutes to fill four drawers of a filing cabinet. At this rate, how long would it take two clerks to fill 16 drawers?

   (A) 4 hrs.
   (B) 4 hrs., 20 min.
   (C) 8 hrs.
   (D) 8 hrs., 40 min.
   (E) none of these

The answer is E. The correct answer is not given as one of the response choices. The answer can be obtained by first converting 12 minutes to .2 hour, and then setting up a simple proportion:

$$2.2/4 = X/16$$

Solving this proportion, we obtain 4X = 35.2; X = 8.8. This, however, is the number of hours that it would take one filing clerk to do the job. If two clerks are filling the 16 drawers, the job would be completed in half that time or in 4.4 hours, which is 4 hours, 24 minutes.

Responses A, B, C, and D are the result of erroneous computations.

COMPLETE LIST OF ARCO CIVIL
SERVICE TITLES

Accountant—Auditor
ACWA—Administrative Careers With America
Air Traffic Controller Qualifying Test
Air Traffic Controller Training Program
American Foreign Service Officer
Assistant Accountant
Auto Mechanic/Automotive Serviceman
Beginning Clerical Worker
Bookkeeper—Account Clerk
Border Patrol Agent
Building Custodian-Building Superintendent-
  Custodian Engineer
Bus Operator-Conductor
Business Typing
Carpenter
Case Worker
CIA Entrance Examination
Civil Service Administrative Tests
Civil Service Arithmetic and Vocabulary
Civil Service Clerical Promotion Tests
Civil Service Handbook
Civil Service Psychological and Psychiatric Tests
Civil Service Reading Comprehension Tests
Civil Service Tests for Basic Skills Jobs
Civil Service Typing Tests
Complete Guide to U.S. Civil Service Jobs
Computer Specialist GS 5-9
The Corey Guide to Postal Exams
Correction Officer
Correction Officer Promotion Tests
Court Officer-Senior Court Officer-Court Clerk
Distribution Clerk, Machine
Drug Enforcement Agent
Electrician—Electrician's Helper
Emergency Dispatcher/911 Operator
FBI Entrance Examination
Federal Clerk—Steno-Typist
Federal Jobs for College Graduates
File Clerk-General Clerk
Firefighter
Fire Department Lieutenant/Captain/Battalion
  Chief
Gardener—Grounds Maintenance Worker
General Test Practice for 101 U.S. Jobs
Homestudy Course for Civil Service Jobs
How to Get a Clerical Job in Government
How to Pass Civil Service Oral Examinations
How to Pass Clerical Employment Tests
Investigator/Claim Examiner
Librarian
Machinist—Machinist's Helper

Mail Handler
Maintenance Mechanic
Maintenance Worker/Mechanical Maintainer
Mark-up Clerk/Clerk-Typist/Clerk-Stenographer—
  U.S. Postal Service
Mechanical Aptitude and Spatial Relations Tests
New York City Civil Service Job Guide
Nurse
Office Aide
Office Associate
101 Challenging Government Jobs for College
  Graduates
Plumber-Steam Fitter
Police Administrative Aide
Police Officer
Police Promotion Examinations
Police Sergeant/Lieutenant/Captain
Postal Exams Handbook
Post Office Clerk-Carrier
Practice for Clerical, Typing and Stenographic
  Tests
Preparacion Para el Examen de Cartero
Principal Administrative Associate—
  Administrative Assistant
Principal Clerk/Principal Stenographer
Probation Officer—Parole Officer
Railroad Clerk
Rural Carrier U.S. Postal Service
Sanitation Worker
School Secretary
Senior Clerical Series
SF 171: The Federal Employment Application
  Form
Special Agent Treasury Department
Special Officer—Senior Special Officer—Bridge
  and Tunnel Officer
Staff Analyst—Associate Staff Analyst
State Trooper/Highway Patrol Officer/State
  Traffic Officer
Supervision
Track Worker
Traffic Enforcement Agent
Train Operator—Tower Operator—Assistant
  Train Dispatcher
Transit Electrical Helper
Typing for Everyone
U.S. Employment Service General Aptitude Test
  Battery
You as a Law Enforcement Officer